GOD INTERVENES BETWEEN A PERSON AND THEIR HEART

KEY LESSONS FROM THE PROPHETS

Fadwa Wazwaz

© Copyright 2020 by Fadwa Wazwaz - All rights reserved.

It is not legal to reproduce, duplicate, or transmit any part of this document in either electronic means or printed format. Recording of this publication is strictly prohibited.

Interior Design: Patti Frazee
Cover Design: www.lockandkey.me
Cover Photo: EyeEm.com, Photographer Aaron Davis
Editor: Marcia Lynx Qualey

ISBN: 978-1-7347975-0-3
ISBN: 978-1-7347975-1-0 (ebook)

Library of Congress Cataloging-in-Publication Data: 2020905484

Printed in the United States of America

Little Wonders Publishing
Brooklyn Park, Minnesota 55443

In loving memory of those who are forever in our hearts.

To Prophet Muhammad, upon him peace and blessings, God's Chosen One, and also to Amenah Abdel Jawwad Wazwaz, my beloved mother, who loved him tremendously. She raised us under very difficult circumstances, with very little support and few resources, working hard to teach us the faith through her resilience and character in the face of life's challenges and difficult health struggles. In loving memory of my father, Muhammad Abdur Rahman Wazwaz; my paternal grandfather, Abdur Rahman Ibrahim Ali Wazwaz; my maternal grandfather, Abdel Jawwad Ibrahim Ali Wazwaz; my paternal grandmother, Sabriya Abdul Khaliq Abu Turki; and my maternal grandmother, Hamdeh Muhammad al Jamal, without whom I would not exist. Also to all the Prophets of God all the way to Prophet Adam, upon them peace. Finally, to Maryam Laid, my beautiful daughter who I hope will find this book beneficial and write her own book and share her wisdom.

Table of Contents

Stories of the Prophets as a Force for Healing 1
   Know Thyself 5
   My Image, Honor, and Reputation 8
   Transforming Anger 12
   Journaling and the Quran 16

Re-framing the Why 19
   Moving Beyond Confirmation Bias 21

Why Study Islam? 25
   What Do We Mean When We Talk About Faith? 27

Adam: Lessons on Repentance and Forgiveness 31
   The Awakener, the Resurrector,
   the Arouser, the Dispatcher 31
   Of Adam, Eve, Satan, and Angels 34
   Why Satan? 40
   How to Fight Satan 45
   Rationalization and the Healthy Heart 46
   How Do We Fear God? 49

The Resolute Prophets and Dealing with Rejection 55
   What We Can Learn from Rejection in Art 56
   Seeing People for What They Are: Corrupter or Reformer 59

Noah and "The Most Abject Among Us" 63
   We Are Not in Control 65
   Speaking Truth to Power Is Not About Results 67

Abraham: Lessons on Truth 73
   Submission 73
   Submission, Awareness, and the Facts 76
   Rejecting the Signs 78
   Surrendering to the Knowledge Embedded in Your Heart 81

Jacob and Joseph: Love and Projection 93
- How We Tell "The Most Beautiful Story" 93
- The Dream 94
- Seduction 98
- What Joseph's Story Tells Us About Sexual Harassment 101
- Joseph and the Misinterpretation of Shame 104
- Hijab Is Not About Oppression or Seduction: It's About Trust 110
- Seeking God the Protector 115
- When Is It Time for Forgiveness? 117
- The Reunion: Deception Has a Short Lifespan 125

Solomon and David: Lessons on Gratitude and Wisdom 131
- What Is—and Isn't—Bravery? 131
- Lessons from the "Let's Be Great Again" Syndrome 135
- Solomon and Bilqis: Healthy Power 141
- Experiencing Humility and Power: In the Footsteps of David and Solomon 151

Moses: Lessons on Power and Oppression 157
- Muslims and the Elephant in the Room 157
- Opening the Windows to the Stories of Moses 159
- How Do You Know You're Really Fighting Oppression? 160
- Nurture Thyself 164
- Growing the Moses Within 173
- Speaking Truth to Power 175
- Two Names of God: The Patient and the Just 178
- New World, Old Habits 185
- Fighting the Pharaoh Inside Us 189
- To Always Be in a Humble State 192

Jesus and Mary: Lessons on Humility 197
- Jesus in the Bible, Jesus in the Quran 197
- Seeking God al-Wahhab, and Seeking God ar-Razzaq 200
- Mary, Hagar, and the Importance of Independence 204
- Judging Others in a Trial 206
- Having Conversations Across Differences 208

Muhammad: Beautiful Prophet, Beautiful Messenger 213
His Birth 213
The Importance of Listening 217
Trust and Trustworthiness 221
The First Revelation 226
Let Aisha Speak for Aisha 229
Believing His Wives 233
Husband and Prophet:
Resolving Conflict, Creating Choices 238
Taif and Rejection 241
What We Learn about Muhammad from Taif 245
Healthy Power: Enforcing Boundaries, Removing Barriers 248
The Story of At-Tufayl Bin Amr Ad-Dawsi 250
Muhammad and Aisha: Dealing with Slander 252
Aisha and Her Co-wives: Who Repeated the Rumor? 256
Welcoming Nobility 258
Making Peace: Between Fantasy, Reasoning, and Denial 261
The Light, the Illuminator, the One Who Reveals 264
Seeking Greatness or Following Conviction? 268
Lessons of Badr and Uhud 274
Beautiful Names 276
Muharram, Ashura, and Stopping Cycles of Violence 281

Praise is for God Alone 285
A Torch to Light the Way 288
Amenah Abdel Jawwad Wazwaz:
How to Praise God in Illness? 293

Sources 299
Acknowledgments 301
About the Author 303

STORIES OF THE PROPHETS AS A FORCE FOR HEALING

O you who have believed, respond to Allah and to the Messenger when he calls you to that which gives you life. And know that Allah intervenes between a person and their heart and that to Him you will be gathered. (Quran 8:24)

My journey to comfort with my faith, and with its healing powers, has been a long one.

I was born in Jerusalem, into a large Palestinian family. My dad was a fan of Egyptian President Gamal Abdel-Nasser. My father approved of science and progress, and he disliked religious groups. My mom, on the other hand, was a deeply faithful woman. When I was very young, we moved to Chicago, and that's where she raised her ten children.

My parents had their love story: They fell for each other at first sight, they said. He went out of his way to stand up to her family. They fell in love even though they were worlds apart: My father wasn't formally educated, but he was intelligent and well-read. He'd suffered as a young man at the hands of people of faith, and he never moved past this suffering. My mom, meanwhile, was illiterate and faithful. She couldn't read about her faith, but she passed down to us what she'd understood of Islam, which was knotted up with the good and the bad of her society.

They are both socially conservative, from very conservative families. However, my mother is more religious and has always been a devoted, practicing Muslim.

My path was full of twists and turns. But after I graduated from the University of Minnesota, I committed myself to helping build and strengthen the United States' Muslim communities, as well as our ties to other marginalized communities.

We children took after my father in that we loved to read. And there was truth in his story: He had suffered, and there was important truth to be found in books and in reflection. My mother had understood something, too. But I couldn't accept the religion as she understood it, where women weren't respected.

I didn't want to wholly reject the religious community like my father, nor did I want to embrace everything just as it was given to me, as my mother had. This was my starting point: discovering the Prophet's appreciation for women as strong partners in society, and how he nurtured the society around him to appreciate women in a healthy way. My father is Muslim, but was more inclined to Gamal Abdel Nasser, the late Egyptian president. He never liked Islamic movements such as the Muslim Brotherhood.

That's how I come to this project: to read, to consider, and to weigh ideas—but then to embrace them fully, with my heart, through God. This book is both for Muslims looking to learn more about their faith, who want to connect to their faith, as well as for the rest of creation. The stories of the prophets are key, because through them we can see how our own stories measure up.

The expectation is not that we'll be prophets! It is, instead, to help us to grow and check ourselves. Instead of engaging in a blind faith, studying the stories of the prophets keeps us open and nurtures a sense of openness as we engage ourselves and others.

The aim of this book is to create a connection to the prophets, using them as a benchmark, an ideal. By reflecting on their lives, their stories, and their deeds in the context of our own lives, we can help heal ourselves and move forward. We shouldn't feel ashamed about the ways in which we haven't lived up. Instead, we should use these stories, and our faith, as a force for healing.

Many Muslims are suffering a crisis of faith. After all, the modern world can feel overwhelming. The stories of the prophets can help illuminate our hearts and the world around us.

It was 1992, and I was living in Chicago, when one of my younger sisters divorced her husband. This brought our family head-to-head with the Chicago court system. Until that time, I had believed that the US legal system would protect women and stand by their rights, and I was shaken by how people with money could use the court system, and how deep-seated prejudices against women—of the sort that had manifested in my family—could manifest in the justice system, too.

At that point, I went on a journey of understanding how power and oppression work, guided by the Quran, workshops, and individual healers. Eventually, I found the deep relationship between holistic healing and Islam.

God Intervenes Between a Person and Their Heart: Key Lessons from the Prophets is a journey in healing, inspired by the life experiences that challenged me, and questions that I had to work through as a Muslim growing up in the United States.

Some of the core questions in this book are my own, while I've received others through a life of public writing and speaking, as people have sometimes asked tough questions. This book invites the reader to look at the stories of the prophets afresh. What are the ways in which the Quran can help us make decisions in our lives? How can the Quran help us to look at things anew? The first few sections will discuss anger, how we transform anger, and healing.

The sections that follow will explore how to create a connection to the prophets.

Although I am not a doctor of Islamic Studies, I take my qualifications from the public speaking that I've done, the writing that has challenged me, the people who have questioned me, the healers I have questioned, and the projects I've been engaged in, such as "Engage Minnesota," as well as writing for the Minneapolis Star Tribune, St. Paul Pioneer Press, and other venues.

For his part, Shaykh Qays Arthur is a teacher who is in a unique position to give us insight into the relationships of the prophets. Arthur looks at Islam through multiple lenses, as he is from a Christian background, but became a Muslim. In our discussions, he once said that, when he moved to Jordan, he noticed that the Christians there could recognize Muslims. Not just by seeing them, but by recognizing the connectivity between the prophets.

But in the United States and Europe, he said, when people hear about Islam, they hear it as a totally new religion, alien from Jewish and Christian belief systems.

Muslims can make the situation worse, he added, if "we treat the Bible and Christianity as alien to our faith or when we look upon ourselves as some new, independent community as opposed to simply believers in God's final Prophet (peace be upon him) who continue in the legacy of the prophets of the Bible (peace be upon them all)."

The prophets addressed here thus range from Adam to Moses to Muhammad. Some people have asked me how Islam can stake any claim to Adam or Moses. After all, those people reason, early prophets "belong" to other religions.

To this I would say: How does anyone lay claim to Moses? Through God.

One thing I've learned as a Palestinian born in Jerusalem is that the world's biggest religions share a great deal of connective tissue. Here in the United States, we often don't see the bridges between the "us" of a secular or religious Judaism and Christianity and the "them" of a secular or religious Islam, which is often painted as a complete new and foreign practice.

Yet that isn't the case. The religions do have a different narrative at times—different ways of seeing Moses, Joseph, Jesus, and others—but there are also stories that connect us. Moses offers a compelling way of looking at power and oppression, both in his own time and in ours. Joseph and Jacob help us understand love and projection, and we can learn a great deal about truth and wisdom from Abraham.

These are exactly the points of connection that I want to develop and underline.

I have long written about these individual stories, but now I want to weave them into an overall picture that brings the stories of these ancient figures to life. I want to work with mentors who will help me to give voice to varied stories—not just mine, but the voices of others in Minnesota and other Muslim communities around the United States. I want us to enrich our understanding of each other and the conflicts that exist—and how we can see our way past them into a place of many, many stories.

This book will not focus on the differences between monotheists and polytheists or Islamic Law, but rather on ethics. After all, our clashes have less to do with religious differences and more to do with our selfish interests. We can disagree with polytheists or atheists; however, this disagreement should not rationalize abuse in either direction.

I also hope to promote a sense of self-knowledge—and, to do that, I must also know myself. Then, ultimately, by connecting and reconnecting to ourselves, by connecting to our communities and beyond, I hope we will create a ripple effect of positive transformation.

I would like to share this work in the spirit of those Muslim scholars who strove their hardest to benefit and open themselves to being benefited by others. Imam ash-Shafi' shared his works and knowledge by saying:

Never do I argue with a man with a desire to hear him say what is wrong, or to expose him and win victory over him. Whenever I face an opponent in debate I silently pray - O Lord, help him so that truth may flow from his heart and on his tongue, and so that if truth is on my side, he may follow me; and if truth be on his side, I may follow him.

As I worked on this book, I recited the following prayers of Prophet Muhammad, upon him peace and blessings continuously:

Oh Allah (God), show us the truth as truth and enable us to observe it and show us falsehood as falsehood and enable us to avoid it.

I seek refuge with You from misleading others or being misguided, or slipping or making a slip, or wronging others or being wronged, or feeling important or being made ignorant.

In that spirit, I pray this work is of benefit to people, and I pray for forgiveness if there are unintentional mistakes, slips, or ignorance, and I hope it is brought to my attention for correction. I pray to God that He forgives me for any mistakes, and if, in His knowledge, anything I share is in error or false, that He elevates the truth and correction, and lets it prevail over this work. I pray that He grants me and others the grace and humility to accept it, and also to follow it.

Know Thyself

The unexamined life is not worth living.

—Socrates

Throughout history, Islam has had many different manifestations. The core principles are the same, but the manifestations have been rooted in a particular time and place. As we look around the world now, there are places where Islam has a very East African or very Latin American manifestation.

Are any of these "wrong" or "right"? No. They are all the same religion, but Islam opens and gives breathing space for each individual culture.

There was a very famous Muslim traveler in the 14th century CE named Ibn Battuta (1304-1369 CE), who traveled thousands of miles through Africa, Europe, and Asia—from Timbuktu to Bulgaria to Beijing—and is recognized as one of history's great travel writers.

Wherever he went, he felt at home in the community's Islam. In China, the expressions of Islam incorporated Chinese symbolism. In India, there was the Taj Mahal. In West Africa, Ibn Battuta found different expressions that were very much a part of the local culture.

In each case, Islam didn't come to alter the culture or the differences of the land. It came to promote basic principles: protection of life and property, justice and faith, and the few maxims that are a matter of consensus. All other things can be found in, and integrated into, a local culture.

Nowadays, some Muslims have a cultural blindness or a cultural phobia. Yet all these manifestations of Islam are equally true. Indeed, the one that's false is the one that is blind to itself and trying to purge out other cultures. These are the ones like ISIS, that push one particular culture and say there is "one" Islam.

Cultural connectivity

Being Muslim should not disconnect a person from their family, their community, or their culture. Islam should be part of a larger cultural connectivity and an appreciation for diversity. Part of this is knowledge of ourselves, our own culture, and the fact that we each have a culture. You can't appreciate others if you don't know who you are.

I, for instance, am a proud Palestinian. From this place, I also love Somali culture, Mexican culture, and many others. Knowing yourself, and your own culture, provides a lens through which you can gain a genuine appreciation of and respect for others.

False sense of self, false sense of culture

There is a danger in not knowing oneself and one's culture—it leaves a person open to being defined entirely from the outside and being told what to think. People who have a false sense of self can be drawn into both narcissism and the sort of self-doubt that urges us to surround ourselves with people who give only praise and don't help us define and strengthen our boundaries.

One question for us to ask ourselves is: Have you ever apologized?

There was a time when I was surrounded entirely by people telling me I was right. Then, when I was in the wrong, my friends—who had helped me build up a false sense of self—would stand by me and hype me up. After a while, I felt that something was wrong. I made a U-turn in my life and turned to God.

God finally brought me to the realization that I was wrong. My friends had told me all along that I was fine. But, in that crowd around me, no one had my best interests at heart, and no one helped me to be mindful of myself, my origins, my boundaries, and how I might be harming others.

These were religious people who were led by the ego, and whose ego pushed them to manipulate religion to be in the service of their own self-interests. There are those who preach loudly about God, but the "Mecca" of their hearts is ruled by the idols of ambition, fears, insecurities, arrogance, delusion, a desire for greatness, an attachment to foolishness, and ignorance. These idols become a tool for Satan to use to execute his plans. In the end, such individuals—even if they talk a lot about religion—become Satan's wolfpack rather than a guiding light to God.

Those who are led by the ego can sound like true worshipers, but God is just a tool to fulfill their ambitions. When I separated from these people, I was able to use my time to get to know God genuinely instead of being a tool, a fool, or a hyena in the hands of a Pharaoh in religious clothing.

After that, I had to build different connections in order to better know myself and better explore the direction I wanted to go.

> First, you have to get to know yourself, and one of the ways of doing this is to take active participation in those things that interest you, learning about why they interest you, whether that interest is healthy, and in the process learning about who you are as a person deep down inside. When you can learn to trust your own thoughts, your own heart, and understand your own weaknesses and strengths (and exercise your strengths so that the weakness become more obedient), then you are in a position to be patient when patience is necessary. "If you hear words that hurt you, then bow your head before them and they will miss you" (`Ali ibn Abi Talib). They will miss you when what they say no longer has any influence over you, and they will miss you because you would have learned with whom to spend time and with

whom politeness is sufficient. When you are at peace with yourself, then you will find it to have some degree of control over your ability to concentrate because your mind will not be preoccupied with what others think.

—Hwaa Irfan

Certainly, we don't want the people around us to be hypercritical. But: Do they give genuine, sincere advice? Or do they always have your back, no matter what? Certainly, that feels good. But it might not be the best way for you to learn more about yourself and the world around you.

My Image, Honor, and Reputation

When you are hurt by people not showing you favor, or by them directing their criticism towards you, then return to Allah's knowledge of you. If His knowledge does not satisfy you, then your misfortune through your dis-satisfaction with Allah's knowledge is worse than your misfortune through the presence of their harm.

— Ibn Ata Allah al-Iskandari

What is image? Image is our perception either of ourselves or of others. It lacks understanding, depth, and breadth—it's a snapshot, if you will. Carl Jung said that perception is projection. What does this mean? We all have a shadow self, a hidden personality that we do not like. When we are listening and engaging others in a reflective mode, we are aware of that personality and don't disown it. We work on it continuously and repetitively. That's what we're invited to do during the month of Ramadan, and we can take it with us the rest of the year.

However, when we disown parts of our personality, we project them onto other people in a scapegoating way, in order to feel better about ourselves and to avoid spiritual growth. When we obsess or become fixated on a particular group or individual, and use that image to engage them, that is projection. To avoid it, we must stop and ask ourselves the following six questions:

1) Do I know them beyond that perception?
2) How much effort have I made to know them as a human being?
3) How much of my time is spent psychoanalyzing the other's flaws?
4) How often do I find myself pointing out their flaws and suggesting they fix them?
5) Do I find myself feeling good after telling them to fix their flaws?

6) How well do I receive advice from this "other?"

Now pause and reflect: How are the flaws that characterize this "other" representative of you? How much of the bad that you see in this little-known other, if you were to be really honest with yourself, exists in you?

Sometimes, in our clash with others, there are messages and lessons that support our own growth. Hwaa Irfan, a healer I deeply admire and respect, said it best in one of her counseling responses to an individual. The italics are my emphasis.

> Throughout life we are always discovering ourselves, because we learn about ourselves through others – it is through others we learn to reach our higher selves. *By this I do not mean their perception of us, but the lessons, and challenges through interaction helps to stimulate and awaken our compassion, understanding, and intuition, our ability to give unconditionally, and sacrifice. We can learn where to invest our energy, where not to, and when to be a little patient, because everyone has their own struggle.*
>
> To give you an example, one time when I was being finally served, the cashier was being really cold, to the extent he wished that I did not exist. I asked myself, I did not do anything to this man, and he does not know me, then just like that I asked him if I have done anything wrong. He suddenly "awoke" from whatever state of mind he was in, and *heard someone (me) communicating with him as if he was a human being.* He then proceeded to tell me what had upset him.

One thing I have learned from healers' counseling advice is that the oppressor is usually obsessed with their own image. This obsession is so strong that such a person goes to great lengths to protect the image, disregarding the damage done to their soul. The possibility that they could be wrong, or contributing to a problem, is hidden and ferociously resisted. They put themselves in a position where they can give advice, but not receive it.

Such individuals do a lot of talking and plotting and planning behind the scenes. A genuine conversation is not just making loud noises in the air or behind walls, because conversation requires reciprocity. An honest conversation requires all parties to be open to the contributions of others.

What does honor have to do with image?

If you seek honor in your own eyes, this is egotism, and it can harden and fossilize. If you seek honor in the eyes of others, this is a sense of inferiority, and it can make you feel bound by the crowd, such that you will seek acceptance over growth. To do honorable deeds without seeking praise either from one's ego or from others is true honor. This is the honor Islam teaches, and the one the prophets practiced. To arrive at this stage, you must graduate from the first two stages and recognize the true experience of being honorable.

This does not mean that we should disclose our sins, since Islam teaches us to hide them. However, we should repent, and we will know that genuine and authentic repentance took place when we don't become fixated or obsessed with a particular group or individual who we see as flawed or inferior, such that we project our sins onto them to feel good about ourselves.

At times, as human beings, we err, fall, and clash with one another. Problems arise. When we engage others through the process of reflection instead of projection, without holding onto any negative feelings, biases, prejudices, or assumptions, then the event as it actually happened manifests to us. The chaos of everything around us will settle, and each will see how the clash happened and how each contributed to the situation.

Hwaa Irfan described the process in the following manner:

> We can learn much about ourselves from the challenges that bring out our impatience, our bigotry, our lack of compassion, our need to control or to be a victim of circumstance, our ability to give and receive, and our ability to accept our own selves thus others. We are presented with an opportunity to realize what is really important, and that we are not perfect, and that we have a few issues of our own that we need to work on, or to better ourselves so that we may help others. *If we are impatient for example, we ask ourselves why are we so impatient, but we do not ask and answer the question ourselves. How can we answer the question, when we still think, and perceive as before. When we think and perceive a situation without change, nothing actually changes, so we must wait for the answer to present itself to us. This will come to us in many ways, but in that process changes will be taking place within us to ready us for the answer, and to be open to that answer. By doing so, we learn more about ourselves, and are more ready for the next stage in our jihad an nafs (struggle of the soul)!*

At times, the clash turns enmity to a new friendship, or the friendship blossoms. Other times, some obsess with their image and choose to remain where they are at and one has to decide to forgive, move on and wish them well.

What does reputation have to do with image?

Reputation is what people expect us to say or do. What you do when no one is looking is in reality your true reputation. Moreover, what you do or say to another, that no one will call you to account for, is also a reflection of your reputation.

A case in point is interfering in the private lives of others. When you interfere in the privacy and personal lives of others, your reputation is harmed, albeit with your own hands.

Prophet Muhammad, upon him peace and blessings said, "Verily, from the perfection of Islam is that a person leaves what does not concern him." And if we do not project, we engage in spying, false assumptions, and distort what we see and hear.

In a story regarding one of the righteous rulers, Umar ibn Al Khattab, it was reported that he spied on Muslims by entering their home without permission and caught them engaging in an activity not accepted by Islamic teachings. Umar accepted the reprimand by the Muslims that he engaged in three sins: entering the home without permission, spying, and not saying salaam or peace. In today's terminology this translates to violation of one's civil, privacy, and human rights.

Prophet Muhammad, upon him peace and blessings said, "Verily, if you seek out people's faults, you will corrupt them or almost corrupt them."

As much as we want to and like to rationalize spying on others for religious or security reasons, we must realize it does more harm than good. How one treats fellow human beings is a true reflection of their reputation.

Oppressors in essence are more obsessed with their image than being truly honorable before God. They can give advice, but unlike Umar, a truly honorable ruler before God, they cannot take it from others or in particular, from people they see as their inferiors. That is not honorable at all.

Transforming Anger

> *Who spend [in the cause of Allah] during ease and hardship and who restrain anger and who pardon the people - and Allah loves the doers of good[.]* (Quran 3:134)

The life of Martin Luther King, Jr. has important lessons about how to grapple with and direct our justified anger.

King did have big dreams. But he was never dreamy or in denial: He was focused, awake, and angry about the injustices inflicted on African Americans.

Yet he had to move beyond just being angry. He had to nurture himself and others to grapple with the reality of their pain. Although we focus on the legacy of King's "I Have a Dream" speech, his life was a journey toward growth and understanding, not a dream.

King had a particularly complex understanding of anger. He said, in a tribute to W.E.B. DuBois printed in Freedomways in 1968, he wrote that "there had developed beneath the surface a slow fire of discontent, fed by the continuing indignities and inequities to which the Negroes were subjected." He added that "the supreme task is to organize and unite people so that their anger becomes a transforming force."

This is a skill we can use with all of our angers: whether it's anger about Palestine, or about prison brutalities in the US, or about other injustices. Anger is only a starting point. After that, you have to say no to yourself.

Once we've recognized our anger, we need to balance it. It's important not to go to the extreme of abusive anger. We want to recognize that there are injustices taking place, but we also need to deal with these injustices in a way that will help us anchor one another.

After all, our anger is really about the oppression, not about those who are doing the oppressing. At times, we lose sight of that. Anger is not for the self or for the tribe. It needs a higher consciousness so that it can be directed against the institutions of war and injustice rather than against individuals. We should not use our anger to enable our abuse of others.

As Dr. King showed us: Acknowledge that there is anger, but call yourself out if your anger becomes abusive.

And, as to personal matters, King admonished himself, "You must not harbor anger."

Here, I'm talking about a kind of anger that flares up when a person's rights are transgressed by another or an interlocking system of people. This is when somebody transgresses your boundaries: when you're raped or abused, when your land is taken away, when there is systematic police violence, when you're stripped of your dignity.

Even in a situation like this, some people manage, by the grace of God, to deal with their anger gracefully and well. I have tremendous respect for such people. They know how to reason with themselves during times of anger. They have a strong sense of boundaries, which prevents them from harming others. They are in control of their emotions. These are qualities we need to seek in our leaders.

But some of us—myself included—need to strengthen ourselves when dealing with anger. Sometimes, I admonish myself with the wise words of others:

> Whoever holds back his anger, Allah will conceal his faults and whoever suppresses his fury while being able to execute it, Allah will fill his heart with satisfaction on the Day of Standing (Judgment).
>
> — Prophet Muhammad, upon him peace and blessings

> Temper is a weapon that we hold by the blade.
>
> — Sir James M Barrie

> Holding on to anger is like grasping a hot coal with the intent of throwing it at someone else; you are the one getting burned.
>
> — Buddha

> Anger: an acid that can do more harm to the vessel in which it is stored than to anything on which it is poured.
>
> — Seneca

> He who speaks with a sharp tongue cuts his own throat.
>
> — Unknown

> It only takes a spark, remember, to set off a forest fire.
>
> — James 3:5-5

What if someone is angry at us?

Often, when an individual or group recognizes and coalesces around their anger, they voice their pain and suffering to others through the lens of anger. We need to listen with empathy and decide whether there are grounds for that anger. Where is it coming from?

Nobody likes an angry person. It can be frightening or just unpleasant. Often, we don't want to hear the angry person; we just want to shut them out. But anger sometimes comes from hurt, pain, abuse, and transgressed boundaries. It's up to us to explore: Are there boundaries being transgressed? Sometimes, we're so comfortable with our privilege that we don't want to hear that it's transgressing the rights of another human being.

Other times, the person we see is not angry at all. At times, the lenses we look through encourage us to see others as angry. Maybe the person who seems angry isn't. Maybe we just don't want to see them in truth. There are some deep-seated prejudices that make people see an "angry black woman" or an "angry Arab" when a person might be expressing something else entirely.

But, if it really is anger, where do we go with it?

A Muslim counseling site once got the question below from a Muslim woman who was experiencing psychological abuse from her family, her husband, and her husband's family. She felt like a servant for her husband and her entire family. She wrote:

> I am feeling useless. And I hate everyone and everything. I pray to Allah but Allah doesn't listen to me. I don't know who to ask for help or where to go. I am not normal as I'm full of hate. My day starts with hate and ends with hate. It is destroying me. But I can't do anything.

This woman doesn't need closed doors, mental institutions, terror groups, or pills. She needs what Martin Luther King Jr. offered: to steer her anger in the right direction, into a transformative force.

The counselor, Abdul Lateef Abdullah, answered her, in part:

> You see people doing things that you cannot stand and it makes you angry, al hamdu Lillah (Praise God)! You recognize them as something that you do not want for yourself and for your loved ones. So, are you going to be just like them or are you going to be different? If you follow the path of hatred,

you will become just like them or worse ... You have been given a gift and that gift is awareness. You can see all the negatives and consequences of what everyone around you is doing. That is the most important first step that is required in order to transform, and without it, transformation is impossible. So, what are you going to do with this gift?

God, after all, isn't some giant slot machine. You can't put in your coin and expect a jackpot. God doesn't exist to respond to our demands.

We are the ones who must make the first move. God says in the Quran that He will only change our external conditions if we change our internal conditions first. We have been given the gift of free will, here in this life, so we can make choices.

Abdul Lateef Abdullah tells the woman to stop hating because it is destroying her. The first place any change must happen is in the heart. First, we must turn to God with a pure heart before we can hope to help those around us enact change. She doesn't need to wait for anyone else: She, like all of us, needs to take the first step, because she's the one who's been given the gift of awareness and insight.

To continue to simply live in rejection of what is happening is denial. Accept it, try to understand it, and then try to change it.

Once we have surrendered ourselves, and accepted things as they are around us, then it's time to start over. We have to stop seeing things not as we want them to be, but as they are. We need to seek knowledge and insight so that we can understand what is happening around us. Start living life for the sake of knowing, worshipping, and serving our Creator, and thus start fulfilling our life's purpose and potential.

Hatred will destroy us. Once we have made another choice, to embrace God and the reality of the situation around us, then we will recognize that we do have choices.

Instead of turning anger into corrosive hatred, anger has to be a way to organize the community and the self. We have to challenge the injustices that we're facing together.

What I like about Abdul Lateef Abdullah's response is that he is not condemning her—he's telling her to do something about her situation. She can't just close her eyes and make it stop. These injustices actually are happening. From this point of recognition, she now has to figure out a healthy way to set boundaries so she can push the people who are transgressing her rights back within their boundaries.

And so it is with anger: We must let it be a stimulus to promote growth in ourselves and those around us.

Journaling and the Quran

Until what remains unspoken is written, the wound that determines your whole life will never heal.

— Hwaa Irfan

The tools of psychology and the tools of spirituality often work together, and, when we fit them in our hands, we see they are the same tools.

Keeping a journal can help us see ourselves, come closer to God, and read the Quran. I began writing a journal in 2000. Separating ourselves from the immediacy of our thoughts and feelings can help us take a step back and see ourselves more clearly. A journal doesn't have to be written in daily, but it does need to be as honest as we can make it. This journal is only between the writer and God.

An honest journal helps us not only in understanding ourselves, but also in understanding the voices of the prophets, upon them peace and blessings, and the Quran. As you look at your journal and the Quran, you can better see the parallels and develop your awareness.

Deny it or turn it into art

Once you have been wounded—as all of us have been who live on this earth—you have to make a choice. Some people choose to deny and suppress their wounds. Others turn them into art.

This art doesn't have to be a performance for others; it can be instead a private art of writing. Most of all, writing a journal helps you not to suppress or deny your emotions. An excellent way to begin is by coming up with questions. What's important isn't to answer the questions, but to focus on the questions themselves.

Later, you can bring this questioning self to reading the Quran. Then, as you read, you're not engaged in rationalizing, but instead you're open to what's in front of you in an honest way. In this state, when you're reading the Quran, you can find yourself inside the Book's other voices.

You may be in a situation where you think you're right, and think you have everything under control. But once you write it all down, you might realize you have questions. You can bring the openness of these questions to reading the Quran.

The inner voice

We shouldn't assume to know another person's internal reality. After all, we're not telepathic! Only God knows our internal realities, and, unless we are paying close attention, our internal realities can be blocked even from our own sight. But if we're not repressing our realities, and we're working hard to journal honestly, then a healer can help us respond to our internal stories.

Once, a man came to Prophet Muhammad, upon him peace and blessings, and asked whether, if someone committed murder, would they be forgiven? The Prophet answered, "No."

Yet another person came to Prophet Muhammad, upon him peace and blessings, and asked if someone committed murder, would they be forgiven? The Prophet answered, "Yes."

What matters here is the person's internal story, which a good healer can be alive to. The first man was seeking a green light to murder, while the second had made a grave error and was working toward repentance and repairing the harm he had created.

What matters here is to understand the inside story. That's what a journal helps us do, and we can bring that to a healer to help us move forward, repent, and heal our lives.

Journaling and positivity

In logging the moments of our life, sometimes we find ourselves backsliding: committing the same wrongs, feeling the same pain. This can cause a person to feel depressed. That's why it's just as important to have moments when we also log our blessings, our gifts, and our strengths. Don't allow yourself to only journal the negative! If you also focus on blessings and gratitude, it will help you continue on the road of healing and growth. It will help you to accept your imperfections as well as your weaknesses, and to avoid falling into the trap of self-hatred.

But, as we go, we also need to beware false gratitude.

False gratitude is when we're saying all the right words, but we don't really believe it. True gratitude is shown by Prophet Solomon, who smiled with a gentle, warm gratitude when he came across the troubles of ants.

At length, when they came to a (lowly) valley of ants, one of the ants said: "O ye ants get into your habitations, lest Solomon and his hosts crush you (under foot) without knowing it." So he smiled, amused at her speech; and he said: "O my Lord! so enable me that I may be grateful for Thy favors which Thou hast bestowed on me and on my parents and that I may work the righteousness that will please you: and admit me by your Grace, to the ranks of your righteous Servants."

Prophet Solomon wasn't looking down on the ants, and he wasn't intoxicated by promoting an image of gratitude. He was genuinely and cheerfully grateful for what he had.

False gratitude is when we look down on others who might be deprived of what we have and pump ourselves up with the feeling of "gratitude," as though our gifts mean we are better than others. We must always recognize these gifts come by the grace of God.

If you see somebody who's not so smart, you don't ridicule them. Intelligence is a blessing, a gift from God. When you see someone deprived of what you've been given, rather than looking down on them, we should feel grateful, and we should ask God to enable us to use the gift in a way that pleases Him.

RE-FRAMING THE WHY

I pointed out to you the stars and the moon and all you saw was the tip of my finger.

— Tanzanian Proverb

When I have given talks about Islam to audiences in the United States, I've been asked some of the same questions again and again. It's not just me: Many Muslim speakers have been deluged with the same roster of questions. Many of these are not questions—not if we define a question as an indication of a real desire to learn. Instead, these are fearful accusations.

Five of these so-called questions that I hear most often:

Why aren't Muslims condemning terrorism?
Why are women oppressed?
Why isn't there liberty or free speech among Muslims?
Why does the Quran promote violence and hatred?
Does Islam want to take over America?

None of these questions can be addressed directly without talking about the assumptions that generate them. As to the first, if the questioner were sincere, then a simple google search would clarify the point.

In the second, we can talk candidly about women's rights and roles in any society. But often those who frame the question in this way are treating Muslim women like a museum artifact, particularly when asking us to explain why many wear a hijab. In much the same way, people might ask a Sikh about his turban. If asked in innocence, there is nothing really wrong with the question. But there is the underlying assumption that the Sikh must prove his humanity, must explain or justify his sartorial decisions to the disapproving majority.

The third question, about liberty and free speech, assumes that Muslims are one big monolithic group and that they follow one leader, whether this is Khomeini, Nasrallah, Osama bin Laden, or the goons of ISIS. The last two assume that there is a sentient creature called "Islam" that not only promotes violence and hatred, but is plotting to take over a nation.

As I fielded these questions, at first I thought they were coming only from a fringe group, and that they could be safely disregarded. But these questions also come from the mouths of otherwise moderate and thoughtful Americans. Thus, rather than getting into the details of these questions, we need to fix the frame.

When answering these questions, we could give facts and evidence. But facts and evidence will only take us so far: as has been discussed elsewhere, all of us have a "confirmation bias" toward what we already believe. Often, we are unable to listen to facts that contradict our beliefs.

The more I have waded into answering these questions, the more I feel you can't always target the person who's asking. Instead, you have to target the people who are around them.

I'll add that it is important to reach these people. These questions aren't coming from the fringe, and we can't just be speaking to people who invite us, treat us nicely, and look at the facts. We also need to speak to the crowd that's insecure.

How to do it?

First, it's important not to respond to an "us and them" question with an "us and them answer." Just as Muslims aren't one big group, neither are Christians, atheists, Buddhists, Jews, or any other collection of humanity. Even Islamophobes aren't an undifferentiated group.

As for where to go next with these questions, it depends on the audience. At times, you can tell that the person asking the question is troubled, and you have to use compassion. They may well be someone who wants attention.

In one case, I encountered a woman who was full of angry questions. I sat down with her, and we talked for a while. Afterwards, she thanked me, that was when I realized that she'd really just been afraid of Muslims, who she'd been taught to fear. I came across another man who was simply confused. When a person is being deluged with all the nonstop nonsense that comes from talk radio, it's understandable. So there are people, like these two, who will be changed just by sitting with Muslims and engaging in conversation, particularly if the root of their angry questions is confusion and fear.

At other times, as with someone who is highly educated, it may be that the person wants to see the Muslim community as inferior for one reason or another. In most of these cases, neither sitting with them nor the facts will help.

In this situation, one of the best ways to approach a questioner is to help them see themselves. It's usually not helpful to go tit for tat, as Muslims or scholars of Islam sometimes do in conversation with people like Richard Dawkins. This is bound to go nowhere, only allowing everyone to flex their argumentative muscles.

There is also another sort of person who "misunderstands" Islam, particularly an opportunistic lawmaker, and this sort needs to be fought against. In this case, it's best to find allies in an effort to marginalize them and their unethical behavior. This is when it's important to have many groups helping to push this person to the sidelines, to portray them as someone who's hateful, and to reveal them for who they are. It's particularly important to have allies who come from the opportunist's community, and not to make it a situation of "us vs. them."

We found just such a situation in the rise of Republican presidential candidate Donald Trump, who wasn't ignorant, fearful, confused, or needing compassion. He was a person making mischief here on earth, and we must come together to prevent such people from getting into power.

Certainly, we don't want to harm the mischief-makers, and we don't want to act out of rancor or hatred! When you treat your enemy the way they treated you, you're not helping society in any way. Instead, we need to promote stability and the rule of law.

While such people promote division and hate, we need to promote unity.

Moving Beyond Confirmation Bias

This is life. For good or for ill, we generate these incredible stories about the world around us and then the world turns around and astonishes us...Look out at the vastness and complexity and mystery of the universe and be able to say, wow I don't know, maybe I am wrong.

— Kathyrn Schulz

Sometimes, one of the most important ways of turning to God is accepting there are things we don't know.

At one point in his life, the scholar Shaykh Ramadan al Buti exerted himself, and exerted himself, but he still couldn't understand a text he was reading by the scholar Ibn Ata Allah. He badly wanted to know what the author had meant. But instead of jumping to conclusions, giving up, or seeing the text as he wanted to see it, Shaykh al Buti prayed that God would inspire his understanding.

As part of his effort, Shaykh al Buti even visited Shaykh Ibn Ata Allah's grave in Cairo and prayed. Then, just like that, it came to him. Instead of blundering ahead of his understanding, or papering over what he didn't grasp, Shaykh al Buti turned to God.

The world is enormous. Even though humanity has discovered many things in the last few millennia, there are still just as many things we don't know. When we are confronted with something we honestly don't know, we can go two different ways. We can either try to rationalize, putting an intellectual wrapper on our misunderstanding, and making it fit with what we already believe. Or we can open our hearts to God's wisdom and light, turning in to God to say I don't know before we turn outward to say, but I want to understand, as we remain open to God's inspiration and understanding.

God is very generous and very near. If we really want to understand that which we don't know, we shouldn't try to box up the people around us. That's how stereotypes and misunderstandings are created. Instead, we should remain open to our lack of perfect knowledge, and open to God's gift of understanding.

Against confirmation bias, toward leadership

When something new and different appears before us, we can't simply know what it is with the tools already at our disposal. We have to research and learn new things in order to understand them. One role model in this is Bilqis, who was ruler over a nation called Saba' and had great wealth and power before she had heard the news about Islam.

Prophet Solomon, upon him peace, sent her a letter, urging her to accept Islam—about which, at that point, she knew nothing. But instead of likening Islam to sun worship or something else she already understood, Bilqis kept her mind open. She consulted, engaged, sought advice, and verified her hypotheses by talking to Solomon.

When he first entered her city, Bilqis was biased against him, because she'd previously had a bad experience with kings. But instead of simply assuming he was a king like other kings she had met, Bilqis listened to the evidence as it was presented before making up her mind.

A more recent example of this is that of New Zealand Prime Minister Jacinda Ardern, whose country was rocked by a terror attack on the Muslim community in March 2019. Instead of assuming she already knew what to do or calling for more of the same "thoughts and prayers," Ardern opened herself to advice, reached out to listen to people, and was a leader who was open to her community. Like Bilqis, Ardern was a leader with wisdom in a time of crisis, and she rose in the eyes of both men and women, Muslims and others, across the world.

Confirmation bias, confirming bias

Others recently leapt on the bandwagon of assuming—either in reality or for political gain—that Rep. Ilhan Omar must be anti-Semitic because she has criticized Israel. Rather than opening themselves up to her words and taking advice, they immediately jumped to a conclusion that supports their privilege.

There is another story in the Quran that talks about confirmation bias. Here, instead of believing a rich and privileged man was in the right—the man with 99 ewes—David opened himself to listening, and he sided with the man who had a single ewe.

> Has the Story of the Disputants reached thee? Behold, they climbed over the wall of the private chamber; When they entered the presence of David, and he was terrified of them, they said: "Fear not: we are two disputants, one of whom has wronged the other: Decide now between us with truth, and treat us not with injustice, but guide us to the even Path.. This man is my brother: He has nine and ninety ewes, and I have (but) one: Yet he says, 'commit her to my care,' and is (moreover) harsh to me in speech." (David) said: "He has undoubtedly wronged thee in demanding thy (single) ewe to be added to his (flock of) ewes: truly many are the partners (in business) who wrong each other: Not so do those who believe and work deeds of righteousness, and how few are they?"... and David gathered that We had tried him: he asked forgiveness of his Lord, fell down, bowing (in prostration), and turned (to Allah in repentance). So We forgave him this (lapse): he enjoyed, indeed, a Near Approach to Us, and a

beautiful place of (Final) Return. "O David! We did indeed make thee a vicegerent on earth: so judge thou between men in truth (and justice): Nor follow thou the lusts (of thy heart), for they will mislead thee from the Path of Allah." Indeed, those who go astray from the way of Allah will have a severe punishment for having forgotten the Day of Account. (Quran 38:21-26)

Often, we side with the powerful, the rich, those who look like us, and those who come from the same place as us, because this supports our biases. It is only normal to have biases. But instead of accepting our biases, we need to turn inward and turn to God, waiting and listening, leaving ourselves open to truly hear. God intervened between Prophet David, upon him peace, and his heart. The Prophets are divinely protected from sin, and as soon as a thought not pleasing to God emerges, it is repelled immediately by God. God clears Prophet David, upon him peace, from false accusations that circulate about him in other religious traditions. His rank remains of those near God. Likewise, when our hearts are pure, we will experience the intervention of God when our hearts are invited to disobey.

WHY STUDY ISLAM?

Not to know is bad; not to wish to know is worse.

— Nigerian Proverb

Shaykh Qays Arthur is not the man many Americans have in mind when they think of a "Muslim shaykh."

Arthur was born in the small South American nation of Guyana, which is wedged between Venezuela and Suriname. He's now in his mid-thirties and comes from an "essentially Catholic background," he says. But now, he "studies and teaches Islam in Jordan and is passionate about God, His final Prophet Muhammad, His other prophets (peace be upon them all), the Sahaba (companions of Prophet Muhammad), and Muslims in general and Arabs in particular."

Arthur has much to teach a serious student of Islam, but why should we bother to learn? After all, there are so many things to learn about in this world: quantum entanglement, the history of Suriname, the science of climate change.

Studying Islam may not be for everyone—just as studying quantum entanglement might not be for everyone. But those who are going to appear on talk shows to talk about quantum entanglement, or write editorials suggesting quantum-entanglement policy, or even tweet, should ground their comments in a serious study.

Islam, like quantum entanglement or the history of Suriname, can't be understood at a single grasp. It requires serious study. An honest study of the religion should force us to consider the call of the message, asking ourselves whether it is indeed a true invitation from God to humanity. We should not just study it as a phenomenon.

This is not to say you shouldn't criticize Islam. But if we don't study Islam, then how can we have integrity in our critique of Muslims? For hundreds of years, there has been nonstop Western criticism of

Islam, almost always divorced from any serious knowledge or study. This nonstop criticism of Islam and Muslim communities has the effect of dehumanizing Muslims.

Richard Dawkins, for instance, wants to criticize Islam. But his criticisms lack serious understanding.

Islam, like many of the sciences Dawkins studies, cannot be understood by looking only at the surface level. It needs to be understood from several perspectives, including the spiritual. And if you are going to criticize something, the ethical thing to do is to call yourself to account to study it.

Those who want to know what's going on with Islam—who want to criticize or to comment—should first seek to study. Muslims, for our part, should be open to those who want to learn. After all, once you promote the study of any field, you're opening the doors for ethical people to engage in the conversation.

Shaykh Qays Arthur is in a unique position to give us insight into Islam, which he will do later in this book. That's because Arthur is looking at Islam through multiple lenses. First, he is of a Christian background who became a Muslim, which means he sees the connective tissue between the religions, as mentioned earlier.

For myself, I sometimes give public presentations on the prophets, and people are sometimes alarmed to learn that we also believe in Adam and Moses! I get emails from readers, saying that these are not my prophets. Many American Christians are not aware that we're connected at that level.

Among Arab Christians, there is generally a connection to the other "People of the Book." When I speak to Palestinian Christians, we can relate on matters of religion. But with a Western Christian, it's like I've just arrived from Pluto. Or they might speak to me like I'm an artifact in a museum.

There are certainly both similarities and differences between Christianity and Islam. But beginning that conversation is very difficult, because, in most people's minds, Muslims are complete aliens. The first step to learning about Islam is to understand how we can connect the big monotheistic religions.

What Do We Mean When We Talk About Faith?

The dwellers of the desert say: We believe. Say: You do not believe but say, We submit; and faith has not yet entered into your hearts; and if you obey Allah and His Messenger, He will not diminish aught of your deeds; surely Allah is Forgiving, Merciful. (Quran 49:14)

What is faith? It's not something we can see draped around someone else's shoulders, or reflected in their eyes.

None among us can perceive the shape or quality of another person's faith. This quality—faith—is invisible to all but God. Although sometimes, if we look hard in the mirror, we can see the light of our own faith.

We humans have a tendency to take things, including faith, for granted. Although we can't see or judge another person's faith, one of the things we can do for each other is to encourage questions. We can't measure the faith of others, but we can put together questions about it, and we can take a good look at our own heart.

Faith, I believe, is an invitation

God created Adam and Eve, and it was God's will to bring them to earth. When they neglected or forgot God's instructions, this was not a major sin. It's true, they forgot to show resolve and be mindful of God's commands. But the Adam and Eve story is less about sin and more a demonstration of God's mercy and love.

After all, as the poet Khalil Gibran has said, only in the time of separation does love know its depth. When Adam and Eve were separated from God, that's when they discovered their love, and so they returned to God, seeking mercy and forgiveness.

Satan, too, knows that God exists. Satan, too, was separated from God. Satan was asked to surrender to God's reality and majesty, and he was given an invitation to come back on God's terms. Yet Satan wanted to go back based on a partnership with God. That's how some of us humans also worship God. It's a form of belief that's not faith. It says: I worship you, now you owe me.

We worship God, yes. But God has no needs. This worship is meant as a gift, and we're meant to simply receive it.

All three—Adam, Eve, and Satan—were tested with a separation from God. How do we know that Adam and Eve have discovered faith?

Unlike Satan, after Adam was removed from Heaven, he returned to God asking for mercy. That's an indication of faith, and a recognition of the neediness to God. It is also a recognition that he takes responsibility for his actions. Instead of saying, "Satan made me do it," Adam looked to himself: He had stumbled, and he wanted to right himself. Faith is a recognition of our faults and the mistakes we have made.

How can we know our faith?

Faith is not a set of axioms. It cannot be measured on a stick; it is, instead, a light in the heart. It's a light we feel most when we're tested with loss.

When a person is comfortable, they can say quite easily: "God loves me!" Then, when God tries them with loss, they might make a 180-degree turn and say: "God humiliated me."

That's a lack of faith. In doing that, we place God under conditions, treating God as our servant. In the words of Shaykh Qays Arthur: "When that majesty of the Divine becomes lost on us due to our own perceived self-importance such that we think it is God who must come to us, pursue us, and serve us; that is the root of disbelief, extremism, and misguidance."

If someone has faith, it manifests not as pride in what God has given us, but in an acknowledgment that our accomplishments are not our own. When Solomon faced the queen of the ants, he didn't feel pride in his own stature. Neither did he crush her beneath his feet. He was at first bemused by her selflessness, and by how worried she was for her own kind. Next, he saw the many gifts that God had given him, and how this made him responsible to others who did not have his size or power.

Faith means that, when God gives you something, you see your responsibility. You see that it's a trust, and you see your accountability. What you owe to the world around you cannot be paid simply in lip service, but instead must be paid in action. In Shaikh Qays Arthur's eloquent words: "So faith is an act of the heart, yet it must be manifested in works."

The person who has no faith is filled with pride. If given something, they would not turn to others with aid. Guidance and faith are gifts, and we must respond with gratitude, not with a belief that God is indebted to us. In faith, we turn to God for guidance in any situation, even when we're happy.

But that's for those of us who are being showered with gifts. If we're deprived, God tests us in other ways. Then, too, we must have faith, as the Quran shows in many stories. When we're deprived, we must show patience. And, even when we're deprived, we can use what's available to worship God. What we mustn't do is turn to despair and blame God.

Even if we stumble, or feel our faith waning, we must not despair. Having faith doesn't mean immediate perfection! Recognizing the darkness within us is also faith. What we must fear is turning away from our mirror. Faith fades when a person persists, over time, in failing to take responsibility for their actions, and in projecting and blaming everyone and anyone else, particularly God.

How can we regain our faith?

Faith is not an entirely steady thing. Sometimes, it can be chipped away. To return it to our hearts, we can start out by turning to God. There are prayers for asking God to increase one in faith, just as there are prayers against all the diseases of the heart. If you find that you're struggling with faith and want to increase it, there are verses in the Quran to ask for guidance. That's why we pray five times a day: In the prayer, we can seek guidance.

But it's important, when we look in the mirror, to know that we can never measure the faith of another. Nor do we have the right to condemn another human being. That's something in the hands and power of God. While we uphold the laws and rules around us, none of us has the right to condemn another person.

A person could seem to be practicing their faith very well, almost nonstop, but that doesn't mean they have a "one-way ticket to heaven." That's a reality that only God knows. For those of us on earth, we're always meant to feel midway between fear and hope, with a light in our hearts, always in a state of seeking forgiveness. That's faith.

One of the ways that God describes the faithful is that, before dawn, they wake and seek forgiveness for their sins. The faithful aren't thinking about other people's sins, or ways to punish others. Instead, they're thinking about their own. They also recognize that we humans are needy. None of us are superwoman or superman.

As Abraham once said to Nimrod, who thought he was a very powerful man: If you are so, can you make the sun rise from the west? All of us are contingent, part of the rest of God's universe.

As Shaykh Qays Arthur has said: "Faith is not a right, nor an earned merit; it is a special favor from God. The believers seek it from Him and seek its increase from Him and guard it out of gratitude, and are more concerned about losing it than they are about guarding and losing wealth and treasures."

We should never assume that we're either saved or damned, falling into either self-righteousness or great despair. It's important never to condemn ourselves. If we've made a mistake, it's because we're human! Faith is turning to God and figuring out how to repair the harm.

Faith is not a uniform

Just as there are many individual humans, there are many levels of faith. There is the certainty of the elect, who worship God as though they see Him. But of course not all can have that certainty. Many struggle with their convictions, and this doesn't mean they aren't Muslim. It only means there are different stages and manifestations of faith.

What's important is that faith can't be a show for ourselves or for others.

In the Holy Quran, the last verse of al Baqara chapter, Allah Most High says: "Allah does not tax any soul but what it can bear[.]"

We all face difficulties in life – at home, at the job, family, to personal issues, and in our communities. Our reaction to problems reveals who we are and shows our real character. Problems and difficulties come into our life like mirrors to help us see our true selves. Do you see scheming, unwarranted cunning, deception, or slander? Or do you see prophetic qualities like repentance, honesty, truthfulness, and wisdom?

Faith invites us to wisdom and problem-solving, which requires practice and knowledge. It is a know-how, a skill that is learned and acquired based on the Quran and Sunnah or the sayings and actions of Prophet Muhammad, upon him peace and blessings, practiced throughout Islamic history.

In studying Islam, we begin to read the Quran and we fall in love with the Prophets, but first and foremost with God. We cannot see them, but we have their thoughts, their words, and their actions, which are a window into their hearts and souls. We step through the door of our faith in order to get to know God, and to get to know ourselves at a deeper level.

ADAM: LESSONS ON REPENTANCE AND FORGIVENESS

That is the Knower of the unseen and the witnessed, the Exalted in Might, the Merciful, Who perfected everything which He created and began the creation of man from clay. Then He made his posterity out of the extract of a liquid disdained. Then He proportioned him and breathed into him from His [created] soul and made for you hearing and vision and hearts; little are you grateful. (Quran 32:6-9)

The Awakener, the Resurrector, the Arouser, the Dispatcher

Does man not consider that We created him from a [mere] sperm-drop - then at once he is a clear adversary? And he presents for Us an example and forgets his [own] creation. He says, "Who will give life to bones while they are disintegrated?" Say, "He will give them life who produced them the first time; and He is, of all creation, Knowing." (Quran 36:77-79)

When we say that God is al-Ba'ith, we mean that God calls us forth and awakens us; God raises us from sleep or death; God resurrects us.

God calls us to be spiritually alive and awake, and to bring this light to others. Being spiritually alive means being aware of God's presence such that, even though you don't see Him, God sees you.

Al-Ba'ith means we are alive to God and fostering the Divine breath within ourselves. When we keep this connection awake, we can coexist with nature and also with each other. When we don't, then we can become toxic to ourselves, others, and even to the planet.

This consciousness of God is not shame—we are not ashamed because God knows us. Instead, we are alive and awake. We know that we will be judged one day, but this does not make us ashamed. Instead, it keeps us alert to ourselves and others. Those who are not conscious of God act as though no one is going to call them to account. Being aware of God means being aware that we will face a Day of Judgment. It means being connected to your soul.

One thing that reminds us of this state of awakeness is the Chernobyl disaster. There is a documentary about the nuclear containment zone called "Radioactive Wolves" that shows the containment zone, where people have been barred since the 1986 nuclear accident. Although it was turned into a "dead zone" for humans, the documentary shows the different species that thrive there. In the end, we see how toxic humans can be and how, if we are not in touch with the Divine, we can be more toxic than nuclear waste.

This is just one of the ways in which we can use science as a lens to help us apprehend God.

Science as mischief, science as a lens on God

In our times, science is sometimes used to undermine faith. Some even suggest that there's a "clash" between science and faith. But as with other so-called binary "clashes" (East and West, Islam and Christianity), this is false. Just as we can use science to learn new things about our world, we can also use it to bear witness to God.

Science is also sometimes used by hucksters who want to play with people's minds, as hucksters have always operated throughout human history. In Moses's time, so-called magic was used to manipulate people. For that reason, God sent Moses to truly turn a staff into a living snake, so that people would see that what these so-called magicians were doing was false.

In Abraham's time, people were manipulated with idols. He destroyed idols, and the people saw this caused him no harm. Just so, during Jesus's time, people put their trust in snake-oil treatments. Jesus instead brought them faith, and real healing.

In each of these cases, false gods sought to profit off the backs of the marginalized and oppressed. But God turned it around and used what people cherished as medicine to bring forth the truth.

In our own time, science and technology are the social currency of the day; we're living in a day and age where we want to touch, measure, and feel things before we believe. Science is absolutely something we need, and yet it also can be manipulated.

If we open our eyes, we'll find that God is manifesting His signs, reality, attributes through science. This can help us bear witness that indeed there is a Day of Judgment, indeed there was a pre-eternal realm. We can see things like Chernobyl that help us reflect on the truth of the verses in the Quran.

We certainly shouldn't turn away from science or knowledge! We come more to life through knowledge and through seeking it. Science and the Quran both encourage knowledge, as ignorance is harmful. But although science is a way to know God, we can't use it to replace God or to undermine faith. We need science, but we also need to embrace it with humility.

What does Chernobyl tell us?

Before Adam, there were human-like beings on Earth who did mischief and shed blood. These beings lacked the most important thing we humans have: the Divine breath. The angels waged war on these early beings and cleansed the earth, which was rejuvenated just as Chernobyl was. These beings were toxic, just as we can be toxic if we're not in touch with the Divine within us.

In the Quran, after God has asked the angels to cleanse the Earth, He says:

> Behold, thy Lord said to the angels: "I will create a vicegerent on earth." They said: "Wilt Thou place therein one who will make mischief therein and shed blood?- whilst we do celebrate Thy praises and glorify Thy holy (name)?" He said: "I know what ye know not." (Quran 2:30)

God brought Adam to Earth, and it was a dead place, like Chernobyl. Just so, when we become divorced from God's presence and His attribute of al-Ba'ith, then we can cause major damage to the earth and to each other.

There are many other scientific realities—our ability to communicate with animals, for instance—that help us see God and God's truths more clearly. Yet science cannot be a substitute for faith; it is, instead, a lens to help us see.

And as we see, so we should help others:

> Whoever revives himself from the death of ignorance into the life of knowledge, or whoever helps another to be reborn into knowledge from the dark tomb of ignorance, will then see the manifestation of al-Ba'ith and truly believe it.
>
> —From *The Name & the Named* by Shaykh Tosun Bayrak al-Jerrahi al-Halveti

Ignorance is a disease, and its consequences are many. The powerful and the hucksters can take advantage of ignorance and use them to create an ever-more-toxic world. We are obligated to gain knowledge, and to spread the knowledge we have, to protect ourselves and our world from snake-oil treatments, magic, and false applications of science.

Of Adam, Eve, Satan, and Angels

> *Abu Huraira, a companion of the Prophet, narrated, "Adam and Moses argued with each other. Moses said to Adam. 'O Adam! You are our father who disappointed us and turned us out of Paradise.' Then Adam said to him, 'O Moses! Allah favored you with His talk (talked to you directly) and He wrote (the Torah) for you with His Own Hand. Do you blame me for action which Allah had written in my fate forty years before my creation?' So Adam confuted Moses, Adam confuted Moses," the Prophet added, repeating the Statement three times.*
>
> — Sahih Bukhari Hadith No. 6614

As I said in the last chapter, the Quran tells us that in the time before Adam, there was another species much like people, and they were also made of mud. But there was one essential difference between this species and ours: Although we're both made of mud, these creatures were not enlivened by God's divine breath before going to walk upon the earth.

These people—who were not quite people, but had only our baser characteristics—slaughtered and abused each other without stopping. This species showed nothing in their behavior but corruption and violence, and eventually God sent angels and a djinn named Iblis, or Satan, to clear the earth of their corruption. Satan was among those chosen for the job, as he was a djinn of renowned devotion and ability. Satan was a showcase of faith and knowledge, although he had no true or humble faith.

And so the angels and Satan cleared the earth of this first corruption.

"When that task was finished, Satan's heart swerved as a sense of accomplishment gave way to an astounding arrogance," Shaykh Qays Arthur told me, speaking of this moment. "Satan, in his arrogance, felt that rank belonged to him after all that he had accomplished. He felt a sense of entitlement."

After doing all this, Satan wanted to be put in control of all the earth.

Satan was not one of the angels, the Quran tells us. Instead, he was one of the djinn, another self-aware species. The djinn are made of smokeless fire, and they can travel in the same ways angels can, slipping between earth and the different realms of heaven. Both angels and djinn were made by God's command: Be.

But djinn are unlike angels in an important way: The djinn have free will. Angels are creatures of light who can only appreciate God and do His bidding, appreciating His power and majesty. But djinn are like us: They can choose to be good and live up to their values, or to do evil.

Satan was a powerful djinn, a creature of smokeless fire invisible to human eyes, who felt he'd done God a tremendous favor when he cleared the earth of corruption. Satan took great pride in his gifts. Although he appreciated God's majesty, he did not have any regard for God's love or mercy. Instead, he wanted God's power for himself. When Satan discovered God had made another species of "mud people," in the form of Adam and Eve, he was scornful.

These "mud people," the first of whom were Adam and Eve, were not like the earlier mud people. Although both species shared the same material, and they had some of the same instincts toward venality and violence, there was a key difference. This was the breath God gave our species, which gifts us the possibility of gratitude, love, generosity, mercy, and the ability to repent our wrongs: all of our better traits. The moment the divine breath entered Adam, he said, "Thanks be to God." This shows how gratitude had already made a home inside him.

Both the djinn and the angels were surprised when God asked them to prostrate themselves before Adam, upon him peace, as the rank of the prophets is above that of the Angels.

At first, even the angels scorned Adam and Eve, and they were surprised by God's command. The angels saw these new creatures as the same as the first mud people. After all, we had many of the same attributes of these earlier creatures. Yet the angels didn't challenge God. Instead, they asked Him: Why is Adam being given such a powerful station? Why should we bow before him? The Angels asked about Adam before they were commanded to prostrate towards him. Once the command was given, they immediately fell prostrate.

The angels, unlike Satan, didn't debate this issue. They asked, and He explained that He knew things they did not. God explained to the angels that Adam and Eve were learning creatures, who would be able to develop and nurture themselves and advance.

So the angels accepted this, and they said: Glory be to You, we only know what You taught us.

The angels realized their mission was to anchor Adam and Eve, and to remind humans of their values and their mission. They did not question this, but rather surrendered to it. This is when God showed them the beauty of Adam and Eve, who were able to learn things and know God at a very intimate level. Unlike the angels, who only knew the power and majesty of God, Adam and Eve would be able to know God as a forgiving God, as a merciful God, and as a loving God.

And the angels glorified God.

Satan cannot be moved

Satan, however, was not flexible. He would not listen or admit what was before his eyes, and he could not be budged in his opinion of Adam. Satan believed he knew better than God, and he debated the point without ceasing. In the end, he refused to prostrate before this new creation. He held up his head and said he was better than Adam.

At this point, Satan was truly a "disbeliever," which means a being who refuses to admit of a truth they know, living so as to deceive themselves and others. Despite his knowledge of God's truth, he refused to submit because of his sense of entitlement. Satan did not go so far as to say that the fire from which he was made was greater than the divine breath. However, he did say that "fire is better than mud."

In his disbelief, Satan didn't simply make a mistake. He lied to himself, to God, and to all the world around. He believed, overwhelmingly, that he'd earned a station with God, and that God was indebted to him. Because of his arrogance, knowledge, and power, Satan became the world's arch-deceiver. He became the world's most pathological liar, who twists and distorts in order to fit his own will.

Satan was always thus, certainly. But this conflict brought it out.

Before it, Satan had an outward "showcase of faith," and this brought him both self-satisfaction and a sense of entitlement. Satan worshiped God and felt a sense of success and power, which allowed self-deception to creep into his smoke-and-fire heart. Many Sufis say you either worship God with a gaze toward Him or a gaze toward your ego. Satan was always gazing at his ego. He was not really worshiping God, but using his relationship with God for power and prestige.

After this willful disbelief, this refusal to admit the facts of the world, Satan didn't once think of asking God's forgiveness. Instead, he blamed God for his own disobedience and vowed to attack Adam from all sides to make him go astray. Why did I purge earth of corruption, Satan asked, if God was so determined to allow Adam and Eve, and all of their muddy progeny, to sow discord and evil until the Day of Judgment? After Satan refused to prostrate himself, he asked only for power—the power to tempt Adam and Eve, and to prove God was wrong, until Judgment Day.

When making this request, Satan called God by his names of power. He threw down this gauntlet as though calling God to a duel. He wanted to show he had more knowledge than God, that he had more wisdom than God. Also, if Satan was going to be banned from heaven, then—he decided—he was surely going to take Adam and Eve with him.

God granted Satan's request, although God didn't leave Adam and Eve unprotected. God told them Satan was an enemy who had vowed to bring them down. Satan is an enemy to you, God told them. Do not admire him.

From that point, Satan embodied the sin of pathological lying. He is much like a person who reaches a certain stage of lying, when they can't turn back, and continually keeps lying. Like other liars, he dragged others down with him.

Whispering the breath of evil

We on earth absorb the social ills from the world around us. These ills have an impact on our hearts, and from there, we begin having venal and vicious thoughts. As a djinn, Satan has powers humans do not, but he cannot force us to act. His power over us is to call. Satan can notice when we're likely to be weak, and he can whisper his suggestions.

Of course, Satan doesn't come right up and say: "Hello, good morning, it's time to disobey God!" He has slippery and deceptive tactics to sway us against our values, and he uses our despair and self-hatred.

For that reason, we must be mindful when venal and vicious thoughts enter our minds, and we must repel them immediately. Or, if we do act upon these thoughts, we should repent as soon as we can, as this is one of our great gifts. The mere remembrance of God drives Satan away.

In his tactics, Satan is like those people who use religion, knowledge, and charisma to control and overpower others, knowing that they're doing wrong.

It's important, as this moment, to remember we can't judge the whole world of the djinn, just as we can't judge any things in a realm we cannot see or touch. God commands us to stay away from djinn, and not concern ourselves with their world. They're a set of beings that God alone will judge. They have free choice and suffer from the results of their choices, but they are not tainted by their association with Satan. Each must be judged on their own merits and defects. Like us, they're judged by their own choices.

Adam and Eve were told to concern themselves with their own lives and choices, and to live up to their best selves, for themselves and for their communities. After all, they could do all this with the help of God's divine breath. The divine breath connects us to God and allows us to know God intimately. The divine breath opens the door to knowledge of ourselves, which helps us live up to our values and to receive the many gifts God will shower upon us.

Fall and repentance

Could Satan repent? His spine was too stiff, and he was too mired in pride and lies. He was given all possible opportunities, and yet he refused. He did this while knowing the unseen, while in the company of the angels, and yet he refused the truth.

Instead of seeking mercy and compassion, Satan vowed to bring down Adam, Eve, all their children, and their children's children.

So Satan found Adam and Eve, who were still present in heaven, and he whispered and whispered. Adam and Eve had been given the sacred law, and they were strongly advised to stay away from Satan. But they were weak and neglected this focus. Their fall didn't come because they had broken the law, but because Adam listened to Satan. He was neglectful, and he didn't have strong resolve. So Adam fell from heaven to earth, along with Eve, and here we are today.

Adam's intention was not to disobey God, the Quran tells us. He was simply not mindful that Satan was an enemy. Satan came to him as a sincere adviser, and Adam looked up at him in a childlike way.

God knew Adam and Eve were weak. After all, our ancestors were made from mud. Yet we cannot underestimate the value of the divine breath God gave us, because even though we're made from a lowly substance, we also have what can save us. Just so, we can either cling to the muddy things that abase or humiliate us, or we can cling to the divine breath and climb up our spiritual ladder.

Adam and Eve fell. But there is good in this, too. As the poets say, it is in the time of separation that love knows its depth.

Immediately as Adam fell, he turned to God and repented. He didn't say if, or but, as Satan did. He didn't blame Satan. He didn't even mention Satan's whispering! And Adam wasn't worried about his loss of power, in leaving heaven, but about the potential loss of his relationship with God. He knew that, without the divine breath, and the connection to God, he would be nothing. So he turned to the divine breath within himself, and he turned to God.

Anything good that we do, all acts of compassion and mercy, come from that divine breath.

"All three—Adam, Eve, and Satan—were tested with a separation from God," Shaykh Qays said to me, about this moment. "How do we know that Adam and Eve have discovered faith? Unlike Satan, after Adam was removed from God's sight, he returned to God asking for mercy. That's an indication of faith, and a recognition of the need of God. It is a recognition of our own responsibility for our actions. Instead of saying, 'Satan made me do it,' Adam looked to himself: He had stumbled, and he wanted to right himself. Faith is a recognition of our faults and the mistakes we have made."

After the fall, Adam and Eve came to know another side of God. Those in heaven, such as the angels, can know only God's majesty and power. This is like knowing the stars and the planets, and gazing out at them in admiration. We are able to know God intimately, as the angels cannot.

God brought Adam down, but God also offered guidance. Adam and Eve needed that guidance, and after it, they knew themselves a little better, and they also knew God a little better. It is very hard to know God if you don't know yourself.

At this point, Adam and Eve started to increase in knowledge, not just of creation, but also of themselves and of God. In this way, they became more prepared to return to heaven.

Reflection lessons

In this section, we've talked about where Adam and Satan parted ways. One of the two was one was able to admit he was wrong, while the other was not. Faith begins with repentance and seeking forgiveness, a key to our relationship with God and with others around us.

Why Satan?

> *And [mention] when We said to the angels, "Prostrate before Adam"; so they prostrated, except for Iblees. He refused and was arrogant and became of the disbelievers.* (Quran 2:34)

People often express confusion about Satan: Why did God allow this powerful djinn to trick Adam? Why does God continue to allow Satan to target those of us who are trying to do right in the world?

Why didn't God stop Satan then, and why doesn't He stop Satan now?

At times, when people ask this question, they are blaming God for their slips, implying that a good or just God would not allow Satan to exist. But to answer the question of "Why Satan?" we must also ask the question "Why humanity?" Angels and djinn existed long before God created humans. So why create humanity at all? God created humans because angels couldn't know God the way humans do. God has said that He created humanity so that we might know Him in a different way. We can discover the aspects of God that can only be discovered by beings who have the freedom to choose well or badly. As God said: "I was a hidden treasure, and I wanted to be known."

We can say it's our purpose in life to get to know God. But how do we get to know God's hidden treasures—His intimate, loving reality? It is through our flaws and failings.

Identifying our weaknesses

Just as the angels call us to God, so Satan calls us away from God. And God gives us the choice: We can listen either to the angels or to Satan.

In calling us away from God, Satan also does something for us—he identifies our weaknesses. While this can cause us to stumble, it can also help us see our weaknesses, which humans naturally tend to hide from themselves. Satan follows us wherever we go, seeing whatever we do. As he watches us, he learns how to call each and every one of us away from our faith, using our particular weaknesses. Perhaps our weakness is for flattery, or for alcohol, or perhaps we have a temper. Whatever Satan sees, he uses it against us.

The story of Adam and Eve began when Satan identified their weakness.

God, too, knew that Adam had weaknesses. He didn't leave Adam and Eve alone to discover that Satan was their enemy. Instead, God told them clearly: Satan is an avowed enemy. Satan had taken a vow to come from every direction and cause humanity to slip.

At the point when God told Adam and Eve that Satan was coming, they should have prepared. They should have identified their weaknesses, become mindful of them, and taken steps to assure these weaknesses couldn't be used against them.

Even if someone comes and cheats us, or takes advantage of us, it doesn't mean we aren't to blame in some measure. Perhaps someone cheated or took advantage of you. They did wrong. Yet there are still lessons to be learned about what conditions allowed you to be taken advantage of.

In the case of Satan and Adam, Satan played on Adam's desires and his ignorance. Satan is what we would now call a pathological liar. The Quran refers to him as the archdeceiver. He lied to the Angels, and he lied to himself, and he also lied to Adam.

There are people in the world who are like this. Like Adam, we might want to believe the best in everyone. We might want to believe that everyone has our best interests at heart. But, as the years pass, we will find that there are people who are unwilling to stop abusing others. No matter what punishments or admonishments they receive, they won't stop. Some people—such as Pharaoh—have made themselves irredeemable, and they refuse any mercy. We have to be prepared for those sorts of people. Just as God warned Adam, God has warned us, and we must take precautions and not listen to those who wish us ill.

Does Satan humble Adam?

Some people suggest that God was humbling Adam before raising him up—that we have to be knocked to the bottom before we can be redeemed. But the fall isn't meant to humble Adam. Indeed, people cannot be forced into a position of humility. If people could be humbled just by being brought low, then Satan would've been humbled long ago.

There are many people who hit rock bottom, and yet they don't become humble. No matter how many bottoms Satan hit, he never became humble.

And such is the situation in our world, too. There was once a homeless man who had hit bottom in his life, and he asked if he could stay in a mosque. They agreed, and the man was allowed to stay. But instead of being grateful, examining his life, and turning to God, this man vandalized the mosque and attacked the people in it. He mocked and ridiculed them. When he was asked to apologize, he scoffed and said, "God has to send me a sign that I should apologize."

God already sent the Quran to all of us. And the Quran tells us: If we transgress, then we should apologize.

But some people refuse to apologize and return to God. When some people reach rock bottom, they aren't humbled by this state. Instead, they try to bring everyone else down with them. These people are choosing the path of Satan—to be brought low, yet still be arrogant. Satan doesn't grapple with his behavior, get to know himself, or turn to God. Instead, he has decided that, until the Day of Judgment, he will keep trying to bring humans down. Just so, when some of us feel the shame of being brought low, we grow angry and upset and try to drag others down with us.

Humility doesn't come from the mere fact of being knocked down. Instead, humility is a positive emotion that comes from our decision to repair the harms we have done and return to God. Humility is when we stand back up again, repent, and turn to God.

Humility is when we decide not to blame others for where we are, but to grapple with what we've done. After all, others may have harmed us—as Satan surely harmed Adam—but God is already aware of other people's contributions to our harm. Just so, Adam didn't spend time blaming Satan.

Adam had two choices when he fell: He could try to drag others down, like Satan did, or he could return to God. Adam and Eve chose humility, and they chose to return to God:

> They said: "Our Lord! We have wronged our own souls: If thou forgive us not and bestow not upon us Thy Mercy, we shall certainly be lost." (Quran 7:23)

In life, things will make us slip. But, just like Adam, we can always get back up again.

There's a story about a man who made his ablutions, washing himself for prayer. Once he was finished, this man headed out to the mosque. On the way, the man fell and became dirty. So he went back home, washed, and set out again. This second time he set out, the man also fell and became dirty. But instead of being discouraged, he went home, washed, and set out a third time.

This third time, a stranger came to light the man's way. As it turned out, this stranger was Satan. Why would Satan light the man's way? Satan explained: The first time the man got back up again, God forgave the man's sins. The second time he got back up, God forgave the sins of the man's whole family. The third time, Satan grew afraid that, were the man to fall again, his whole village would be blessed. Thus Satan brought a lamp so as not to risk it.

Humility didn't come because the man fell. Humility was when the man stood up and tried again.

So it is for us. Every time we fall, we have two choices: We can follow the call of Satan, and stay down and curse what's happened to us, snatching at other people's ankles and trying to pull them down. Or we can follow the call of God's angels and stand back up. We can recognize our problems, realize we need help, and try again.

When Adam fell, he didn't blame Satan or rationalize his behavior. He didn't blame God. Instead, he stood right back up again and returned humble, to God, saying along with Eve, "Our Lord! We have wronged our own souls: If thou forgive us not and bestow not upon us Thy Mercy, we shall certainly be lost."

When we fall, we need to work on ourselves with compassion and mercy, and we train ourselves to become stronger.

What are rules good for?

Why did Adam fall? I used to think that Adam, upon him peace, fell because he forgot the sacred law or violated it by eating from the tree. I used to think Adam's fall came because he failed to follow the letter of the law.

But Adam's fall wasn't about disobeying the law. Adam was a good-hearted person, and he saw others through the lens of his good-heartedness, expecting them to be like himself. When he saw Satan, he also expected Satan to be good. He expected Satan to have others' best interests at heart.

The reason Adam had to leave heaven was not because he violated the law.

The scholar Dr. Abdul Lateef Krauss Abdullah has said: "The few rules that we have in Islam are not meant to suppress or oppress. They are healthy boundaries that are designed to protect us."

So what did Adam do wrong?

When God said, "Don't speak to Satan," God said this because God knew that Satan was a pathological liar. God also knew that Adam wasn't aware of these things, as Adam was a trusting, good person who was not aware of the deviousness of Satan.

Yet, at this point, Adam should have taken precautions. If someone told you there was a dangerous virus spreading through the community, then you would take precautions against it. You would get a vaccination, and wash your hands more often, and perhaps stop going into crowded public places. But Adam took no care to protect himself from Satan. This was his fault and his responsibility.

The laws of Islam are meant not to suppress us, but to protect us. Listening to God—and avoiding the temptations of Satan—isn't about following rules so we can avoid going to hell. It's about respecting ourselves and others, returning to God, and creating a loving relationship with God.

How to Fight Satan

And if an evil whisper comes to you from Shaitan, then seek refuge with Allah. Verily, He is the All-Hearer, All-Knower. (Quran 7:200)

The way to fight Satan is to keep standing up again and again, just like the man on his way to the mosque. But it's also to understand ourselves and seek help when we need it.

Sometimes, when people sin, it stirs up a negative energy inside them, and they start plotting how to bring other people down. This is the psychology of the oppressors who are following in the footsteps of Satan.

Sometimes, when people sin, it stirs up self-hatred. Sometimes, we come to think God hates us, and we attack ourselves spiritually, just as an autoimmune disorder will attack the body. It's important to remember that, no matter how we have slipped, God is always waiting for us. God is always waiting for us to return to Him and to seek His beautiful names and realities. We can say:

> O Allah, O Lord, O Omnipotent, O Most Powerful, O Most Firm I ask You, through Your ability and power, to bolster my inward and outward strength, giving me the ability and strength to perform the things which You have charged me to perform which pertain to the rights of Your lordship.
>
> —Imam Haddad

We can't judge others' efforts to stand back up. Instead, when someone knocks us down, we can simply get back up again, and die in a continuous state of struggling to rise. We must keep getting up, keep praying, keep making an effort to repair the harm we've done.

Instead of normalizing hatred, anger, or self-hatred, we want to normalize getting back up again and turning to God.

Why do there have to be punishments at all?

As I said before, God is not trying to humble us, just as He wasn't trying to humble Adam. God gave many gifts to Adam in heaven, and Adam appreciated them. But humans sometimes respond better when there is something at stake.

A coffee shop tried an experiment. In order to cut down on waste, they offered customers a 25-cent discount for bringing in their own mug.

Few customers took them up on it. But then, as an experiment, they adjusted their prices down by a quarter, and those who didn't bring in a mug had to pay an additional 25 cents. Essentially, the pricing structure was the same, but this time it felt like a punishment.

People responded quickly to this penalty in a way they didn't to a reward—that is simply human nature. It is hard for us to get out of a habit, sometimes, unless we feel there is a penalty.

The penalty that Adam was given—leaving heaven—was meant to motivate him, and thus to motivate humanity, to do the right thing. Adam had enjoyed heaven. Adam didn't negate it, like Satan, and he didn't say, "I don't care." But he understood the penalty, and what he wanted afterwards was to return to God. He understood that, from then on, we were meant to take precautions against Satan, and not forget that Satan wishes us ill.

Rationalization and the Healthy Heart

It was We Who created man, and We know what dark suggestions his soul makes to him: for We are nearer to him than (his) jugular vein. (Quran 50:16)

Despite the very real knowledge that human science has allowed us to build about our bodies and ourselves, we still know very little about the brain. One of the things we do know is that many of the decisions we make that seem logical are in fact made from a different seat of cognition. We'll call this the heart.

Certainly, logic is both important and useful. When humans can perform acts of serious critical thinking, we can do powerful things. Yet, often we think we're being logical when in fact we're just arguing—using the tools of the mind, but speaking right out of the heart. One of the most important ways to exercise our intelligence is to see these tools for what they are. And it's especially important to know when to pause and look around.

Psychologists and cognitive scientists have found that the human mind doesn't use "pure" reason, but rather that it conjectures and rationalizes in order to fit information that we receive into familiar boxes. The mind can certainly seem to spin gold from straw, creating edifices that look like sound intelligence. But these gardens and buildings of thought come not from neutral intelligence, but painted with the colors of the heart. Sometimes, when we're attempting to understand something new, the most rational thing to do is hit pause. To look at ourselves before we look at the world around.

No one can get away from rationalization and conjecture, from spinning arguments to suit our worldview: that's how our brains seem to work. The important thing is to be self-aware and to know when we don't have sufficient information for a ruling or opinion.

This is the reason Islam encourages self-knowledge. As some Muslim scholars have said: The one who knows himself, knows God.

Know thyself

By knowing a little about the human brain, we are able to open up. One way to gather more information is to listen to statements and arguments with less resistance. Usually, we filter out whatever comes to us that doesn't fit our rationalizations. But sometimes, we need to let go of that type of cognition, which feels rational but is instead rationalizing. Once we let go, we can move to the deeper seat of cognition: the heart.

It's the heart that drives the mind in one direction or the other.

This doesn't mean we're the puppets of our subconscious minds, as Shaykh Qays so aptly said in a recent discussion. "Subconscious rationalizations are part of how and what we think. There is no need to assume that what we 'really think' is an objective reality outside of or apart from them." The state of brain science doesn't suggest that we're puppets, or that we're easy to manipulate, but rather it shows us "the ephemeral nature of physical reality and the wondrous way the human mind deals with it."

This also means that the state of our hearts affects whatever data, whatever information we receive. To grossly oversimplify: If we are in a healthy, balanced state-of-heart, a set of data will look one way. If we are in a miserable, proud, arrogant state-of-heart, the data will appear differently.

This heart of ours must be constantly tuned and weeded, like a garden, so that it doesn't grow hardened and corrupt.

> So do not claim yourselves to be pure; He knows best who it is that guards against evil. (Quran 53:32)

The purity—or health—of our hearts takes constant self-cultivation. The Quran doesn't suggest that we're born into sin. But when we enter the world, we are surrounded by the world's diseases and social ills, and these affect our state-of-heart. These diseases can be greed, racism, sexism, arrogance, pride, and more.

Satan provides a key example of rationalizing from a diseased heart. His heart was full of arrogance, pride, and a sort of proto-racism: Satan felt that he was better than Adam, as he was made from fire while humans were made from clay. Satan looked down on Adam and refused to accept Adam's status as chosen.

Satan was dealing with the same facts as Adam. But, because of his arrogance, he could not accept new information. Instead, he rejected Adam's importance, accusing humans of ingratitude—projecting and rationalizing, since Satan himself was ungrateful.

Even though Satan appeared to have faith, and to be thinking rationally, his actions weren't based on reason. Instead, they were based on a projection of the state of his heart.

A purification of the heart, or a process of making the heart healthy, is something we must seek from God, just as we seek God's guidance. None of us can fully identify our own faults and diseases—but we can ask for help. One important thing: We should never do this from a position of self-hatred. After all, we're human, and whatever society one comes from, there are social ills. There are issues that affect the state of our hearts.

It's important to be as aware as possible of the biases that we've absorbed, that have grown inside us. Our hearts are wonderful sponges, absorbing the love around them, but they're also terrible sponges, in that they absorb surrounding diseases.

Prayers can help bring our state-of-heart back to health. Faith is the first level of this self-care. The second is to ask for forgiveness. A healthy heart isn't filled with arrogance or blame for others. Instead, a healthy heart is self-critical, sees itself as part of a community, and looks to make things right.

None of us should be complacent or self-satisfied, or claim that our heart is "purely healthy." Keeping a healthy heart is a daily exercise of cultivation, getting rid of diseased elements such as arrogance and pride. These might disappear for a while, but just as you must always take care of a garden, so you must care for your heart. We must be constantly looking for those weeds. Constantly watering and cultivating.

What if I fail?

When we find difficult traits within ourselves, we don't need to be ashamed. Sometimes, as we struggle to help our heart toward health, we fail. What if our inclinations are too strong? What if our failures cause us to be depressed and to feel like a failure?

In this struggle, there is no "success" and no "failure"; there is only the struggle. We must recognize that we all have weaknesses toward certain unhealthy traits. Indeed, these traits may have positive manifestations—such as self-confidence—that need to be kept in check so that they don't grow harmful—for instance, into arrogance. This takes a great deal of effort, training, and practice. It takes a lot of effort to sit down and look at oneself.

A first step is to recognize that this will take both time and continuous effort.

Religion is not just about commands and prohibitions. The Quran is very clear about what religion is about: It's about God, and our relationship with Him. So what is important is not that we "fail" or "succeed," but rather that we have made our continual best effort in our relationship with ourselves and with God.

If need be, repentance cleanses the heart. Repentance is akin to pulling out the weeds that are overgrowing the diseased and unbalanced garden of our heart. Repentance isn't just admitting wrongdoing, but it's also repairing the misdeed.

The first step—the one never taken by Satan—is to admit fault. Don't use the part of our brains that can rationalize and justify. Instead, feel the wrong. Acknowledge and own up to it. Then turn to God and ask for forgiveness: ask to cleanse your heart.

How Do We Fear God?

Say, "O My servants who have transgressed against themselves [by sinning], do not despair of the mercy of Allah. Indeed, Allah forgives all sins. Indeed, it is He who is the Forgiving, the Merciful." (Quran 39:53)

When some people think of "fearing God," they imagine God as a fearsome torturer. This "God" is a towering, vindictive being who is just waiting for them to make a mistake.

In fact, it's the opposite. The God who we fear is patient and loving. This God gives us opportunity after opportunity to repent, feel remorse, change our habits, and grow. Punishment comes into the picture only when it becomes evident to God, and to everyone around, that an individual is not receptive to growth.

Indeed, God gives us many opportunities to see our actions through other eyes. Pharaoh was surrounded not only by the slaves who he dehumanized and oppressed, but also by people of light and goodness who lived in his own home. These were people who he respected: namely Asiya, his wife, and her adopted son Moses.

Pharaoh also had a pious, wise advisor, and there were others in his kingdom who tried to steer him toward a better way, to the intertwined love and fear of God. But none of these good people were able to have an impact on Pharaoh. His arrogance and narcissism were simply too deep-seated.

So, yes, God is loving, merciful, compassionate, and patient. Yet this cannot be all. Because there must also come a time for justice.

We shouldn't fear God because we believe that God is vindictive. God doesn't care only about a select elite—God is compassionate and cares about everyone. Instead, we fear God because God is majestic. This majesty should bring about not our quavering, but our humility. It should help us to authentically know our own limitations.

Fear of God as a positive

The fear of God is indeed a positive force, nudging us always to do right. It's this fear that compels us to get to know others, in spite of our differences. This fear also presses us to be humble and not to transgress the boundaries of others.

For instance: At times, when marginalized groups express anger and rage, it can hit our ears in a difficult way. Maybe the way in which people express their anger sounds harsh, and it is hard for us to hear. But the fear of God should force us to hear the pain and struggle of groups that are calling out, such as those in the contemporary "Black Lives Matter" movement.

Indeed, the fear of God should humble us so that we can hear these marginalized communities in pain. This is particularly true of those communities that are saying: I need you to hear me right now, I need you to listen!

The fear of God is a healthy fear. Just as our body sends us a message of pain when it's ill, telling us that we need to tend to it, the fear of God should send us a similar message when we are about to cause harm to others.

The ability to disobey

In the Quran, Satan is not an angel. Instead, Satan is a djinn, and he—like other djinn and humans—has the power to obey or disobey God. If Adam is the father-leader of human beings, then Satan is the same for the djinn. Once, Satan was an avid worshiper of God.

Then along came this newcomer, Adam, who wasn't made from fire like the djinn, but instead from lowly clay. Satan didn't want to know Adam. He felt that, given all that he'd done, God owed him something.

The angels recognized that Adam was a special being. Satan was also invited to that journey, to recognize the special aspects of Adam, but he rejected it. Satan felt that, because he was made of smokeless fire he was better than Adam. Moreover, Satan did not fear God.

Satan was very worshipful, but he had no fear. It was this lack of fear that made him violate the boundaries not just of God, but also of Adam. Indeed, Satan made an oath to God that he would spend the rest of his life trying to bring Adam down.

Where he should've felt fear, Satan instead felt entitlement.

Mindfulness in faith

The outward show of faith shouldn't bring us self-satisfaction or entitlement.

In any action, we should be mindful and conscious of why we're doing it. These acts are, after all, not just for our singular selves. They are also for God and for everyone with whom we're connected. Indeed, when we act for God, we become aware of the boundaries of ourselves and others.

A person can feel enlightened, but unless they're aware of the boundaries of others, that's not true self-knowledge. It's instead a sort of narcissism.

It's not uncommon for religious people to worship the command of God instead of worshiping God. But if we really feel that God is king, then there should be a fear of being held accountable inside us. It doesn't matter who we are—what faith, or of no faith at all—we must feel an accountability for transgressing the boundaries of others.

If we realize that our actions aren't only for ourselves, then we'll be aware of that.

What is a disbeliever?

A disbeliever isn't just someone who doesn't adhere to faith. Disbelievers are people who know the truth, and yet they conspire to hide it because it's of benefit to them. So they will actively fight the truth through distorting it, brainwashing people to reject it, turning them away from knowing the truth and following it.

These are disbelievers. The following verses best summarize their inward state:

> We know that you, [O Muhammad], are saddened by what they say. And indeed, they do not call you untruthful, but it is the verses of Allah that the wrongdoers reject. And certainly were messengers denied before you, but they were patient over [the effects of] denial, and they were harmed until Our victory came to them. And none can alter the words of Allah. And there has certainly come to you some information about the [previous] messengers. And if their evasion is difficult for you, then if you are able to seek a tunnel into the earth or a stairway into the sky to bring them a sign, [then do so]. But if Allah had willed, He would have united them upon guidance. So never be of the ignorant. Only those who hear will respond. But the dead, Allah will resurrect them; then to Him they will be returned. (Quran 6:33-36)

Fear embedded in love

There isn't only a question of why we fear God, but also of how we do it. We shouldn't fear God from a distance, or while running away. We should have a fear of God that's deeply embedded in love.

If you dislike and fear someone, then you most likely want to escape them, since we want to run away from people we hate. If you have a bad opinion of God—perhaps you imagine that God is just waiting to throw a thunderbolt and smack you for some ill deed!—then you'll most likely be running away from Him.

Instead, we must embed our fear in love. In this case, we run to God. To understand this, it helps to think of someone who you love very much. If that person, who you care about, is displeased or angry at one of your actions, then you don't run away. Instead, your love for them forces you to care about their opinion. It's our fear of displeasing this beloved that makes us attentive, and that can help set us right.

So: We shouldn't just fear God because we're afraid of hell or punishment. Our relationship with God isn't one of an abuse victim with an abuser. We should also be afraid of displeasing a beloved, and this is something we can only do when we're fostering a relationship with God.

Fearmongering and having a paranoia of God is not the same as fearing God.

Those who truly fear God are those who know and love God.

Fear and anger

Fear of God should most certainly not be rooted in anger. At its worst, this creates a situation that is ripe for brainwashing.

A person might be angry about Palestine, for instance, or the situation in Somalia, and theirs might well be a legitimate anger. But first that person needs to nourish their self-knowledge, and also their connection and relationship with God. If the relationship with God is not built, then others can easily come along, validate their anger, and lead them astray, as ISIS has done.

Certainly, this lack of self-knowledge isn't just a state that religious people can manipulate. Anyone who is stuck in a situation of free-floating anger, without a strong relationship to self and God, could be ripe to follow a demagogic and destructive leader.

Instead, we need to develop our relationship with God, our knowledge of ourselves, and let ourselves be guided by a fear that is deeply, deeply embedded in love.

THE RESOLUTE PROPHETS AND DEALING WITH REJECTION

Say you: "We believe in God, and in that which has been sent down on us and sent down on Abraham, Ishmael, Isaac and Jacob, and the Tribes, and that which was given to Moses and Jesus and the prophets, of their Lord; we make no division between any of them, and to Him we surrender." (Quran 153:84)

The verse above is not talking about the rank of the prophets. There is no contradiction in our belief that the Prophet, God bless him and grant him peace, is leader of all other prophets and seal of prophethood. This particular section of the verse is talking about how we, the believers, don't deny that the prophets of God are all prophets, nor do we distinguish them in this respect. They were not all at the same rank, nor did they face the same degree of persecution. Some had greater resolve than others, and Prophet Muhammad, upon him peace and blessings, had the most perfect character.

The five resolute prophets—Jesus, Muhammad, Abraham, Moses, and Noah; upon them peace and blessings—all experienced tremendous rejection.

Rejection can take many forms. It can be directed at a person, in the form of a failure to recognize and accept an individual's being or ideas. Or it can be collective, a rejection of a whole faith, ethnicity, culture, identity, or community.

All of us will experience some rejection in our lives, whether it is fair or not. How did the prophets deal with it?

Noah, for instance, was asked to call people to God solely by talking with them. The Quran tells us that, after 950 years of telling people about God, Noah found only 80 people who had listened. Yet he persevered in the face of constant rejection, calmly, with only minimal results to show for all his efforts. Other resolute prophets persevered in the face of humiliation, disgrace, and physical attacks. Throughout this, they continued to believe and to endure with hope.

Another of the prophets who experienced great rejection was Jonah. The Quran tells of how Jonah lost hope of ever being heard and left town. When he was swallowed by a whale, he realized that this had happened because he'd lost hope. But he never gave up trying.

Sometimes, the fruits of the prophets' work materialized only after they had left a place. But whatever happened, they persisted, continually calling people to their ideals, and also giving people space to reject them. Giving people this space can often be critically important.

What We Can Learn from Rejection in Art

It is not for the swan to teach eaglets to sing.

—French and Danish Proverb

I want to talk about two very different artistic portraits of rejection. They are William Golding's classic novel *Lord of the Flies* and the film *12 Angry Men*, originally written for TV by Reginald Rose and made into a film that appeared in 1957.

In William Golding's *Lord of the Flies*, rejection is absolute. In the novel, a group of boys is stranded alone on an island, and their lives quickly descend into violence and rejection. Anything that deviates from the violence at the center of the group of boys is destroyed. There is no talking, no persuasion.

In *12 Angry Men*, we get a different, more hopeful picture of persuasion and rejection. In this movie, a court case was raised against an 18-year-old Latino, and it was up to twelve white male jurors to decide his fate. The hero of *12 Angry Men* wasn't persuaded by the case against the teen defendant. But he didn't try to force his views on the other jury members, even when he was initially rejected.

Instead, he persisted, slowly and calmly, in calling his fellow jurors to their own values.

Importantly, Juror 8, our protagonist, gives the other jurors the power to reject him. His is not a voice that controls. Instead, his is a voice of conscience: a voice that invites, because it's speaking out of love.

Manipulation vs. persuasion

The prophets dealt with rejection in much the same way. Their guiding lights are important, since we all experience some rejection in our lives.

Sometimes, rejection is fair and healthy. And if you're pressuring someone else, such that they're not able to reject what you're calling them to, then that's manipulation. But Juror 8, like the prophets, didn't manipulate his fellow jurors. Instead, he created an open space for them to walk into, where they could see different views.

For those of us facing harsh rejection in our lives, especially group rejection like racism or Islamophobia, we need to understand how the Lord of the Flies works. But we also need to understand how the voice of conscience works in *12 Angry Men*, and how it stands up against rejection.

In *Lord of the Flies*, there is no space, no calling-to, and all the voices feed on fear and despair. Those who would stand against violence don't have the mental and emotional strength to convince others to come to their path, or to isolate the sadist's voice.

Lord of the Flies takes us on the journey of the worst that can happen, and it ultimately portrays a negative view of human possibility. Just so, in 12 Angry Men, there are people with sadistic tendencies who want to rule. But in *Lord of the Flies*, there is no possibility of pushing back, and boys end up with mob violence and murder.

Golding's novel shows us the worst that can happen when we face groupthink. Ultimately, the novel lacks hope and the light of faith.

12 Angry Men, by contrast, shows how a strong conscience can win out. Here, Juror 8, played in the film by Henry Fonda, began as a lone voice saying there isn't sufficient evidence to determine guilt. The others, each for his own reasons, wanted to find the teen guilty. Some were lazy, some wanted to get home, and some were prejudiced.

But by offering them space and by taking a stand, Juror 8 brought the first voice over to his side. After that, he simply asked to be heard, to have a discussion about his ideas. In this way, groupthink can be defeated: by taking one layer at a time and getting people to reflect on their own values and principles.

At first, none of the other men, outside of Juror 8, wanted to take a risk and stand out. Most people can only speak out when they feel themselves in the comfort of a group. But when the first man comes to see Juror 8's point of view, it makes it easier for everyone else to defect from groupthink and to join the space of open discussion.

Holding people accountable to their own values

It's also important that Juror 8 isn't trying to convince his fellow jurors of something entirely new. Instead, he's presenting them with the values of the American judicial system and holding people accountable to their own ideals.

In this, the judicial system is no different from a religion or other institution. If voices of conscience do not speak to the group, and hold the group accountable, then the worst of human behaviors can emerge. In any place, there are women and men who have deep-seated prejudices. Some of the jurors have unreliable judgment. Some are fearful and ignorant and impatient. All of these normal human permutations threaten to taint the group's decision-making ability.

Yet what I like about the film is that, instead of simply showing how sadistic humans can be, it shows a process of growth within the group, as a single voice of conscience succeeds, over time, in winning over racist, ignorant, and biased people, by urging them to listen to their consciences and to uphold their values.

But it's not easy

At the moment when the jurors are beginning to reach a consensus, that's when the worst voices come out. Those who are lazy or ignorant are much easier to win over than the voices of extreme prejudice. But how Juror 8 deals with them is by not engaging them. If you engage these voices, they will feed on that.

Instead, Juror 8 turns his back on them.

If you engage the voices of extreme prejudice, then you give them attention, and that hurts society. If you isolate the voices of extreme prejudice, then they have to come to terms with that.

Henry Fonda makes an excellent Juror 8, as he never portrays the voice of conscience as someone alone, bitter, or angry. He never said, "If you guys don't accept me and my views, you're all evil." Instead, he said, this is the voice of my conscience. I must stand by it, but I'm giving you a choice to have another voice.

The voice of hope, like the voice of faith, continues to invite and engage. This is very different from the voice of manipulation, which takes advantage of those rejected by society. We may be rejected, but faith should help us deal with this rejection not with anger, but with hope, wisdom, and persistent engagement.

Dealing with rejection is part of life and part of faith. But we should always have hope, and never go the road of the *Lord of the Flies*. We want to stand up in the way Juror 8 did. In this moment, people might be against you, and they might mock you. But you want to still take that stand and continue to help them see.

Seeing People for What They Are: Corrupter or Reformer

When it is said to them: "Make not mischief on the earth," they say: "Why, we only want to make peace!" Beware, they are the ones who make mischief, but they realize (it) not. When it is said to them: "Believe as the others believe:" They say: "Shall we believe as the fools believe?" Nay, beware they are the fools, but they do not know. (Quran 2:11-13)

When it comes to justice and corruption, the illuminating verses in the second chapter of the Quran are key. How can we tell the difference between those who are good, and those who make mischief while proclaiming, "Why, we only want to make peace!"

As with any group of humans, throughout history, there has been unity and disunity amongst Muslims. There has been corruption and reform; there have been periods of making peace and honoring justice; and there have been coups such as those of the Abbasids and Fatimids. There is no Utopian or "Great Again" period to which we can return. That is the nature of the world and of change. But there are ways to be more and less just; there are ways to be someone who does good on earth or makes trouble and pain.

Shaykh ash-Shaarawi gives an excellent example of water that comes from the sky to benefit humans, plants, animals. This water—which might be any mercy or sustenance sent from God—irrigates the land and fills up springs and wells for people to drink and take to their homes.

Beware the corrupter, welcome the reformer

Let's imagine the first person who arrives at this well. They see it, drink from it, and allow others to drink from it. This is a good person. This person is not going to push others away. This person simply uses what is available. They don't build anything or go out of their way to help others, but they also don't pollute or cause harm to the well. That way, when it rains, the well is filled again. This person allows the mercy of God to fill the well. This first person doesn't ease access, but they also don't prevent anyone else from reaching the well.

The second person who arrives at the well is another sort entirely. This is a person who sees the well and throws dirt or pollutes the springs, so that it becomes harmful or can't be used. We can call this sort of person a corrupter. This person closes off the well, or prevents access, so that the water doesn't reach others. They might keep it only for themselves, they might require steep payment from others, or they might make the water less healthy.

The third person who arrives at the well uses their intelligence, which is a gift from God, to take the well and create additional benefits from it. They might ease irrigation for farmers or create better and cleaner ways of drinking the water for people and animals. They might expand the well so it can hold more water, or create new access points for elders and people with disabilities.

The reformer removes impurities, such as earth and rocks, as they build upon the natural foundation to assist and support every living thing in need of water.

Two sorts of corrupters

To extend Shaykh ash-Shaarawi's metaphor, there are two types of corrupters down at the well. Among the corrupters, there are those who are ignorant and can be educated. If we point out what they are doing, and how it harms others, these corrupters can see themselves differently and change their behavior.

But there is another type of corrupter who is an expert at self-deception. This person, as we read in the verse above, claims to be working toward peace. God responds to such people by first using the word "beware." This is a stern warning meant to alert us to the seriousness of the matter, to command attention from listeners.

Education doesn't help this sort of corrupter, since they see themselves as reformers.

Listening vs. distraction

How do you tell the difference between a reformer and a corrupter, if they both believe they're doing good? Reformers call people to listen, while corrupters create distractions. Corrupters also present their evidence as sensory, vague, and obscure.

It was Carl Jung who said, "perception is projection." That is, corrupters, such as Islamophobes, already have a perception of those who they hate, and they search for information to fit that perception before projecting it out to the world. They accuse others of hate because of their own hatred.

Corrupters play with people's perceptions and senses in order to create falsehoods.

These are the ones who create mischief, the Quran tells us, but they know it not. God tells them to beware, and to believe as the believers do. But they respond in the negative:

They say: "Shall we believe as the fools believe?"

What do these corrupters mean when they say "fools"? For them, a fool is someone who has low social status. When they used the term "fools," they were not thinking in terms of knowledge, evidence, facts, or critical thinking, but rather in terms of class, race, or other forms of social status.

Even during the time of Prophet Muhammad, upon him peace and blessings, people rejected the truth when it wasn't delivered by those with privilege and popularity.

God responds that they indeed are the fools who do not know. Real foolishness has nothing to do with social status, but is instead about carelessness and recklessness. Faith requires knowledge, proofs, science, analogy, investigation, and verification. It is not just the smoke, mirrors, and rationalizations of the corrupter.

With these warnings, God distinguishes the corrupters from the reformers. The former are people of irreverence, duplicity, conjecture, and stereotypes. The latter are people of serious study, knowledge, clarification, and verification.

Faith against corruption

Who benefits from corruption and falsehood? Usually, it is people with unchecked power and privilege who benefit from fencing off the well.

Faith, then, comes to give the true definitions of corruption, foolishness, falsehood, and reform, thus finding a new, middle way between oppressor and oppressed. Here, we don't want to completely obliterate abusive power and start a new cycle of abuse or revenge. Instead, we want to elevate those who are oppressed, and confront their oppressors.

Faith does give light to the underdog because it offers light and elevation to all—the oppressors and the oppressed. However, faith sides with whomever is right (in submission to God). Classism is rejected by the faith, as it leans towards groupthink. We see this from conservative snobbery and leftist proletarianism alike.

It's also important to remember the corrupters who don't act out of malice and can be educated and brought to the light. These are people such as the magicians during Pharaoh's time. Once they understood they had been working on the side of corruption and evil, they used their skills to open doors for the oppressed.

Pharaoh, on the other hand, could not be educated, even by Moses. He asked, Should I believe what slaves believe, and thought them to be fools just because they were of a lower social status. How people perceive the oppressed is an important distinction between reformers and corrupters. Do they see them as oppressed, or do they see them as fools? Do they see a refugee as a foolish person?

Faith destroys classism, and a person of faith educates—first themselves, and then people around them. We are all equal in the eyes of God. A person of faith is interested in helping creation, not in using others to climb the social ladder.

NOAH AND "THE MOST ABJECT AMONG US"

He said, "My Lord, indeed I invited my people [to truth] night and day. But my invitation increased them not except in flight. And indeed, every time I invited them that You may forgive them, they put their fingers in their ears, covered themselves with their garments, persisted, and were arrogant with [great] arrogance. Then I invited them publicly. Then I announced to them and [also] confided to them secretly And said, 'Ask forgiveness of your Lord. Indeed, He is ever a Perpetual Forgiver.'" (Quran 71:5-10)

All the prophets did not come to us to dismantle and destroy abusive power and oppression, but to organize the oppressed and build their own power grounded in faith. Yet dismantling oppression never means becoming the oppressor. Islam does not aim to turn us into fighters against abusive power. Rather, the prophets came to humanity to enjoin us to worship God and witness His power and strength. This calling necessitates facing enemies among both individuals and groups that impede these teachings. Pushing these enemies back within their boundaries is a means, but not an end. The Prophet Noah, upon him peace, for his part, spent hundreds of years calling people to the message of God and fighting against the oppression of vulnerable groups.

The majority of the weak and vulnerable were with the arrogant, in whom they sought protection, and their fate was tied to their arrogant protectors. But the minority groups among the powerful were with the prophets, and their fate was that of those protected by God Most High.

Noah knew very well that abusive power benefits from and relies on the mechanisms of oppression. He also knew that abusers look down on the oppressed.

So when Noah appears in the Quran, he is bringing God's truth around the world. Yet the powerful scorned Noah, seeing him as a mortal human like themselves. They sneered, as they saw a mortal being followed not by the rich and powerful, but by the vulnerable and oppressed.

> We do not see in thee anything but a mortal man like ourselves; and we do not see that any follow thee save those who are quite obviously the most abject among us; and we do not see that you could be in any way superior to us: on the contrary, we think that you are liars! (Quran 11:27)

The powerful here are looking for angels, not for fellow human beings. They scorn the idea of being associated with the vulnerable and marginalized. Not one among them asks Noah: "Where's your evidence, where's your argument? Let's study it and see if it's true." Instead, the mere fact that someone of a "lower" social station might approach them angers the powerful.

Noah says they shouldn't worry, because he doesn't mean to force anything upon them. He asks, "Can we force it on you even though it be hateful to you?"

All he's asking of them is that they take the message of God into consideration. He tells the assembled that he asks no benefit; this is a message many of the prophets repeat.

As he speaks, Prophet Noah doesn't draw from his own feelings, opinions, or desires. He is instead working from a sense of responsibility and accountability before God. He can't turn his back on the unprotected or oppressed. He is embracing all, as God would want.

He asks the powerful, "O my people, who would shield me from God were I to repulse them [the powerless and marginal]? Will you not, then, keep this in mind?"

But the powerful and those who follow them have no desire to listen. Instead, they tell him, scornfully, to bring violence or go away. Abusive power doesn't respect facts, evidence, or sad stories. It respects only power that can keep it in check or knock it down.

The powerful of the city say: We'll consider your argument, but only if you can bring us down. They, with their false sense of power, spread their arms and say: Bring it on.

How does Prophet Noah, upon him peace, respond? Does he believe God is wrapped around his little finger, such that he can call out, and God will come and knock others down? Certainly not. Noah can only shrug and say, "Only God can bring it upon you, if He so wills, and you shall not elude it."

Like all the prophets, Noah strives to present an argument without trying to overpower or manipulate or threaten. He's resigned to the fact that he can do his best and no more. Speaking truth to power is exerting yourself within your boundaries and values while leaving the results to God.

Prophet Noah called people to faith in God, and the powerless and marginal here refer to those who accepted his call and believed. However, it is important to note that not all marginalized groups accept the call to faith.

In 950 years, Noah was able to convince only 80 followers. Still, he persisted. He persisted, even though his very own son didn't accept the message, which clearly caused Noah grief.

We Are Not in Control

> And Noah called to his Lord and said, "My Lord, indeed my son is of my family; and indeed, Your promise is true; and You are the most just of judges!" He said, "O Noah, indeed he is not of your family; indeed, he is [one whose] work was other than righteous, so ask Me not for that about which you have no knowledge. Indeed, I advise you, lest you be among the ignorant." [Noah] said, "My Lord, I seek refuge in You from asking that of which I have no knowledge. And unless You forgive me and have mercy upon me, I will be among the losers." (Quran 11:45-47)

Surely one of the hardest things for any parent is to let a child go down a path the parent knows is wrong. And yet, as parents and as the faithful, sometimes we must let our children walk off.

When the flood came, Noah's son didn't want to board the boat. Rather, he rejected the invitation to faith, wanting to stay behind with his powerful friends. Noah could not convince his son otherwise. Noah pleaded with God to save his son, saying "verily my son is of my family!"

Indeed, when we use the word family, we think of blood ties. Yet God told Noah that his son's actions were unrighteous, and thus his son had chosen his own family among the ignorant.

God certainly did not tell Noah to go after his son and drag him back to the right path. Sometimes, people justify the extremes of their violence and anger by claiming the support of Islamic law. So-called "honor killings" are among the worst transgressions against humanity, and they are a horrible malpractice of Islam.

We can guide our children to the very best of our abilities. But this guidance must have boundaries, just as it does in all other human relationships. Guidance—of children, of employees, of citizens—should never cross the line into overpowering control.

God shows us this repeatedly in the Quran. Even family members of the prophets can take the wrong path. And the prophets must love them, while also letting them choose their own way.

Family isn't destiny

Even those who have prophets as parents may not be righteous. Indeed, every person will be judged on their own merits. Each person must examine themselves as an individual, and righteous parents don't give anyone a free ticket. Everyone has to consider the message of truth for themselves; everyone has to investigate it; and everyone has to turn to God and focus on their sense of responsibility

> As the Prophet Jonah said, "If they charge thee with falsehood, say: 'My work to me, and yours to you! Ye are free from responsibility for what I do, and I for what ye do!'" (Quran 10:41)

We have a responsibility to stop our siblings and neighbors from hurting others. In the case of harm, we are obligated to push people back within their boundaries. If a family member is a murderer, for instance, we have to stop them. Yet we will not be asked about others' sins. We will only be asked about our own.

Noah's son tells his father that he intends to follow the oppressors instead of those who are rightly guided. He was an accomplice, perhaps, but he didn't do any harm, and thus Noah had to let him go.

At times, for any of us, family members can be a trial and a tribulation. But we must call ourselves to account and not be obsessed with running after other people's sins.

What's left for us to do? We must have a good opinion of the individual at all times and keep making prayers. Having done this duty, we have to let go. We can call people to the truth, but what other people do is not in our control. Whatever God wills, that is in God's domain.

Speaking Truth to Power Is Not About Results

And there came from the farthest end of the city a man, running. He said, "O my people, follow the messengers. Follow those who do not ask of you [any] payment, and they are [rightly] guided." (Quran 36:20-21)

In the Quran's thirty-sixth surah, a man named Habib an-Najjar (Habib the Carpenter) appears. Habib an-Najjar was a very charitable man who was known to have given half of his earnings to those in the community who needed help.

But Habib an-Najjar was not a wealthy man, nor was he one of the city's notables. Instead, he was a very sick man who suffered from leprosy and lived at the outskirts of his city.

When we first hear about Habib an-Najjar, he arrives from the outskirts of town, running to come to the defense of the prophets. He does not arrive laureled as a hero. He's neither powerful nor strong. And although he's a kind man, he is not acclaimed, talented, or famous.

Instead of being well-regarded for his charity, because of his altered appearance, people heaped mockery and ridicule on Habib an-Najjar, which was why he lived at the outskirts of town. That's where he was when two messengers arrived with word from the Divine and were denied. A third messenger was sent to confirm that they were indeed sent to the town by God.

The people in power—the city's notables—denied these prophets because they were not angels, but were instead fellow humans. They couldn't believe these two could have something special to impart, as they didn't come robed or jeweled.

But they couldn't have been angels, as angels can't be seen by the human eye, since they are made of light. Also, angels wouldn't be the right messengers for humanity, as angels don't experience the pain, suffering, and struggles that we do.

The notables of the city were rigid in not accepting the message. But when the prophets spoke, Habib an-Najjar came running. He heard the prophets, and he was deeply moved.

He wasn't the only one to have heard the prophets' message. The powerful of the city also heard, and they were clearly shaken by it. They called the prophets liars and ordered them to stop speaking. The prophets, for their part, said that they had only come to speak and give "clear notification."

Yet the powerful of the city wanted the prophets to stop. "Indeed," the powerful said, "we consider you a bad omen." The city's leaders ordered the prophets to desist, or else "we will surely stone you"—not just killing the prophets, but torturing them to death. The prophets, for their part, used only words, reminding the people of the truths that they could feel buried in their souls.

We must ask ourselves: Why were the city's wealthy and powerful so agitated? Why did they want to punish the messengers, threatening them with torture and violence, instead of responding with speech?

The prophets stood their ground. They told the men and women of the city that a message of justice seems like a bad omen only to those who know they are transgressing the boundaries of others. "Your omen is with yourselves."

This is when Habib an-Najjar arrives. He arrives late perhaps, coming from the outskirts of the town, hurrying to speak to his fellow townsmen, who seem on the verge of stoning the prophets. He comes, the Quran tells us, "running."

The man doesn't run in because he is relying on the prophets as heroes or saviors. He doesn't bow or grovel before them. Instead, he shows that he respects their message.

Habib an-Najjar speaks eloquently about the prophets' message, calling them rightly guided and reminding his fellow townspeople that the messengers asked for no compensation, no payment. "And why should I not worship He who created me and to whom you will be returned?"

Since Habib an-Najjar shared most of his wealth out of love for his people, he easily understood the heart of the prophets' message. His heart was innocent, and thus it could not only receive the message, but it gave him the courage to share the message, with genuine concern, and to benefit all humanity.

Yet after his eloquent appeal, the man is killed.

After bearing witness that there is none worthy of worship except God, Habib an-Najjar was mercilessly killed by the people of his town. One account says the people began to stone him while he was saying, "O God, guide my people for they do not know," and that they continued to stone him until he died a violent death. Yet he was still praying for them. Another account states that the people stamped on him until his intestines came out.

While being tortured, he said: "I believe in your Lord, so listen to me."

Some say it was the angels who told Habib an-Najjar to "enter Paradise," in order to give him spiritual strength. Others say it was God, because the man was killed and was thereafter granted heaven and the honor of being a witness.

Yet even after he made it to heaven, this man's main concern remained his people! It's thus we know he was speaking out of genuine love for his people. Even in heaven, he continued to think about his people: not out of obligation, but out of love.

"Would that my people knew," he said. "That my Lord (God) has forgiven me, and made me of the honored ones!"

Counter oppression with faith, forbearance, and patience

Habib an-Najjar clearly fights against the oppressive ways of his fellow townsmen. But he doesn't respond to abuse with abuse. Instead, he responds with faith, patience, and understanding. He doesn't arrive at the center of town with weapons. Instead, he remains connected to the vulnerability he experienced all his life, and he speaks with both courage and faith.

One of the things we can find in this man's story is that, when you're fighting abusive power, it's important to worry about your soul. One of the worst things to happen, while fighting abusive power, is to your soul. While fighting abuse, it's important not to embrace the spirit of that abuse.

The first lesson in fighting abusive power is what not to do, and we should never assume we're immune from becoming an abuser. We should never lock ourselves in a love-hate relationship with the oppressor. When fighting oppressive power, we should be wary of focusing on any particular abuser—any particular individual. Instead, we should fight the oppressor's actions.

In this surah in the Quran, there are no names. We don't know the abusers' name. Neither do we know who in the town has ordered the prophets to stop speaking, nor who orders this innocent man's death. These men are not held up as "bad guys" who need to be vanquished. What's important isn't targeting an enemy, but rather targeting the abusive behavior.

Moreover, Habib an-Najjar didn't fight his neighbors in a spirit of enmity and defiance. After he arrives in paradise, the man says, "I wish my people could know." He doesn't say, "Aha! I won!" Instead, in his heart, he still wants them to see what is right and to act according to what they see—even though these people had ridiculed him and driven him to the edges of town.

Should we, as Habib an-Najjar did, tolerate rejection?

There's no reason for us to desire rejection. We all want to belong and be accepted! Yet rejection still happens, particularly in unjust societies, just as Habib an-Najjar was rejected in his unjust town.

The important thing is that we don't destroy our souls just to gain acceptance from an abusive power. When Habib an-Najjar came running from the outskirts of town, he didn't come to fight for the acceptance of his fellow townspeople. He wasn't angling for them to declare him right or handsome, or to apologize for the damage they had done to him. He came to speak his truth to power with courage, faith, and dignity.

Ultimately, his words shook the town. For this, the town leaders killed him. He didn't speak to their egos, but directly to their souls. When you're speaking truth to power, you're speaking directly to people's souls, reminding the soul of its truth and reality. His words, coming from a place of vulnerability, stirred the people, and for this reason they felt threatened.

Did he fail?

We might notice that this man didn't lead a revolution in his town. If his eloquence convinced any of his fellow townspeople in his lifetime, we don't hear of it. But speaking truth to power is not about results. If we aim at results, then we'll start to engage in backward reasoning. And if we have a result in mind, then we're opening the door to oppressive tendencies.

When we start with the result and work backwards, we may be so attached to a particular result that we start on the path to evil actions. This attachment drives many to dump their values and rationalize all sorts of torture and abuse in the name of achieving a particular goal. Instead, we must remain open to possibility. The result that's aimed for by the people of *ihsan*—believers who act according to what pleases God—is God's acceptance of their deeds and aims, not the control of other people. Hence, the believers never fail, even if they are not followed.

Faith is about handling uncertainty

Faith is never about controlling the wave of life. Instead, it's about facing this wave and acting in accordance with our values. This doesn't give us any guarantees, but rather leaves us open to uncertainty. Faith teaches us to always have hope and faith in God's promise. But we don't know when that promise will be realized. In the meantime, we have to speak truth to power in a way that's rooted in our values.

Thus, Habib an-Najjar—the man who came running—did not fail. He ran in to help, and he did exactly what his faith called him to do. He spoke according to his values, and he appealed to his fellow townspeople's consciences. The townspeople were so sure of themselves, in their power, that they couldn't even allow him to speak his few words.

Here, Habib an-Najjar acts as a witness for God against oppression. He is a witness for the messengers, and a witness for God on the Day of Judgment.

We're all going to exit this world; Habib an-Najjar made his an honorable one. From a faith perspective, he won. He was an innocent who wanted what was best for humanity, and he died with honor.

ABRAHAM: LESSONS ON TRUTH

Indeed, I have turned my face toward He who created the heavens and the earth, inclining toward truth, and I am not of those who associate others with Allah. (Quran 6:79)

This section discusses the difference between rationalizing and truth-seeking in the light of lessons from the Prophet Abraham, upon him peace.

Submission

Submission or surrender to God is an idea that's much-misunderstood, sometimes purposefully so. Both words have mostly negative meanings in current usage. A woman is "submissive," for instance, if she doesn't think for herself. We "surrender" when we are weaker than the other party, usually unwillingly.

Yet the sense in which we submit or surrender to God is something entirely different.

This submission means making ourselves not hardened, but vulnerable, and it means opening ourselves both to self-knowledge and self-awareness. It urges us to understand all the unconscious forces that are at work inside us, and how we can be used, manipulated, and hyped. Most of all, this submission urges us to remember that we are dying, vulnerable beings.

Two verses from the Quran help us remember this. The first is Quran al-Waqia: 80-86:

> A Revelation from the Lord of the Worlds. Is it such a Message that ye would hold in light esteem? And have ye made it your livelihood that ye should declare it false? Then why do ye not (intervene) when (the soul of the dying man)

reaches the throat. And ye the while (sit) looking on. But We are nearer to him than ye, and yet see not. Then why do ye not. If you are exempt from (future) account. Call back the soul, if ye are true (in the claim of independence)?

We are indeed not independent beings, as we often feel ourselves to be. We cannot get on alone in this world: We need each other's friendship, technology, and resources. Sometimes, we rely on each other in healthy, vulnerable ways, aware of our fragility. Often, we rely on each other but refuse to acknowledge our real state.

It's important for us to remember: We're not independent. We can't do things on our own. We need to have self-awareness as we go about our brief lives.

The other verse is Quran Ta-Ha: 14-16:

Verily, I am Allah: There is no god but I: So serve thou Me (only), and establish regular prayer for celebrating My praise. Verily the Hour is coming. My design is to keep it hidden, for every soul to receive its reward by the measure of its Endeavour. Therefore let not such as believe not therein but follow their own lusts, divert thee therefrom, lest thou perish!

To me, this means: Focus on what you need to do and don't focus on distractions. We can't constantly be in a reactive mode, responding to others. We need to stay focused, stay on mission, and stay on the path of what we're trying to do. At any point, we could exit this world.

Awakening

The moment of reflecting on death is submission to God, but it is also a moment of awakening.

Often, in our contemporary world, we talk about death in a non-reflective way. We talk about the functions of systems: the nervous, circulatory, and respiratory systems, which simply stop functioning from some mechanical cause. The assumption here is that the human being is akin to a machine in a universe that is a machine. But the Quran speaks to the meaning of it all, beyond the mechanics.

Extremists, too, ask you to focus on death. But they're not asking you to reflect on your values, or on the relationship between you and God. Instead, they're scaring you so that you might go against your values.

When we reflect on death, it has to be done calmly, in a way that's not forced, and that doesn't force us outside our boundaries.

Submission to the truth

Submission doesn't mean an obedience. Instead, it means coming to the realization that you're vulnerable, your knowledge is limited, and that the human brain tends to rationalize much more than it uses reason to arrive at conclusions. Submission is a recognition that our ignorance will always be greater than what we know. Submission is about trust, about accepting God's wisdom, and accepting that God is not trying to trick you.

Submission is about choosing not to trust in all of one's own impressions of the world, but instead trusting God, and following God out of choice.

Certainly, we can easily be turned off the idea of surrender. If a religious leader is trying to shove faith down your throat, you might see God in just that way—associating God with a loss of control. But surrender is instead about giving ourselves up to our vulnerability, and about turning to God in that state.

Bilqis, the Queen of Sheba, put the principle to the test: living on the truth, and receiving the truth, above everything else. That included putting it above her position, her culture, and her wealth.

Indeed, there is something called truth, and it has a greater right over us than the things that we do and own.

In a time of crisis

When catastrophe hits, the loudest voices are almost always those of charlatans. Indeed, when our brains are disordered, and when we're afraid, it's the hardest time to recognize the voices of the wise.

Surrender means that we stop. We put the brakes on. We remember: There are consequences to our actions, and we're all mortal beings. Surrender brings you to the point of humility, of thinking about how your actions are going to impact others.

Many of us are prepared to receive a truth that benefits us. Yet many truths don't benefit our desires and opinions. Accepting the truth of climate change doesn't benefit our desire to live comfortably in our current fashion. God Most High gives us the cure to this dilemma: "And seek help through patience and prayer, and indeed, it is difficult except for the humbly submissive [to Allah]."

Submission means really accepting the idea that we might be wrong and contemplating that fact. It leads us to look at the stars and think: Maybe I'm wrong!

Submission means being open to the possibility that we're wrong. Indeed, submission is an open state, and we can't properly listen to God if we're not thinking people.

The moment of dying

Many of us have experienced the death of a loved one.

If you can remember that humbling moment, the moment when someone dies, it's a very humbling experience. When I experienced it, it brought me to my knees. It was difficult to come to the realization that there was really nothing I could do to help that person. I really had no power to help that person who was dying right in front of me.

When we're aware of that, it gives us a strong sense of humility. At its best, this humility compels us to be open. This openness to truth is called *taqwa*, the state of being constantly aware.

Faith calls us not to blindness, but to reality. It asks us to be constantly aware, to be conscious, to think, to listen, to reflect on our vulnerability, and to be awake.

To be asleep is to be sunk in our stubborn attachment to our desires. This blinds us to climate change, to racism, to oppression, to how meat is being processed, to how our actions affect the environment. We focus on distractions rather than making choices that really advance our societies and humanity as a whole.

Submission, Awareness, and the Facts

> *In their hearts is a disease; and God has increased their disease: And grievous is the penalty they (incur), because they are false (to themselves).* (Quran 2:10)

Sometimes, we become married to a particular fact or set of facts. It happens to all of us! We researched this fact, we checked it, and we hold it in our hands. This fact defends our beliefs, for one reason or another, and usually this seems like enough. Often, we don't have the strength to look past the facts that we have gathered.

But the way in which we see these facts often has to do with our self-awareness and self-honesty. Two of us might see the exact same fact and set it in two different contexts, and thus see it quite differently.

For instance: People who are anti-Semitic might dig up the fact that some Jews, in the 1930s, found reasons to support Hitler. Those people will further use that fact to delegitimize the sufferings of Jews or perhaps even the entire Holocaust. While the first fact stated is real, a person must consider not just its fact-ness, but also what they're using it for—in this case, to support their hatred and to delegitimize the sufferings and deaths of millions.

Facts aren't everything. Periodically, we also have to check our hearts. Because if there's a disease in our hearts, it will shape how those facts are seen. If we don't have a sense of self-awareness, or at least try to gain a sense of self-awareness, then the disease will increase. In that case, we will cling even harder to our facts and become more belligerent in arguing their merits, instead of stepping back to look at other ways of situating these facts.

Submission and self-knowledge

Surrendering to God is about being awake to the reality that you cannot trick or deceive yourself, just as you cannot trick or deceive God, as God knows the secret depths of our souls, our hearts, and our minds. How can we receive higher truth from God when we are false to ourselves? It isn't possible. Surrender and submission are about self-accountability.

This accountability isn't always visible to the naked eye. But you know when you've done something wrong, and when you have to repair the wrong. Of course, any of us can come up with a great story to justify the wrong thing we've done. But between you and yourself, or between you and God, you know what that truth is. We can lie to ourselves, but ultimately we will be harming not just others, but also ourselves.

This wrong—the harm we have done ourselves—can change the way we see things, and it can cause us to see ill in others. The wrong reinforces itself until we sit down, submit to the truth, and repair the harm.

Two individuals, one fact

I know two young women. Around the same time, both of them did something to violate their personal values in relation to an attractive young man. These needn't be your values, but it's important that these two women transgressed their own values.

One of them repented, called herself to account, and went on to privately repair the harm. The other wanted to argue that she did nothing wrong, so she found a way to explain it away.

When I met with both of them in a shop, all of us saw a third young woman. The woman who had not repented her behavior judged that third woman harshly, saying, "I guess she's trying to get his attention."

The woman who'd looked at herself and repented didn't see things that way. "I think she's just looking at hummus," that woman said. "I don't think she's paying any attention to him."

All three of us were seeing the same set of "facts"—a young woman in a grocery store near a handsome young man—but we interpreted the fact in different ways. Indeed, the young woman who'd explained away her behavior saw the world through a lens of harsh self-deception.

Self-accountability

Submission or surrender is not at all about blindly following a set of beliefs. Indeed, quite the opposite: At its best, it's about submitting to critical thinking and self-accountability.

We don't need to announce our mistakes or failings to the world. But we do need to go through the internal process of setting things right, and of putting our beliefs and actions into alignment, because this affects how we see the world.

It was normal that Meccans with a vested interest did not want to change. It's normal that they did not want to see the things that Muhammad, upon him peace and blessings, was telling them. On the other hand, it was extraordinary that Bilqis was able to set aside her interests and approach the reality around her with a humble heart.

You might get a crowd to support you in winning an argument. But in the end, you have to be honest with yourself. Are you only arguing in this way, or choosing the facts around you, to support your vested interests?

Rejecting the Signs

> *And they rejected those Signs in iniquity and arrogance, though their souls were convinced thereof: so see what was the end of those who acted corruptly!* (Quran 27:14)

We know when we are rejecting something because we're not convinced of it, when we're rejecting something because we know we did something wrong, and when we are just arguing because we don't want to admit wrongdoing.

Once we commit a sin, if it's not repaired, we keep increasing the sin, just as we increase the diseases of the heart. True faith, above all, requires integrity.

Sometimes, this means being uncomfortable. Sometimes, recognizing a wrong can make us feel embarrassed or depressed. We might not feel it in the moment. It's much like Wile E. Coyote walking off the cliff. He continues to walk for a while, on seemingly empty air, before he falls.

When we feel ourselves falling, it's only natural that we want to protect ourselves. We can see the trial as a falling or a call to purification.

Purification is a sign of God's love for a believer and a sign of faith in their heart. We do not want to be in the category of the hypocrites, "those are the ones for whom Allah does not intend to purify their hearts."

Saying "I don't know"

> *Nor canst thou be a guide to the blind, (to prevent them) from straying: only those wilt thou get to listen who believe in Our Signs, and they will bow in Islam. (81) ...Until, when they come (before the Judgment-seat), (God) will say: "Did ye falsify My Signs, though ye comprehended them not in knowledge, or what was it ye did?" (Quran 27:84)*

If someone asks me a question—for instance about Judaism or Christianity, and I don't really know—part of self-accountability is saying that I don't know, and I can't comment on it. For some commenters, they offer nonstop criticism of Islam, yet they have never read the Quran or made a deep study of the religion. This, too, is a form of self-deception.

Most of these commenters, I'd hope, wouldn't talk about an area of science that was completely foreign to their studies, such as an anthropologist going on television to talk about computer science, or vice versa. Yet people often have difficulty saying, "I don't know."

The Prophet, upon him peace and blessings, worked with people who were atheists. These people were not attacking the faith, they were simply not convinced. These atheists would come and speak with him, out in the public square, and they would ask questions.

Yet some people who are hardcore critics refuse the words, "I don't know," and they attack as a form of self-deception.

They fall into a state of heedlessness because they choose to run away, to escape and avoid the steep road to understanding. It's not because they don't have the capacity to understand, but because they chose to turn away or cover up the truth.

Looking in the mirror

Ultimately, the Quran is meant to be a mirror. It's not a cut-and-paste tool in order to defend Islam. It's a text that helps you look at yourself, to know yourself first of all.

In this way, you can start to see your blind spots.

When I was reading the Quran, I used to get confused:

> Here is a troop rushing headlong with you! No welcome for them! Truly, they shall burn in the Fire! (The followers shall cry to the misleaders:)
>
> "Nay, ye (too)! No welcome for you! It is ye who have brought this upon us! Now evil is (this) place to stay in!" They will say: "Our Lord! Whoever brought this upon us, Add to him a double Penalty in the Fire!"
>
> And they will say: "What has happened to us that we see not men whom we used to number among the bad ones? Did we treat them (as such) in ridicule, or have (our) eyes failed to perceive them?" Truly that is just and fitting, the mutual recriminations of the People of the Fire!
>
> Say: "Truly am I a Warner: no god is there but the one Allah, Supreme and Irresistible. The Lord of the heavens and the earth, and all between. Exalted in Might, able to enforce His Will, forgiving again and again."
>
> Say: "That is a Message Supreme (above all)[.]"
>
> (Quran 38:59)

I wondered: Why is God angry with both groups? Why do both the misleaders and the misled both get punished? But over time, I realized that the first group wasn't simply innocent. They were misled by their own self-deception.

Those who are blindly attached to a hateful leader even when presented with facts are also guilty. They were not really misled, but instead they were engaged in self-deception. They were so absorbed in the evil with others that it led them down the road of perdition. They never thought: Maybe I'm wrong, and maybe I have to repair the harm.

Science and truth

Science is a great way of moving forward in particular disciplines. Yet we always have to be in a state of wonder, because science is a tool and a methodology, and the people who are scientists are also human beings. It's good for us to engage in science while also reminding ourselves that we're human.

It's good and healthy to come up with discoveries based on the truth that has reached us. But we should also stay, when possible, in a state of wonder.

Surrendering to the Knowledge Embedded in Your Heart

The hidden well-spring of your soul must needs rise and run murmuring to the sea; And the treasure of your infinite depths would be revealed to your eyes.

—Khalil Gibran

You might be wondering: If I surrender, what exactly am I surrendering to?

God is not asking you to surrender to a teacher, or anything outside yourself. God is also not asking you to surrender, or submit, to thin air. God is asking you to look within your heart, to the embedded knowledge in your heart, and to surrender to that knowledge that already exists inside you.

We hear about this because the Prophet Abraham, upon him peace, once came to a decisive point in his life. He believed in God, but there was so much he didn't know about how life, death, and the world around him worked. He came to the physical limitations of his knowledge, and, as he did, Abraham felt a murmuring in his heart. He wanted to know how these things worked.

At this point, Abraham didn't look outside himself, as that is not where the journey begins. Feeling the murmur of questions, he turned inward to God, seeking guidance and seeking to know.

We will continually have murmurs in our heart. First, we must turn with those murmurs to God, asking God to help us, to satisfy the murmur. Certainly, from this point, we can also use all the tools we have to look out at the world: our intellect, our skills, and our science. But looking inward is the foundation. Without the right roots, we can't build in the right direction. We have to turn to our hearts, because that's where the roots of our knowledge are, and our heart is its proper platform. In turning to our hearts, we surrender to God.

Whatever crossroads or question you face, whatever the murmuring in your heart, it is important to start off with God's embedded knowledge. It guides us, and we can always return to it, particularly when we keep our heart healthy.

Building without foundations

Science certainly can be built on the foundation of a healthy heart. But it can also be built on other, more dangerous foundations.

For instance, some contemporary scientists dangerously promote Islamophobia in a way that's scientific, much as scientists once and currently promote eugenics or racial superiority as "scientific." These are particularly dangerous propositions, as, in the current era, scientists are often viewed as people whose worldview is beyond reproach, and whose opinions are infallibly intelligent.

Faith does value reason, but faith asks us to use our intelligence as a tool, not as an end in itself, or as a tool that might take us in the direction of our anger. After all, whatever our hearts might be, they are never transparent. What we seek and strive for privately influences how we see and receive in the world. A scientist who nurtures racist fears in his heart will see racial hierarchies in his science. Just so, a scientist who nurtures a fear of Muslims may see a "clash of civilizations" and an "enemy Islam."

The state of our heart influences what we can hear. For instance, US Pres. Donald Trump sees women as sexual objects to exploit and objectify, and that influences how he can perceive the world. Women can go to many lengths—could make amazing, stunning arguments about how they are thinking, feeling creatures—but he won't be able to hear these arguments until he comes to terms with himself.

God will judge us by our hearts

And that which is (locked up) in (human) breasts is made manifest. That their Lord had been Well-acquainted with them, (even to) that Day? (Quran 100:10-11)

Pharaoh ordered his minister to build a massive structure, called a sarh, up into the sky. Pharaoh wanted to reach the heights of the heavens to rip the cover off this God that Moses worshiped, because he thought Moses was lying.

Pharaoh did build great things. From our vantage now, he might seem only to be a tyrant, but that is not how he was seen in his time. He was also able to build great things.

Yet inventing the wheel doesn't necessarily make you fit to determine its ethical usage.

Pharaoh, like so many others, believed that by striving to figure out how everything works, he would also know what everything means.

Submission is not humiliation

Many people see "submission" or "surrender" as relegating oneself to insignificance, as being humiliated and downtrodden. But submission or surrender is not about insignificance. It is about being in harmony with the truth, seeing ourselves as part of the world, and seeing how we have responsibility toward others.

Those who don't submit often want to reserve the right to play by their own rules, and to declare that no one has any rights over them. One example of this is, again, US Pres. Donald Trump, who was obsessed with the "great" things that he had done, and didn't want anyone to lay requirements on him: not women, not citizens, not his own party.

The Quran says that we must come to agreements: We are living in a world together, so we have to live in harmony. When we surrender, we are surrendering to the understanding that we all have rights of our own as well as responsibilities to one another.

These responsibilities don't mean that we need to go out and change everyone into copies of us. Faith means that we should be spending time cultivating ourselves, not attacking people who don't believe as we do. If we are out attacking others, it probably means that we don't really believe in what we're doing. We are not here to prove someone else's faults.

We're here to take care of our family, our environment, and the people around us. Such is the knowledge embedded in our heart, and we must find that knowledge, discover it, and turn towards it.

The importance of hajj: Reconnecting to Abraham's story

When the Prophet Muhammad, upon him peace and blessings, went on hajj, he reconnected with the story of his ancestor, Prophet Ibrahim (Abraham), as well as Hajjar (Hagar) and Ismail (Ishmael). Along with Noah, Moses, Jesus, and Muhammad, Prophet Abraham was one of the five resolute prophets. Peace and blessings upon them all.

When those of us who follow in his footsteps go on hajj—the pilgrimage to Mecca and surrounding areas—we also commemorate and reconnect to the stories of Abraham and his family, just as we reconnect to ourselves, to God, and to the stories of all the prophets.

Although hajj commemorates the prophet Abraham and his story, it also encompasses the stories of all those who came after him, the children of both Isaac and Ishmael. The act of going to Mecca on pilgrimage involves both physical and mental activity, and it is a complete act of worship: of the body, mind, and soul.

According to the Quran, "Pilgrimage thereto is a duty men owe to Allah; those who can afford the journey; but if any deny faith, Allah stands not in need of any of His creatures." (Quran 3:97)

Those who are able to perform the hajj, financially and physically, are expected to do so at least once in their lifetime.

Mt. Arafat: A holy site from the time of Adam and Eve

It's understood that, when Adam and Eve first came down to Earth, they were separated. They spent some time traveling on Earth before they met at Mt. Arafat, the name of which stems from the word to know, the meet again, to reconnect.

First, we reconnect to the story of Adam and Eve. It was they who started the foundations of the Ka'aba, although they did not complete it.

When Hagar and the infant Ishmael arrived in the area, it was nothing like contemporary Mecca, which is filled with buildings, lights, and cars. It was, instead, an uninhabited desert.

Hagar came to Abraham late in his life. She had been a slave of Abraham's wife, Sarah, who in turn sent Hagar to Abraham in the hopes that Hagar could bear her husband a son. Abraham had long been ridiculed by his family for not producing a son, and Hagar did indeed bear him one.

It is important to realize that this story is very specific to its time and context. If a man, today, dreamt that he should bring his wife to the desert and leave her there, with her infant, that would be a criminal act. But Abraham was a prophet, and the messages he received came directly from God. What's more, we have the story as it's being told by God to Muhammad.

When God tells this story, it is a story of love, truth, sacrifice, and sincerity. As an expression of immense love, this story helps increase our faith.

Abraham's vision

Just as Abraham was celebrating the arrival of his first son, he received a command from God: To take his wife Hagar and the infant Ishmael to the wilderness of Mecca—known as "Paran" in the Biblical account.

When Abraham took Hagar and Ishmael to Mecca, she asked him: Why are you leaving us in this desolate place, with no one and no companion? She repeated this question many times, yet Abraham did not reply. Finally, Hagar asked him whether he had been ordered by God to do this.

Yes, Abraham told her.

And so Hagar answered, in faith and in submission to God's will, "If God ordained this, then He will never get us lost."

Abraham then left them. Soon, Hagar and Ishmael, alone in the desert, ran out of water. It was pitch dark, and the baby was crying, and yet Hagar continued to exert herself in a search for water. She ran—seven times—between two hills called Safa and Marwa, in her search for water.

This effort on Hagar's part drives home to us what faith is: a complete exertion. Hagar did not sit still, beside her infant, and pray to God for help and deliverance. She kept the faith, but she also did everything she could to get water for her son. When she had exhausted herself—at that very moment she witnessed a miracle. Young Ishmael was crying and kicking the ground with his heels. The tiny baby's kicks revealed a small spring of water, which came from beneath his feet.

Hagar rushed to contain the water, so that it wouldn't be lost among the sands. In doing so, she made the well now known as Zamzam, which is over 3,000 years old.

As birds can sense where water is, they guided people to the desert, to where Hagar and Ishmael could be found beside the well. Slowly, people began to camp in the surrounding area, and Hagar and Ishmael were beloved by them, and connected to them.

One of the ways contemporary Muslims reconnect with Hagar's story is by making seven rounds of the hills of Safa and Marwa. It's a reminder to all of us that miracles are witnessed after we exert and exhaust ourselves, not before. It also reminds us that, while we may not comprehend God's wisdom in all things, we need to have a good opinion of God and trust in His planning.

Also, it's important to remember that our story is part of a bigger one, written by the best of authors, God. We should act based on our faith and values, but also trust in God's divine story. Hagar did not know her story would be an inspiration for thousands of years to come, and an inspiration to millions of pilgrims from around the world, both during the main hajj and the smaller one, called the umra.

This African woman, Hagar, is a guiding light for both women and men in their journey to connect with themselves and with God. Even the Prophet Muhammad, peace and blessings upon him, followed in Hagar's footsteps.

Completing the Ka'aba

And remember Abraham and Ishmael raised the foundations of the House (With this prayer): "Our Lord! Accept (this service) from us: For Thou art the All-Hearing, the All-knowing. Our Lord! make of us Muslims, bowing to Thy (Will), and of our progeny a people Muslim, bowing to Thy (will); and show us our place for the celebration of (due) rites; and turn unto us (in Mercy); for Thou art the Oft-Returning, Most Merciful." (Quran 2:127-128)

When Ishmael was a young man, he and his father Abraham, upon them peace, finished building the first house of worship to God, the Ka'aba. What Adam had begun, Ismail and Ibrahim completed.

After that, God commanded Abraham to call all people to hajj. Naturally, Abraham asked God: "O Allah! How shall my voice reach all of those people?" But God told him his duty was only to give the call. God would make sure it reached all the people.

So the Prophet Abraham climbed Mt. Arafat, the mountain of connection, and called in his loudest voice: "O People! Verily Allah has prescribed upon you hajj, so perform hajj."

Since that call was made from a heart full of sincerity and truth, people answered. Each year, there have been more, and now we witness God's plan and power, as we see millions of people, from different countries and backgrounds and means, going to perform hajj, answering the call Abraham made thousands of years before.

> "And proclaim the hajj among mankind. They will come to thee on foot and (mounted) on every camel, lean on account of journeys through deep and distant mountain highways." (Quran 22:28)

Sacrifice and Ishmael, the faithful son

When Ishmael was a young man, Abraham was called by God to another difficult command.

> "O my son! I see in vision that I offer thee in sacrifice: Now see what is thy view!" (The son) said: "O my father! Do as thou art commanded: thou will find me, if Allah so wills one practicing Patience and Constancy!" When they had both submitted their wills (to Allah, and he had laid him prostrate on his forehead (for sacrifice), We called out to him "O Abraham! Thou hast already fulfilled the vision! Thus indeed do We reward those who do right." (Quran 37:102-105)

This was clearly a trial for elderly Abraham. He was old, and this was his only son, his right arm and his helper. Again, Abraham did not understand the wisdom of God's plan. But he was not an ordinary man who lived for his desires, and this was not an ordinary vision. No human will ever have such a vision again.

Abraham didn't leave his son out of the decision, but instead he explained to him what he'd been told by God. And Ishmael echoed what his mother had said years before: "Do as your God commanded."

Just as with Hagar, this is not a story we are meant to imitate in its details. Instead, it's a story about righteousness and the strength of faith.

Ishmael had now reached an age where his parents needed his companionship and support, and, just then, Abraham was commanded to sacrifice his first and only son.

The test and sacrifice

As a basic rule, a vision or a dream for a prophet is not like one for us, as it is a command from God.

— Jamal Badawi.

We are not prophets. If we had a dream telling us to sacrifice one of our children, surely we should go see a doctor, as our dreams are not commandments from God. It is also important to remember that we have this story not from Abraham, but from God, relayed to Prophet Muhammad, upon him peace and blessings.

After Ishmael's response—telling his father to do as God commanded—Abraham took his son to a place now called Mina, near the city of Mecca. Thousands of years later, this is the location where pilgrims sacrifice a lamb or other animal.

Abraham was about to fulfil God's command when an angel came from the heavens carrying a large ram for him to sacrifice in place of his son. The whole family thus passed a test and became guiding lights for all of humanity to come after them, helping us to understand the difference between having hope and faith in God. Abraham stood firm just as Jacob did when his son Joseph, and then his son Benjamin, were both taken from him.

We all love something that competes with our love of God: a spouse, a child, a career, a home. That object of love is our weakness and our test in life. When we are separated from what we love, it is normal to feel sad, as Jacob was over his sons. But while we may not understand the wisdom of the trial, we must continue to have a good opinion of God and to remain hopeful that God will reunite us with our beloved, either in this world or the next.

After Abraham's test, he and Sarah were rewarded with a second son, Isaac. From that branch came Jacob and many other prophets. From Ishmael's line came the Prophet Muhammad, upon him peace and blessings. Indeed, God promised to bless people through Abraham and to give him a great lineage of prophets through his descendants.

The two weeks of hajj: Reconnecting to Abraham and Hagar's stories

The journey to the holy city is a reminder for us that our entire life is nothing but a journey. Our life is a journey that may be long or short, only God knows.

We have to realize that we are passing through a journey in our life that has an end and that our ultimate destiny is to go back to God and stand accountable for our lives.

— Jamal Badawi

When I went on hajj, someone recommended I read the Quran from beginning to end during the pilgrimage. I recommend people start early, even before getting on the plane, as the place is overwhelmed with crowds and can be exhausting. There are many rituals one must do when performing hajj. Although each group usually has a religious guide, it is sometimes hard for the guide to answer all questions. For that reason, it's important to prepare ourselves for what to expect when traveling and while staying in Mecca and Medina.

The first ten days of Hijrah are the holiest days. Many people who don't go on hajj also participate in the rituals of the first ten days, before the Eid or feast-day comes.

When pilgrims first arrive, they circle the Ka'aba seven times. Abraham built this first house of worship, and we circle because that's how life is: We don't go astray if we just keep turning, worshiping God by turning to him.

After that, we run between the hills of Safa and Marwa seven times, to reconnect with Hagar's story.

The ninth day is the Day of Arafa, or the Day of Knowing. Those who are not on hajj can fast, although for those who are on the pilgrimage, it's too strenuous to fast. The Day of Knowing is a day of remembering. It reminds us of our responsibility and mission on earth, of our end, and of the Day of Judgment. It reminds us how we will stand accountable before God, and it is a practical manifestation of the Islamic principles of fraternity and equality before God.

Pilgrims, now in the millions, gather around the mountain known as Arafah or Arafat. This is a very holy site: the place where Adam and Eve met, the place where Abraham was taught about hajj, and a place where we all return to knowing God.

On the tenth day comes the Eid al-Adha, when pilgrims sacrifice an animal in memory of Abraham's sacrifice, giving a certain percentage—or all of the animal—to those who can't afford their own. Jeewan Chanicka explained Abraham's sacrifice in his hajj reminders with the following words:

But it wasn't his son that was slaughtered. It was his attachment. It was his attachment to anything that could compete with his love for God. And the beauty of such a sacrifice is this: Once you let go of your attachment, what you love is given back to you, in a purer, better form. So let us ask ourselves during these beautiful days of sacrifice, which attachments do we need to slaughter?

After the Eid, pilgrims go from Arafat to Muzdalifa, where they sleep outside, on the ground, to reflect on their connection to the poor and homeless.

From there, pilgrims go to Jamrat al-Aqaba, to throw stones at the pillars to remind us how Satan came and whispered to Abraham not to follow God's command. So we visit Jamrat al-Aqaba and throw stones, just as Abraham did.

After that, pilgrims return to the Ka'aba. Just as we begin with the Ka'aba, we end with the Ka'aba. We do it as a farewell, after which it's possible to travel around and see other sites before going home.

Many ways of connecting with hajj

Not every believer can travel for the hajj. Some don't have enough money, and others aren't physically able.

My mother was a stroke patient, and she had various ailments that made it impossible for her to go on hajj again. It was up to me to remind her of the day, as she became aphasic after her stroke and could not recall the day of the year. It is important to include Muslims who are disabled or sick on this day and not to forget them.

One way is to make a sacrifice on the behalf of a family member who cannot go themselves.

One year, after making a sacrifice on my mother's behalf, I visited her. As she was aphasic, she could understand but was unable to find the words to communicate clearly. Through charades, my mother was able to tell me about a dream she'd had in which a live sheep was coming to her. I smiled after understanding her dream, and I told her I had not forgotten to make a sacrifice on her behalf. She smiled, too, as she felt included. When her health was strong enough, we allowed her to fast on this one day. She could not read, so we made sure she could listen to the Quran on tape.

Part of remembering those in need is not just providing sustenance, but also including them in the spiritual community.

Opening a new chapter: Returning from hajj

When pilgrims return, we join a new chapter in our lives.

At times, people will expect those who went on hajj can no longer make mistakes. Or perhaps we might have that expectation of others. But one thing the hajj teaches us is that we don't ever arrive. We keep facing hardships, and we keep making mistakes. What's important is to remember the importance of accountability, repentance, and seeking guidance and aid from God.

The story of creation begins with Adam, upon him peace, making a mistake out of neglect. And human history is, in many ways, a series of people making mistakes. The best expectations we can have of ourselves is to repent often and to be accountable. And if someone seeks their rights from us, we must work to address that.

JACOB AND JOSEPH: LOVE AND PROJECTION

And he raised his parents upon the throne, and they bowed to him in prostration. And he said, "O my father, this is the explanation of my vision of before. My Lord has made it reality. And He was certainly good to me when He took me out of prison and brought you [here] from bedouin life after Satan had induced [estrangement] between me and my brothers. Indeed, my Lord is Subtle in what He wills. Indeed, it is He who is the Knowing, the Wise." (Quran 12:100)

How We Tell "The Most Beautiful Story"

We relate to you, [O Muhammad], the best of stories in what We have revealed to you of this Qur'an although you were, before it, among the unaware. (Quran 12:3)

Many people use love as an excuse to abuse others. Joseph faced a lot of abuse from people who loved him—or at least claimed they did. Joseph's stories help us to better understand the difference between love and projection.

Everything we know about God comes from the angels, who were sent to messengers, who in turn told stories to humanity. Stories are made of words following other words. Listening to a story is to follow a chain of experiences. Some stories can be exaggerated and bloated with untruths, but others are filled with wisdom. Good stories not only inspire us, but also strengthen our emotional and spiritual well-being. Stories can nurture us as individuals and as communities.

Often, when we tell each other stories, we embellish them to make ourselves out as heroes. But wisdom stories stand out from the others: they help us understand history, psychology, ourselves, and others.

When God shared the story of Joseph, or Yusuf, he shared a story that had many facets. It has lessons about childhood, parenting, envy, false accusations, forgiveness, love, and false love. The story never splits people into groups of "good" vs. "evil." Here, people can be good, but still do evil deeds. And people can do evil deeds, yet over time they can grow and be nurtured back toward their better selves.

Who brings us the story?

The story of Joseph and Jacob comes to us from Muhammad, peace and blessings upon them all. Even before he began to relate the Quran, Muhammad was known for two things: honesty and trustworthiness. He was known for the clarity of his vision and the truthfulness of his words. Those who listened knew he wouldn't tell stories to harm others, nor would he hide aspects of a story because they didn't bring him benefit.

His first wife Khadijah, who knew Muhammad many years before revelation reached him, also knew how trustworthy he was.

Certainly, everyone should tell their story. The act of storytelling itself will challenge us to find the truth. Yet when we're listening to others, we must think hard about whether to trust the truth of their tales, and whether we're hearing from someone who knows.

A storyteller doesn't have to be purposefully spreading falsehoods: They could simply not know, as Prophet Muhammad didn't know until the Quran was sent down to him.

The Dream

> *Joseph said to his father, "O my father, indeed I have seen [in a dream] eleven stars and the sun and the moon; I saw them prostrating to me." (Quran 12:4)*

The chapter of the Quran we know as "Joseph" was sent to Muhammad from God as a whole reality, with all its many details. With some of the stories that come from God, we don't have the full picture. But with the story of the Prophet Joseph, we find a whole living reality, and also the best of stories.

The story thus stands as a proof of Prophet Muhammad, upon him peace and blessings, as God revealed many things that weren't previously known about Joseph and Jacob. For instance, Joseph's paternal aunt loved him so fiercely that—when he was supposed to move from the home of his aunt to that of his father—Joseph's aunt accused him of thievery so that she could keep him a little longer.

But the story really begins when Joseph has a dream. In it, Joseph saw eleven stars prostrating themselves, as well as the moon and the sun. There are many confusing aspects to the dream: When the moon is present, the sun should be absent. And why eleven stars, when the sky is filled with their presence? Why did Joseph see the eleven stars first, and only then the moon and the sun?

Young Joseph related the dream to his father, the elderly Jacob, who well understood the dream. His young son would become an instrument of God and would serve Him in a higher purpose. Jacob knew that the dream was a message not only to his son, but also to himself, and he was being given this insight so that he could remain firm and patient through all the trials yet to come.

Jacob knew all this, but he didn't want to scare his young son. He knew his older sons burned with jealousy, and he knew that if Joseph shared this strange dream, his older brothers might harm him. Thus Jacob told him: Don't share your dream with any of your siblings.

Jacob knew his elder sons were engaged in secret plotting and planning, in scheming in the shadows against his two youngest boys. Those who are convinced of their argument, Jacob knew, would face the world openly. They would speak directly, like Moses, upon him peace. But Jacob's elder sons, who knew they were doing wrong, made their plans in secret. It is said that, when someone plans evil against another, eventually God will use that plan, turning it on the one who is plotting.

Jacob knew all this, and he knew that one day, his son Joseph would be elevated above all his siblings, and even above his father and mother. Thus, the trials and tribulations Jacob was yet to suffer came wrapped in a subtle kindness, a dream to comfort and guide.

Joseph's elder brothers had long been envious both of Joseph and of his brother Benjamin, the two youngest of the family. The elder brothers all felt Joseph and Benjamin were more beloved than them. In truth, the elder brothers knew that these were young children whose mother had died, that Jacob was trying to be both mother and father to them, and that's why he showed them such tenderness. But Joseph was also strikingly handsome, and all of this cut into the elder brothers' hearts and filled them with envy.

The elder brothers knew they were stronger, and, in their hearts, they knew why Jacob offered the younger ones such tenderness. Yet the evil inside them had overtaken their goodness. Thus, they began to plan a solution, a way to regain their previous dominance over their father's heart.

One brother suggested killing young Joseph. Perhaps, another brother suggested, they should allow him to wander by himself until a creature snatched him up and ate him? Another brother suggested throwing Joseph in a deep well.

We can see that, even though the brothers were consumed by envy, they did end up choosing the lesser evil, of lowering Joseph into a well. They did still have goodness inside them, even though the evil overpowered it.

Indeed, with their twisted reasoning, they believed that—if they could get rid of Joseph and regain the center of their father's heart—then they could become more righteous. This logic doesn't add up, and they must've known this, but still they went on.

And here the deceit begins: The elder brother approached their father, Jacob, and told him that they wanted to bring Joseph out with them, so their little brother could play and enjoy his time.

Their father was immediately suspicious.

Why Papa? they asked. Why don't you trust us with Joseph?

Certainly, they knew why, and their insistence that their father should trust them was itself a sign of their untrustworthiness.

But Jacob didn't address the issue directly, as he loved his oldest sons as well. Instead, he said: I'm afraid that, if you take him, the wolves will snatch up Joseph while you're busy.

But the elder brothers insisted, and Jacob worried that their envy would grow even worse if he kept young Joseph at home. In the end, Jacob didn't know what to do. So he put his trust in God, and let the elder brothers take Joseph.

Into the well, another vision

After his elder brothers lowered Joseph into the well, Joseph saw another vision. God inspired this knowledge in Joseph: One day, he would tell his story to his brothers, and they would not be aware of his identity. One day, he would be elevated to a high position.

This strengthened his heart and comforted him. Joseph knew that, one day, his brothers would come seeking his help. One day, the positions of strength and weakness would be reversed.

Meanwhile, at the same time, the elder brothers returned to Jacob, weeping crocodile tears. They came home at night, when Jacob could not see that their tears were false and forced. They stayed in hiding, in the shadows, and rambled as they told their ever-shifting story.

At first, the brothers said that Joseph was playing, and later they said he was watching their belongings when the wolf ate him. They even accused their father, saying, We know you won't believe us! Then they showed him Joseph's shirt, with fake blood on it.

This made the story even less believable. If a wolf had eaten Joseph, why would the wolf leave behind a bloody shirt?

Jacob didn't accept the story, but he didn't have any evidence against his elder sons. He also loved these older sons very much. So, despite everything, Jacob didn't punish them. Instead, he practiced *sabirun jameel*, or a beautiful patience, believing God's message, and believing Joseph would return. For the rest of it, Jacob left the matter to God.

The elder brothers could not help but sneak back to the scene of their crime. By now, others had come to get water, and they found young Joseph, upon him peace. The man looking down in the well was startled by Joseph's beauty, and he thought immediately of how to turn this into a profit.

The brothers, who were watching, now stepped out and sold their brother to the slave-trader for a small price. They sold him quickly, and for little money, as they were afraid of prolonging the transaction, afraid their father would be alerted. So the man bought Joseph with the intention of selling him to al-Aziz, who had no son.

So God has Joseph brought to the king's palace, under The Aziz or The Exalted One, and thus he begins to turn the brothers' plot against them. Here, Joseph grows to adulthood and becomes aware of himself. Here, he reaches his years of adulthood and strength. As he comes of age, Joseph is given the blessing of being able to distinguish right from wrong, as this was his nature.

Seduction

And she, in whose house he was, sought to seduce him. She closed the doors and said, "Come, you." He said, "[I seek] the refuge of Allah. Indeed, he is my master, who has made good my residence. Indeed, wrongdoers will not succeed." (Quran 12:23)

When he reached adulthood, Joseph was no less beautiful than he'd been as a child. Al-Aziz's wife no longer saw him as a child, and she began to see Joseph as a man. She led him deep into the castle and locked all doors leading to the room they were in. Her name was Zuleikha, and she was the most desirable and beautiful women in the palace.

Zuleikha knew that what she was doing was wrong—the fact that she locked all these doors was a clear sign of it. She was the most beautiful woman of her city, and when she approached Joseph with a full heart, he was also a healthy young man. She called him to come to her. She called him a second time, and he responded, "God forbid."

Seeking refuge with God is a powerful thing, as the Prophet Muhammad, upon him peace and blessings, well knew. Once, his new wife was manipulated by others. When Muhammad came to their marital bed, she said, I seek refuge from God from you.

The Prophet Muhammad, peace and blessings on him, accepted this at once, granted her protection, and removed himself. So even between a married couple, this protection is sacrosanct.

Yet Zuleikha did not respect Joseph's words. Joseph ran from her, through door after door, and Zuleikha ripped the back of his shirt while he was running from her. Then the last door opened, and al-Aziz was standing before them.

Zuleikha gathered herself and asked: What could you think of someone who tried to seduce your wife, except that he be punished or imprisoned?

This, again, is a person who is not wholly bad. She didn't choose the worst of the evils available to her, that Joseph be killed, or silenced, or stoned to death. She had goodness in her, but she was driven by love and lust.

Joseph told the truth, saying that she had tried to seduce him. A man from Zuleikha's family bore witness, saying that—if Joseph's shirt was torn from the front, then Zuleikha was telling the truth. Yet if it was torn from the back, she was lying. Zuleikha was forced to acknowledge the truth, and her husband told her to repent.

Through all this, al-Aziz was shamed. Knowing the truth, he was worried about what people would say when they heard his wife preferred Joseph over him. The childless al-Aziz didn't want a scandal, so he turned the other way.

Yet there was good in him, too, as he didn't insist on Joseph being killed. He just looked the other way.

Word reaches the city

The story didn't stay locked up in the palace for long. Gossip reached from home to home, and the women of the city began to talk about the affair. Al-Aziz's wife, who didn't like how she was being portrayed in these stories, grew upset. She planned an event with the notable women of the city, so that she could tell her side.

The women all had food they were cutting when Joseph came into the room, and Zuleikha told them to hold onto their knives.

The women were so moved by Joseph's beauty that they thought he must be an angel. The women cut their hands in shock and amazement.

And so, Zuleikha told them, you cut your hands in amazement at his beauty, so how can you blame me for my actions? Yet again, Zuleikha tried to call Joseph to come to her or be imprisoned, and now she had the notable women on her side.

Yet Joseph responded that prison was better than what the women called him to do.

The men in the kingdom consulted, and they agreed that it was better to keep Joseph in prison for a while. Again, they didn't make a noble choice, but they did choose a lesser harm.

Two other prisoners, who were sent in at the same time as Joseph, saw goodness in Joseph and sought his guidance. Both of them had dreams, and they asked Joseph to interpret them for them. One saw himself pressing grapes, while the other saw birds eating bread from off his head. These men may have done bad things to get themselves sent to prison. Yet they also had goodness in them, which allowed them to see the good in Joseph.

Joseph interpreted their dreams, in order to help lead them to the right path, as he believed they came to him to be guided to God. And so he told them that one of them would later work for the king, while one would be crucified. He didn't tell them which would happen to which, as he didn't want either of the men to become distressed and hopeless.

Joseph only asked that, whichever of them was to work for the king should remind the king of Joseph.

Yet when the man who'd dreamed of pressing wine was released, Satan whispered to him, and he forgot about Joseph's plight. Thus, Joseph remained in prison for many more years.

The king's dream

When Joseph was around thirty years old, the king had a powerful dream, in which he saw seven fat cows being eaten by seven lean ones, and seven green ears and seven dry. He asked all the nobles in his kingdom, but none of them knew how to interpret dreams.

Finally, after the passage of many years, Joseph's former cellmate—who was now the king's cupbearer—remembered him, and he particularly remembered his skill with dreams. And so suddenly everyone in the kingdom, who'd once harmed Joseph, was now in need of him.

Joseph interpreted the dream, which foretold of seven hard years, after which would come a year of rain. They were to store most of their grain and eat only very little of it, Joseph said. Now, the men and women of the kingdom felt a healthy sense of shame and respect as they looked up to Joseph and his important wisdom.

From weakness to strength

> *Thus did We give established power to Joseph in the land, to take possession therein as, when, or where he pleased. We bestow of our Mercy on whom We please, and We suffer not, to be lost, the reward of those who do good. But verily the reward of the Hereafter is the best, for those who believe, and are constant in righteousness.* (Quran 12:56-57)

The King was impressed with this interpretation and requested that Joseph be brought to him. However, Joseph was not as eager to leave the prison. He told his former cellmate to go back to the King and tell him:

> So the king said: "Bring ye him unto me." But when the messenger came to him, (Joseph) said: "Go thou back to thy lord, and ask him, 'What is the state of mind of the ladies who cut their hands'? For my Lord is certainly well aware of their snare."
>
> (The king) said (to the ladies): "What was your affair when ye did seek to seduce Joseph from his (true) self?" The

ladies said: "Allah preserve us! no evil know we against him!" Said the 'Aziz's wife: "Now is the truth manifest (to all): it was I who sought to seduce him from his (true) self: He is indeed of those who are (ever) true (and virtuous).

"This (say I), in order that He may know that I have never been false to him in his absence, and that Allah will never guide the snare of the false ones.

"Nor do I absolve my own self (of blame): the (human) soul is certainly prone to evil, unless my Lord do bestow His Mercy: but surely my Lord is Oft-Forgiving, Most Merciful." (12:50-53)

Now the King wanted him to reach a station of high rank with him. He saw him as someone of good character, generous, and trustworthy. Thus the King told him:

Be assured this day, thou art, before our own presence, with rank firmly established, and fidelity fully proved! (12:54)

The first thing is that he was declared innocent of wrongdoing with the desire that's hardest to control, which is sex. Also he gave his interpretation without demanding his release, and without attacking Zuleikha, or referring to her shame. Now he asks to be the treasurer to ensure the dream he interpreted will be enforced and to protect the community. This was courage on his part to ask for the position, given his dream and vision. Now he was established.

Throughout his first three decades, Joseph faced a great deal of abuse, particularly from people who claimed to love him. One of the things this story shows us is the difference between love and projection.

What Joseph's Story Tells Us About Sexual Harassment

A person will always interpret everything he hears according to the light which dominates their heart.

—Imam Ghazali

During the 2016 presidential campaign, there was a lot of talk about a tape in which US Pres. Donald Trump discussed grabbing women and violating their bodies. The views I share here, about sexual violence and harassment, are strictly mine. They are not a scholarly or legal analysis in the light of Islam, but instead my personal reflections about what the story of Prophet Joseph, upon him peace, can tell us about life today.

The public dialogue about sexual violence against women seems to hit flash points of rage. We go for a while, quietly simmering, largely ignoring the topic. Then something happens, and we dump all the anger and angst out of our systems. While this may be cathartic, it is not necessarily helpful. Instead, things stay much as they were until another flashpoint.

What these flashpoints lack is the nurturing or transformation that can lead us to a better understanding of ourselves and others. Each time there's a fire, an exchange of insults, and a declared winner. Then we await the next crisis without fundamentally changing.

It's true that these exchanges have helped bring about laws and policies that make many sexual assaults a crime. But they have also pushed the disease into hiding. Now lewd, violating conversations about women take place in private, while outwardly people profess to be nothing but respectful.

This isn't a reflection of everyone. However, Trump's tapes do call to mind the aftermath of many other scandalous assaults by people who had one face for the television and another for behind the scenes.

Recently, on Twitter, a woman named Kelly Oxford encouraged other women to write about their experiences of rape culture. Oxford said she was getting 50 stories a minute. Clearly, this indicates a major problem.

We must applaud the women who have stepped forward to share their stories. They help us understand the problem of rape culture, as well as a woman's right to make choices. However, we often remain stuck on the problem. The numerous stories of sexual aggression, assault, and harassment tell us that our solutions have not yet helped to nurture men to a place where they can better respect women.

I pause here to share a part of a story of Prophet Joseph, upon him peace, and to share how this story helps us to move toward a genuine conversation where we—in all humility—nurture each other to a better place.

Each Prophet's story shares with us many lessons that help us in our growth and journey toward God. Part of Joseph's life experience was living under al-Aziz, or Potiphar, and his wife Zuleikha. We know Zuleikha developed feelings for Joseph, upon him peace, and tried to seduce him. When she was caught, she blamed Joseph for seducing her.

When the evidence showed that this very powerful woman was indeed guilty, a scandal emerged, and she encouraged other women to come to her defense. She said that either Joseph could accept her, or he could go to prison. Joseph preferred prison.

Why does God tell the story in this way, so that it seems to validate view that women are temptresses or seductresses, and that men are blameless victims?

Sometimes, it is difficult for us to hear past our deeply held prejudices and biases, and it takes telling a story in a different way to make us see in a new way.

During the 2016 campaign, Donald Trump also attacked Ghazala Khan. After that, some Muslim women started a campaign called #CanYouHearUsNow, highlighting all the great work that they were engaged in. This was indeed excellent work. But did Trump hear them? Well, no. When you can't hear the tenor of your own private voice, you will not be able to hear others—not even God. When you have a false sense of self, you cannot engage or understand others.

The campaign needed instead is #CanYouHearYOURSELFNow? This is also the campaign that's needed for men boasting of their comments about domination over women.

Why Joseph?

So again, the question: Why does God tell Joseph's story in this way, so that it seems to validate the view that women are temptresses or seductresses, and that men are blameless?

God could, instead, have told the story of a woman who was assaulted and violated. But that story would have been blocked by too many unconscious biases. It would've been difficult for many to read—men and women alike.

So instead, God tells us the story of Joseph, upon him peace, who experiences much of the abuse that women do. Back at home, Joseph had suffered abuse from his brothers. He's from a marginalized group. And here, he's being pressured to prove a negative, as women often are, that he didn't seduce al-Aziz's wife.

Yet Joseph doesn't take advantage, and he doesn't succumb.

The "temptress" argument, that "she misled me, it's not my fault," is addressed in the Quran. This argument is never accepted by God. The one who misleads and does not repent will stand alongside the one who is misled and does not repent on the Day of Judgment. Hence, the Prophet said: "I seek refuge with You from misguiding others or being misguided, or slipping or making a slip, or wronging others or being wronged, or feeling important or being made ignorant."

A well-known Muslim scholar of the past, Imam al-Ghazali, said, "If the first inward thought is not warded off, it will generate a desire, then the desire will generate a wish, and the wish will generate an intention, and the intention will generate the action, and the action will result in ruin and divine wrath. Just so, evil must be cut off at its root, which is when it is simply a thought that crosses the mind, from which all the other things follow on."

This is not just Islamic knowledge.

In the ladder of prejudice, we know things begin with talk that objectifies and dehumanizes the Other. Whether this talk is political rhetoric or "locker-room talk" that objectifies women, the reality is that it leads to hate crimes or sexual assault. In some cases, it can lead to widespread violations.

One lesson from Joseph's story

The lesson of Joseph's story is not that women are seductresses. It is, instead, that men can't point to how a woman is dressed, or how she acted, as a rationalization to rape, dehumanize, or portray all women as seductresses. Joseph's story is a way of looking through God's eyes at how a sincere man takes responsibility for his space in the world.

Most importantly, the story short-circuits the rationalization that "she seduced me" or "she asked for it." Even if she did, Joseph can still walk away.

The story shows that God is a nurturer who wants to bring us to a new understanding. The prime minister's wife later recognizes what she did wrong, and is nurtured, and seeks Joseph out of love of God. She no longer sees Joseph, upon him peace, as an object. Instead, she sees him as a human being.

Joseph and the Misinterpretation of Shame

Love who you want, hate who you want, do not oppress anyone.

—Imam Muhammad Metwali al-Sha'arawi

There is a saying attributed to the Prophet Muhammad, upon him peace and blessings, which has been much-misinterpreted. People often translate it as: "Whoever doesn't have shame can do what they like."

But the word here being translated as shame is not *khizi*, which indeed means to put someone in a state of humiliation. Instead it is *haya*, which commonly means life, and is more accurately translated here as "spiritual life."

Shaykh Qays Arthur has argued that "spiritual life" is too ambiguous. The word *haya* covers a range of states, as does the term "shame." The idea of shame does approximate *haya* when used in the statement of reprimand, "Have you no shame?" The shame that one has here is a character trait that inhibits its possessor from gross and sordid conduct which is exactly one of the definitions of *haya* given by our scholars. The proper term in English is the idiom "sense of shame." At any rate some nuance of this kind might be useful for the audience, as we live in an age where *haya* is not very high on people's lists of virtues.

Yet I agree with his understanding that this is too limited. Also, if people can be shamed into the faith, they can be shamed out of the faith. The incorrect emphasis suggests that having shame as a positive thing. But shame is not the same thing as humility or remorse. Shame and humiliation do not lead to positive outcomes. While we must bring harassment and other crimes out into the light, this is not the same as shaming wrong-doers.

Joseph and al-Aziz's wife

When she first appears in the Quran, al-Aziz's wife, Zuleikha is full of internalized shame. This certainly does not lead the Zuleikha who harasses Joseph to act well.

But—if God is to illuminate the issue of sexual harassment—why does He do it through Zuleikha's story? Why should it be the story of a woman in a position of power harassing a man, when most stories are about men harassing women? First, this story is an important marker because Zuleikha is not beyond redemption. She had a desire for Joseph, which led to her want to control and possess him. Because she was in a position of power, she used that in trying to seduce him.

Second, this is also a better way of telling the story, as a man is more likely to be able to relate to a story where a man is being harassed. People in power often cannot relate to stories of harassment or oppression unless they imagine themselves, or someone like them, in that role.

But if we look at these two characters—Zuleikha and Joseph—which one of them is full of *khizi*, or shame? It is not the one who is harassed. It is Zuleikha, who knows that she is doing wrong, and who is filled with shame. When she tries to pressure Joseph into a relationship, she closes all the doors to hide the evidence of her harassment.

Joseph, on the other hand, has led a difficult life. But he is full of *haya*, the spiritual life that is a connection with God. Although Zuleikha stirred his feelings, he listened to his conscience and did what was right: He flung open the doors. He was not ashamed, because he had no reason to be. Zuleikha was the one who had done wrong.

And just so, if we are harassed, we should not feel ashamed. We should open all the doors. We should yell, shout, and call for help. Joseph's actions show that he feels pain, but he is not shamed.

"Opening all the doors," of course, does not negate the right to privacy. We don't have homes with walls because we are ashamed. Instead, we have homes with walls because privacy is a human right, allowing us to have our own personal space and personal boundaries. Saying you don't want to share yourself with others doesn't mean you're ashamed. It means you have reasonable boundaries.

Sometimes, people try to blame harassment on the victim, just as Zuleikha tried to blame her actions on Joseph. Indeed, this is why it's helpful to have the story be about a man's harassment. When men harass a woman, they often say, "Well she was pretty," or they remark on the way she dressed, or how she walked. And when Zuleikha defended herself for having harassed Joseph, she said the same thing: Look at him, he's beautiful.

And although the women around her in the story found this compelling, it's easy for us to see who is the guilty party. If you ask a man, he wouldn't have any trouble saying that Zuleikha here is the harasser, and that Joseph is guilty of nothing. However, men don't often stop to think: We sometimes use the same rationalizations when harassing women.

But no one, neither man nor woman, has a responsibility to share themselves with others, no matter what they're doing in their personal space. If someone says go away, then you go away. People have the power to do what they want in their own personal space.

Opening the doors

After Joseph opens the doors, Zuleikha—like many others whose ill deeds have been exposed—projects her internalized shame onto Joseph. When she's exposed, she responds by rationalizing her actions. She is not completely evil. But she lacks a connection with God, and in this is not fully spiritually alive.

From the Quran:

> When she heard of their malicious talk, she sent for them and prepared a banquet for them: she gave each of them a knife: and she said (to Joseph), "Come out before them." When they saw him, they did extol him, and (in their amazement) cut their hands: they said, "Allah preserve us! no mortal is this! this is none other than a noble angel!" (31)

Although Joseph didn't shame her, she felt the shame, and thus she tried to normalize her actions by staging a "confession" to other women, where she also showed off how handsome Joseph was. I had to do it, she said to them, because of how pretty he is. Fortunately for her, Joseph was a Prophet, and he had no interest in throwing gasoline onto the fire of her internalized shame. While he wanted to set boundaries and bring her actions into the light, he didn't name-call or try to drag her down. Instead, he tried to nurture her back to a connection with God.

This doesn't mean we can be expected to do this to our own harassers—Joseph was a Prophet. If you're harassed or oppressed, you have a right to raise your voice, to yell, to shout, to accuse, to bring someone to a court of law. We don't have to be perfect in this situation; we can accept who we are. When we reflect on the beauty of the prophets, it's not to judge ourselves, but to aspire to that level of closeness to God.

Beyond the oppressor's image

Sexual harassment revolves around consent, whereas the exchange with Zuleikha and Prophet Joseph, upon him peace, was about restraint and the call to fornication. However, my aim here is not to rewrite the story but to derive an understanding that we can use to help society understand why rationalizing sexual harassment is wrong.

Another reason it's important to see sexual harassment from an unlikely source such as Zuleikha is because we sometimes fixate on a particular stereotyped image of a harasser or oppressor. But we shouldn't create a fixed image of the oppressor, as that image can change, while the rationalizations remain the same. We don't want to look at the image, even if a certain sort of harasser has often been a man. This only creates stereotypes and blinders.

Rather than looking out for a particular image, we need to look out for what is being said—the thought process and rationalizations—and this is how we can fight oppression. We want to fight it on the level of thought, not on the level of identity or image.

Queen Bilqis, for instance, realized there were many bad kings. But when she went out personally to greet King Solomon, she had decided not to distrust all kings. Instead, she was looking for particular behaviors.

Due process

Another thing we can argue for is due process. In some cases, due process favors those who are already in power. However, if we throw aside due process—if we don't demand it—most of the victims will be from among the vulnerable and marginalized, as we saw after 9/11.

Due process allows us to step away from our feelings—whether we like Zuleikha more or Joseph more—and to talk about boundaries, rights, and responsibilities. Most of us can respect the rights of those who we love. But *haya* means respecting the rights and boundaries of everyone.

So the saying noted above really means: "Whosoever is not spiritually alive will do what they want." If we connect this to "al-Ba'ith," or the Resurrector, it means that those who believe no one will call them to account will act as they please. This is particularly true of those who have power.

There are many cases of women being harassed, and this is something we need to address. But ultimately it doesn't help if we shame men. People who are shamed will often push back and try to normalize abuse, to make it socially acceptable.

Prophet Muhammad, upon him peace and blessings, was once faced with a harasser who struggled with the problem of controlling his desires. But the Prophet did not engage in shame. Instead, he used a sort of cognitive therapy, helping the man to see his actions from a fresh angle, working with him on the level of thought and showing him the reasons to respect others' boundaries. Ultimately, this man understood and repented.

Shaming someone often leads them to entrench even more deeply in their behaviors. Instead, we want to push them toward facing consequences and genuine repentance.

False and real confessions

When Zuleikha first confessed her feelings for Joseph, it was a false confession. Even though she knew her harassment of him had been wrong, she put it in such a light (he's beautiful!) that it was normalized by the other noblewomen of the kingdom. Just so, many who are in power react to being shamed by rationalizing their abuses.

This is the reason that genuine healers don't use shame or public confessions. Instead, they help people to grapple with their ill deeds and repair the harms done.

Thus it's important not just for doors to be opened, but for the harasser or oppressor to be pushed back within their boundaries.

When using shame, we should remember that it often harms the powerless, not the powerful. When the relationship between Bill Clinton and Monica Lewinsky was revealed, she was the one who was shamed into oblivion and not allowed to be fully human, while he—the one in a position of power—made a public confession and was redeemed.

Zuleikha, wife of the powerful al-Aziz, ultimately did redeem herself, regained her dignity, and became devoted to God. Like Joseph's brothers, she was not irredeemable. Like them, she did not demand Joseph be killed. Those who are evil will often, like Pharaoh, demand that their enemies are slaughtered. But Zuleikha, like Joseph's brothers, sought his imprisonment or banishment instead.

Harassment as a continuing story

No calamity befalleth save by Allah's leave. And whosoever believeth in Allah, He guideth their heart. And Allah is Knower of all things. (Quran 64:11).

Another part of Joseph's story that is often overlooked is that he had a history of being abused, which made him a target. First, he was abused by his aunt. Then, he was thrown in the well. Later, he was put in prison. In order for Joseph to deal with all this trauma, it had to be brought out and purged, and Joseph had to learn to connect to God the Protector before he could face his brothers again.

When Joseph's brothers did return years later, they found him a different person, not just in his material conditions, but also spiritually and emotionally. Joseph always had integrity, but he also relied on himself. In his first trial, he tried to defend himself. But later, he turned to God the Protector.

Part of dealing with the trauma of previous abuse is guilt, and asking oneself: Why didn't I lift up my voice? But Joseph was faced with two situations, one where he didn't speak out, when he was young. And later he did speak up about harassment from al-Aziz's wife. At that point, he could see that when he didn't speak up, it was bad, and when he did speak up, it was also bad.

Now what? All doors are closed, and the only way out is to rely on God.

Joseph didn't plan to gain power and then have his brothers come to him. This was God's plan. But while we could look at this story to better understand the mechanics that underpin harassment, and ways of getting past abuse, there is no one-size-fits-all healing. We cannot take someone else's story, even a prophet's, and make it our own.

Hijab Is Not About Oppression or Seduction: It's About Trust

> *Living Islam means living, modeling, guiding, teaching, and counseling with loving care and concern. It is a life of trust, struggle, and noble effort. Using Islam often takes the form of holier-than-thou judgmentalism that is used to oppress and keep others in line. It often shows its ugly side through allegations that others are not 'Islamic' or 'obedient'; enough. In actuality, the obedience that is demanded is not obedience as a result of taqwa, that is obedience to Allah, but rather obedience to the tyrant and his own fear-based self. When Islam becomes objectified in such a manner, the state of inner unity (that leads to outer unity, i.e. peace and where 'it', i.e. Islam, is 'used' to achieve an objective other than its divinely inherent goal of bringing peace and goodness to people's lives.*
>
> — Dr. Abdul Lateef Krauss Abdullah

If men are responsible for their actions, why do we wear hijab? Hijab, which in its essence means "to conceal," is usually associated with Muslim women. Although other faith traditions promote modest dress, and Muslim men are also asked to dress modestly, most of the noise around this word is directed at Muslim women.

There are two unhealthy views around women wearing hijab. First, that a woman who wears hijab is always oppressed. Second, that women must wear hijab because they are necessarily seductresses, and men cannot follow their own consciences unless women are covered.

Hijab and oppression

Some people believe that hijab is always oppression. Certainly, they realize that not all women who wear hijab are coerced into doing so. But, they say, in those cases there are social and family pressures.

It's true that humans are always subject to social and family pressures. None of us—Christian, Muslim, Buddhist, or atheist—was born alone, on a desert island. None of us made up our own rules from scratch. All of us were raised in some sort of social system, where we were likely subject both to healthy and unhealthy social pressures.

Although there are many negative social pressures, there are also many positive ones. We are pressured to recycle, put on our seatbelts, eat healthy foods, and wear a bike helmet. All these things are good for us as individuals and for the wider society.

There are social norms everywhere. Just because a person adopts a social norm—such as wearing hijab—doesn't necessarily mean they're oppressed. Nor does it necessarily mean they're religious. Some women wear hijab but don't pray or seek refuge in God.

Some women are forced to wear hijab. They might be forced by law, or they might be bullied or shamed into it. Where women are compelled to be obedient to another human, this is oppression, and there are Muslims—both men and women—who speak out against this. Women should not be forced to wear hijab out of fear of a tyrant.

The same is true, for instance, of marriage. The fact that a woman follows social norms and gets married doesn't mean she is oppressed. But if another person tries to control her, and force her into getting married, then that is oppressive.

"Be free"

There is a stereotype about Muslim women that they are constantly repressed, and that all Muslims are dying to pull of their hijab, drink alcohol, and eat bacon. While this might be true of some, it is certainly not a struggle for everyone, and some might simply want to adhere to a healthy lifestyle.

Simply because one can do something doesn't necessarily make it a healthy lifestyle, and we also need to consider the consequences for ourselves and others.

While there are voices within the Muslim community pressuring women to wear hijab, there are also people within the Muslim community forcing women to take it off. In both cases, this is an issue of abusive control.

Seduction, temptation, and covering

Some men believe women should wear hijab because they are "inherently" temptresses. But women should not need to feel responsible for the irresponsible behavior of men. If a man harasses a woman, then that responsibility falls entirely with him, whether a woman is wearing a winter coat or a bikini.

Women are not required to change themselves to fix men's behavior. If men need help controlling themselves, then they should seek it.

So then why wear hijab?

Sometimes, we come up with reasons to fast during Ramadan. For instance, some say we fast so that we can feel empathy with those who are hungry. While fasting might spark empathy for some, that is not why we fast. The poor are not exempt from fasting. Why do they fast, since they are already poor?

We fast because it is a commandment from God. We fast because we are showing our trust in God. We trust that God is All-Knowing, and He commanded us to fast.

Hijab is the same. If you are drop-dead gorgeous or not good looking in the eyes of some, you are required to wear it. We might not know why God has commanded us to wear hijab, but we wear it because we trust God.

> Say to the believing men that they should lower their gaze and guard their modesty: that will make for greater purity for them: And Allah is well acquainted with all that they do. (Quran 24:30)

The command on hijab or modesty is first addressed to Muslim men, not women. God first addresses men regarding modesty or "hijab of the eyes."

In this verse, Muslim men are commanded not to lustfully look at women who are not their spouses or women who are permissible to marry, meaning not relatives. This helps prevent temptation or desire.

Then, in the following verse, women are commanded likewise:

And say to the believing women that they should lower their gaze and guard their modesty. (Quran 24:31)

Being human like men, they must also practice "hijab of the eyes."

We see similar teachings from Jesus, upon him peace, where he says, "You have heard that it was said by them of old time, you shall not commit adultery. But I say unto you, that whosoever looks on a woman to lust after her has committed adultery with her already in his heart."

Hence, while in some communities it is believed that if someone is not making eye contact they are deceitful or lacking confidence, if you see a Muslim not making eye contact with a member of the opposite sex, this is an indication that they are abiding by the Quranic as well as Biblical teaching.

Implementation and application

The verse completes with the following:

> ...that they should not display their beauty and ornaments except what (must ordinarily) appear thereof; that they should draw their veils over their bosoms and not display their beauty except...

'A'isha, the Prophet's wife, upon them peace and blessings, said: "I have not seen women better than those of al-Ansar (the inhabitants of Medina): when this verse was revealed, all of them got hold of their aprons, tore them apart, and used them to cover their heads..."

There was no debate because, first and foremost, Prophet Muhammad, upon him peace and blessings, connected them to God, and he was the perfect man living and modeling Islam. There was trust and noble character, hence women did not debate the issue, as they were focused on pleasing God just as Prophet Muhammad, upon him peace and blessings, taught and modeled to them.

The verse then lists male family members such as husband, father, father-in-law, the son(s), and others, where hijab is not a requirement.

In another verse, we read:

> O Prophet! Tell thy wives and thy daughters, as well as all [other] believing women, that they should draw over themselves some of their outer garments [when in public]: this will be more conducive to their being recognized [as

noble women] and not annoyed. But [withal,] God is indeed much-forgiving, a dispenser of grace! (Quran 33:59)

Every faith has its social and culture norms. When I was working at EDS, we had to dress very sharp and professional. We went through training for two months to help us understand how we were to be perceived, and what was allowed and not allowed both in dress code and in communication. We had a dress code that was very formal and meant to distinguish us from others, as well as to help the customers to recognize us as very skilled professionals and to treat us with respect.

Likewise, there are cultures and social norms in Islam. There is a social ill in every community around the world, whereby women are perceived as sex objects. The #MeToo movement has brought it out in the open, front and center! This issue impacts all communities, including Muslim communities. Hence, women must be known to themselves and others with the image of noble attire to distinguish themselves from this social ill and to rid their communities from it and promote respectful interactions and encourage others to treat them as such. Hijab is meant to visually command respect.

Mercy and compassion

According to Malik b. Anas, Jesus, the son of Mary, upon them peace, said, "Do not speak much without remembering God, for by doing so, you harden your hearts. Surely a hard heart is distant from God though you are unaware. Do not, like lords, look at the faults of others. Rather, like servants, look at your own faults. In truth, humanity is comprised of only two types, the afflicted and the sound. So show mercy to the afflicted, and praise God for well-being."

We learn from this that, if you see a drunk unconscious woman, or a woman who is otherwise unprotected or vulnerable, do not take advantage. In this, we are not speaking of rape, but of wooing and manipulating into illicit sexual behavior. Sexual assault is about power, not desire.

You can look at a woman with God's mercy and compassion, or you can rationalize impermissible actions and reduce her to a seductress. Likewise, the same goes for men who are not rapists, but who may be astray and lacking self-control. You can lure them into sin ("eat your heart out" or "dress to kill"), or look at them with God's mercy and compassion, push them away and pray for them.

The story of Joseph, upon him peace, teaches us that we will be tested in our areas of weakness, so we must all practice and strengthen ourselves with God, first and foremost, as well as anchoring each other with God, to be honorable and noble before God.

Finally, as we wear hijab, we must understand that our focus is on God, not how others wear or don't wear it. This also means we don't look down on others who don't wear it, nor are we meant to feel superior to those who don't wear it. Everyone has their own relationship with God.

May He guide and protect us all.

Seeking God the Protector

And it is He who sends down the rain after they had despaired and spreads His mercy. And He is the Protector, the Praiseworthy. (Quran 42:28)

God "al-Wali," or "The Protecting Friend"

Prophet Muhammad, upon him peace and blessings, once compared a believer to a "fresh green plant, the leaves of which move in whatever direction the wind forces them to move and when the wind becomes still, it stands straight." A believer is "disturbed by calamities," but soon regains their normal state. A disbeliever, on the other hand, is like "a pine tree that remains hard and straight until God cuts it down when He wills."

Some people, such as Pharaoh, are like that. No matter what calamity was sent down on him, nothing made Pharaoh feel compassion or empathy. Nothing made him feel the suffering of others. Pharaoh was as stiff and unmovable as a pine.

Being a fresh green plant doesn't mean we run in every direction. A green plant always stays tethered to its roots. But a green plant is affected by life and life's lessons.

Being a green plant also means not relying solely on one's own strength, but rather relying on the strength and protective friendship of God.

Joseph's lessons in prison

When Joseph first entered prison, he had—up until that moment—relied on his loving father, himself, and on the powerful king. Although Joseph knew he had to rely on God, there is more than one way of knowing.

In cognitive psychology, there are two types of knowledge: declarative and procedural. "Declarative" knowledge about riding a bike, for instance, would come if you'd read a book about riding bikes, watched videos, and were able to explain the mechanics of it to others. "Procedural" knowledge, on the other hand, comes when you've ridden the bike. At that point, riding a bike becomes part of your muscle memory, and part of the knowledge of your heart.

The same is true of spiritual knowledge. We can understand something with our brain, but we still need to work the muscles of our heart and our spirit, in order to strengthen them and understand at a deeper level. This is a knowledge that goes down to our very roots, such that a person might have a stroke and lose access to some parts of their brain, but the knowledge in their heart remains. Just so: A trauma can blow us down, but the knowledge we have deep in our roots persists.

Joseph always understood that God is the Supreme power. But you don't just sit down on a couch and wait for God to serve you breakfast. You have to move, you have to act, you have to try. The only way to develop our spiritual muscles is through experience.

Someone can have declarative knowledge of the faith, but we must also have the procedural. Of course, all of us will fall off the bike now and then. This doesn't mean we're hypocrites, or even that we lack procedural knowledge. Hypocrisy is when we tell others how to ride that bike when we've never tried to get on one ourselves.

Like Joseph, his brothers had knowledge of the faith, but they still struggled with human emotions like hatred and envy. They needed guidance and practice, and Joseph helped them—although not until after he had learned to rely on God the Protector and thus achieved independence from his oppressors.

Independence, integrity, and dignity

Joseph chose to spend several years in prison, strengthening his spiritual muscles, relying on God, and waiting until he could emerge independent, with dignity and integrity.

As his story shows us, it's important for oppressed peoples to have independence from others, and to rely on God. When Joseph emerged from prison, Potiphar and Zuleikha could no longer pull his strings. He didn't owe them a favor, and indeed they were in need of his help. Without this independence, an oppressor could say, "how dare you protest" and "after all, we gave you a job."

But with independence from everyone except God, Joseph was truly in a position to help others, including his brothers. This sort of independence goes both for countries and for individuals. Those fleeing the oppression of domestic violence and those fleeing a colonial oppression both need independence.

Embedded in friendship and love

One of the names of God is "al-Wali" or "God the Protector." This sort of protection is embedded in friendship and love, and it helped Joseph strengthen his spiritual muscles.

Every healing story is different, and we need different relationships with God at different times. Sometimes, a family or an oppressor will respond when we reach out to them, as Joseph's family did. Sometimes they won't, as Abraham's family did not. In all cases, we need to trust in God to guide us.

God knows what our needs are. Sometimes we need God the Protector. Hajar, in her story, needed sustenance. If we have sinned, we need God the forgiving and loving, and we need repentance. God always comes to us based on our needs.

When Is It Time for Forgiveness?

> *They said, "O our father, ask for us forgiveness of our sins; indeed, we have been sinners." He said, "I will ask forgiveness for you from my Lord. Indeed, it is He who is the Forgiving, the Merciful."* (Quran 12:97-98)

When we see people oppressed, trampled on, and violated, and their loved ones murdered, "forgiveness" is one of the first words that often comes to hand. There are thousands of memes and stories that urge people to forgive. Indeed, popular wisdom informs us that the anger people carry is only damaging to them. Offload it, we're told, and everything will be fine.

Forgiveness can be a positive force, of that there's no doubt. But we must distinguish between a harmful "instant forgiveness" and a helpful, spiritually satisfying "sustainable forgiveness." Real, sustainable forgiveness rarely comes quickly, and it cannot be forced, compelled, or coerced. A sustainable forgiveness certainly isn't about quickly offloading anger, which often forces victims to deny their reality—putting them in the same position that they were in when they were first victimized.

Indeed, there are many steps on the path toward sustainable forgiveness. This kind of forgiveness doesn't emerge straightaway from victimization, and it certainly doesn't ascribe to "forgive and forget"!

Many times, when people talk about an easy and instant forgiveness, what they're talking about is erasing everything that's happened to the one who has been victimized. "Let's just move on," they say. But that's not forgiveness, that's denial.

Sustainable forgiveness doesn't mean you let go of your rights or stop talking about the abuse that has happened to you. Instant forgiveness can be a tool that helps the powerful to escape accountability. Real forgiveness cannot.

African Americans, for instance, are often asked to forgive and "move on." But, before forgiveness, there must first be a reckoning with the price that African Americans have paid: from slavery, through Jim Crow, through today's structural racisms and police violence. This story has to be told and understood so that we can move toward restoration and reconciliation. We can't start the forgiveness process without this reckoning.

What might that look like? Instead of trying to push people to "forgive" and "move on," we might talk about fixing the inequalities in our schools that hobble African-American children. At that point, we would be acknowledging the harm done and restoring what it was possible to restore. These steps would push us toward reconciliation and healing.

After that, forgiveness comes naturally, as an end result.

Making the choice to forgive then brings us to a place of grace and acceptance. It helps us come to the realization that some lives are not going to be repaired. Some damage cannot be resolved. Accepting grace means coming to a realization that the good we do comes from God.

This grace validates healthy boundaries and offers release in a true "letting go." Yes, the harm was done. Yes, some reparations were made. And yes, there are some harms you cannot undo, no matter what.

Earning forgiveness

What of the transgressor whose privilege has stepped on someone else's rights? This person now has to learn empathy.

In 2016, the news that a young woman was raped by a young man described as an Olympics-bound swimmer rocked through the US and the world. It touched people both because of the man's light sentence and because of the graceful letter written by the victim. This young woman had wanted to forgive her rapist and move on with her life. However, during the trial, not only was she attacked, but the swimmer-rapist refused to accept responsibility for what he had done. He refused to truly acknowledge her pain or to make such reparations as might be possible.

The swimmer-rapist wanted to compel forgiveness by showing that he was vulnerable, and that his reputation had been harmed. In doing this, he closed off any space for real forgiveness. If he had really wanted to create a space for forgiveness, he would've first admitted both his own transgression and her resulting pain.

Instead, the swimmer-rapist's push for her to forgive and move on—before he had made any reparations—created even more pain and hurt. The promotion of denial isn't a solution. It compounds the problem.

In order to make forgiveness possible, there must be accountability. As this case shows, we are very good at calling the poor and unprotected to account. But people of privilege, and people who can afford excellent attorneys, can often escape this reckoning. A society that holds the poor to a much higher standard of accountability is a society where forgiveness becomes difficult.

We can't make progress until we hold ourselves accountable for our actions, admit wrongdoing, acknowledge suffering, rebuild what we have destroyed, and act together as a community.

Often, instead of doing this, we focus on finding "bad guys" and "thugs" among marginalized communities, such as new Somali immigrants and working class African-Americans. There are certainly people who commit crimes, and they also must be held to account. But this obsession with "bad guys" avoids and evades owning up to the mistakes we've made, for instance in Iraq, with structural racism, with slavery, and with Jim Crow.

When is forgiveness good for you?

Forgiveness can be a beautiful form of spiritual nurturing. It is positive, at a spiritual level, to forgive and move on. But you don't, at any point, have to forgive. When you're engaged in peace-making with another party or parties, it can be mentioned as a choice. But you don't ever want to force someone into it.

Once reparations and acknowledgements have been made, healthy boundaries also have to be re-established, so that the same transgressions don't happen all over again. At that point, forgiveness can empower a person to move on and own their life. This is a form of "letting go" where a person doesn't deny what happened to them.

It is important to remember that forgiveness doesn't mean a person disappears and stops seeking their rights! It doesn't mean that you stop fighting for what belongs to you. It's also important to remember that forgiveness can't be just an easy way to escape pain and suffering, a shortcut to acceptance by the oppressor or the mainstream. There are no shortcuts to forgiveness.

Joseph and his brothers: With recognition comes change

Joseph had been gone for many years when his brothers, who had been affected by the great famine, entered the kingdom where he was now a leader, at the right hand of the king. Joseph recognized his brothers immediately, the Quran tells us. But to them he was unknown.

Joseph made sure his brothers got what they needed. While their supplies were being loaded, Joseph told his brothers to come back, and to bring another brother from their father. By this, he meant that they should bring their half-brother, or his own full brother, Benjamin. Joseph even returned their merchandise to their saddlebags, so that it was still there when they got home, and they had even more reason to return.

The brothers, who once tortured Joseph and sold him off for money, were at this point in a state of poverty. Joseph's generosity, he knew, would guarantee their return.

When they got back home, they worked to convince their now blind and ill father to allow them to take his beloved Benjamin off for more supplies.

They said, "O our father, what [more] could we desire? This is our merchandise returned to us. And we will obtain supplies for our family and protect our brother and obtain an increase of a camel's load; that is an easy measurement."

Jacob, however, was not so easily swayed. The memory of losing his beloved son Joseph still stung in his breast, and he was not ready to lose Benjamin as well. He asked his older sons to give him a promise by God that they would return with Benjamin "unless you should be surrounded by enemies."

The brothers promised, and thus they returned to the city. Immediately upon their arrival, Joseph took Benjamin to his side and told him, "Indeed, I am your brother."

Helping his brothers to see

Joseph knew this was his opportunity to reach his brothers' consciences, and slowly turn them around until they faced their better selves. He started off by prodding them, to see whether they had changed in the intervening years.

Many years before, Joseph's paternal aunt had accused him of stealing in order to keep him in her house. His brothers knew about this, so he hid a cup among Benjamin's bags, and had the brothers accused of stealing. The brothers knew nothing about it, but promised wherever the cup was found, that person would pay the accusers.

When the cup was found among Benjamin's things, his brothers did not defend him, nor did they demand proof. Instead, they fell back on accusing Joseph and said, "If Benjamin steals, a brother of his has stolen before."

Thus Joseph knew that they had not yet turned to their better selves, and he still had work to do. He didn't respond to this, as the Prophet recommends: If someone provokes you, do not respond, but change the situation so that the one who provoked has no power over you.

He held firm, insisting that Benjamin stay. Then the brothers thought of Jacob, and they were anxious for their father. They told Joseph, still not knowing who he was:

> They said, "O Aziz, indeed he has a father [who is] an old man, so take one of us in place of him. Indeed, we see you as a doer of good." (Quran 78)

But Joseph insisted he could not take anyone other than the guilty. Otherwise, he said, "we would be unjust." Here, he dropped the suggestion that those who had previously punished the innocent—such as his own brothers—were unjust.

At this point, the brothers began to despair. Their father had suffered a lot from their ill deeds, and now they would cause him to suffer even more. Although they had done wrong, Joseph's brothers were not beyond help. They went to seclude themselves and deliberate.

In the end, the eldest brother's conscience was pricked the most:

> The eldest of them said, "Do you not know that your father has taken upon you an oath by Allah and [that] before you failed in [your duty to] Joseph? So I will never leave [this]

land until my father permits me or Allah decides for me, and
He is the best of judges." (80)

The eldest brother then sent the others back to Jacob. Now, he spoke differently about justice. Only recently, the brothers had suggested Joseph was a thief and accepted Benjamin might be, too. Now, the eldest said they would only testify to what they had seen with their own eyes:

Return to your father and say, "O our father, indeed your son
has stolen, and we did not testify except to what we knew.
And we were not witnesses of the unseen[.]" (81)

Slowly, the consciences of the brothers were awakened, and slowly they came to reconnect with their souls, to recognize they need to act on their values.

The last time these brothers had returned with one fewer, when they had put Joseph in a well, and then sold him to slavers, they came to their father in the night, with crocodile tears and a shirt covered in blood.

This time, they spoke differently. They told him the story plainly and said that he, too, could investigate the truth of it. This time, they used neither mental nor emotional blackmail. They left themselves open to investigation because, finally, they were telling the truth.

Jacob was still uncertain, as he has suffered a great deal from their prevarications. He answered: "Rather, your souls have enticed you to something, so patience is most fitting. Perhaps God will bring them to me all together. Indeed it is He who is the Knowing, the Wise."

The hearts of the fathers and his sons were not yet in sync, and it is difficult for them to reconcile. But Jacob was patient, and he still trusted in God.

Jacob then removed himself from his sons and he, too, went into seclusion with his grief.

This is an important thing to remember. God has asked Jacob to bear a great deal, but he doesn't ask Jacob to be a stone. God doesn't ask us to pretend we're not moved by the trials of our life. Instead, He asks that we nurture these feelings in the service of God and good. God seeks to strengthen us with these trials, not to torture us.

As I said, the Prophet Muhammad, upon him peace, once likened a believer to a fresh green plant. The believer is disturbed by calamities, but they regain their normal state quickly. A disbeliever, on the other hand, is like a pine tree that remains "hard and straight." This unbending tree is soon cut down.

Jacob did not try to rationalize what was happening, but instead took his pain to God. Then he told his sons to go and help their brothers with all possible effort, as Hagar once gave all possible effort. He told his sons to put their hope in God, not in their capabilities, and yet use all of their capabilities. Jacob still had not given up, and he still had faith that he would be reunited with his sons. He knew that no story is complete until Judgment Day.

Indeed, not everyone sees justice in this world, and not every wrong is righted. Those who are oppressed might be elevated in this world, or they might be elevated in the hereafter, where there will also be an account.

Yet with Joseph and his brothers, God showed how it's possible for the tables to turn on earth.

Now, we can see the growth of conscience inside Joseph's brothers. They returned to the kingdom and addressed Joseph with respect, seeking compassion from him. Those who had once harmed Joseph now humbled themselves before him.

> So when they entered upon Joseph, they said, "O Aziz, adversity has touched us and our family, and we have come with goods poor in quality, but give us full measure and be charitable to us. Indeed, Allah rewards the charitable." He said, "Do you know what you did with Joseph and his brother when you were ignorant?" (Quran 12:88-89)

Joseph asked his brothers if they knew what they'd done when they were ignorant, giving them a way of saving face in this difficult situation. It's said that, at this moment, Joseph gave a characteristic smile. And at this, his brothers knew him. They didn't deny they had been ignorant, but instead asked: "Are you indeed Joseph?"

Joseph didn't attack them, nor did he shame or blame them. He treated them with the same kind generosity with which he had once treated the king's wife, when she wanted forgiveness. His brothers bowed their heads and said, "Indeed, we have been sinners."

The brothers realized God had elevated him over them, and, like the women in the kingdom, they recognized their faults and transgressions.

Joseph was kind to them, and kinder still to his father:

He said, "No blame will there be upon you today. Allah will forgive you; and He is the most merciful of the merciful. Take this, my shirt, and cast it over the face of my father; he will become seeing. And bring me your family, all together." (Quran 92-93)

This story of forgiveness also nurtured the prophet, as when Abu Sufyan finally came to Islam. Abu Sufyan had committed many crimes and had persecuted Muslims. But when Abu Sufyan came to the Prophet, upon him peace and blessings, seeking real forgiveness, the Prophet used the same words: "No blame will there be upon you today."

If a person comes seeking forgiveness, and you keep reminding them of the evil they did, then they might feel they are condemned to that state. Then, instead of moving toward the good in themselves, they might be inclined to move toward the evil. This is different from creating a boundary. Once the boundary is created, there is no need to continually remind a former abuser of what they've done. It's important to give them an exit point from the sin and to allow them to grow, as Joseph allowed his brothers to grow.

Now, finally, in recognizing Joseph, the brothers also recognized themselves. They not only saw what they had done wrong, but also recognized and honored the good in themselves.

It was the eldest brother, the one who had stayed behind, who insisted on taking the healing shirt to Jacob. After all, he said, it was he who had once given his father an old shirt covered with fake blood. "Let me make amends with him by giving him your shirt of reunion."

This is the beautiful forgiveness.

No forgiveness without equality

With this story, God shows us how—slowly—real forgiveness can happen. An oppressed or abused person can't really forgive if they have no other choice. If they are obligated to forgive for social acceptance, then that is not real forgiveness.

It's not forgiveness unless you have real choice. We saw how Joseph refused to come out of prison until the people realized that what they had done was wrong. The decision to remain in jail was to avoid the serious trial of *zina* or fornication at the hands of a powerful and attractive woman who was taken by his extraordinary beauty. He was given two choices: jail, or *zina* and betrayal of his soul. So he chose jail. It was the same with his brothers. The positions needed to change before there was a chance for beautiful forgiveness, before they could recognize themselves and Joseph.

The brothers had to despair of their games, seclude themselves, and then begin a journey of sincere reflection.

Bit by bit, Joseph helped them to see.

In restorative justice, we say that, if the offender comes seeking forgiveness, this doesn't create the right conditions for true forgiveness. Once you've harmed someone, you shouldn't approach the victim. The power between you needs to be rebalanced. So if you want to approach the victim, it needs to be through a mediator the victim trusts, and who will have the victim's back.

God demonstrates the way real forgiveness works. There is always some reversal of power, and forgiveness cannot be demanded. Instead, the brothers had to put themselves in a vulnerable position and publicly acknowledge what they had done, publicly recognize it. Only then could there be a beautiful forgiveness.

The Reunion: Deception Has a Short Lifespan

Sufficient for us is Allah and He is the best disposer of affairs. (Quran 3:173)

When Joseph's brothers came to the realization that what they had done was wrong, they hurried back to their father, Jacob. They told Jacob that his beloved son Joseph was alive and, what's more, that he was working alongside the ruler of Egypt.

After this news, they traveled back together, and the reunion was like you might imagine. They'd forged a tremendous connection, and they had a desire to hold on to each other. Father and son must have shed tears of love.

Prostration as a greeting was permitted in the previous legal codes before Islam. Usually, we are not meant to prostrate to anyone except God. And yet in a few instances—as when God asked the angels to bow before Adam—it happens. Here, Joseph's parents prostrate before him out of love and respect for his station.

> And he raised his parents high on the throne (of dignity), and they fell down in prostration, (all) before him. He said: "O my father! this is the fulfilment of my vision of old! Allah hath made it come true! He was indeed good to me when

> He took me out of prison and brought you (all here) out of the desert, (even) after Satan had sown enmity between me and my brothers. Verily my Lord understandeth best the mysteries of all that He planneth to do, for verily He is full of knowledge and wisdom." (Quran 12:100)

Here, at this moment of reunion, Joseph didn't tell his father what his brothers had done to him. He didn't tattle or get into details, and he didn't bear any grudge that might get in the way of their moving reunion. Instead, to begin a new chapter, Joseph put the blame on Satan.

Joseph, here, has put himself in a position to receive grace. He has forgiven and is generous with others. He doesn't challenge them, but moves them only in small, almost unseen ways.

In this, Joseph is following in the path of God—you cannot provoke him. He didn't get into a duel with his brothers. Instead, he waited for them, and guided them in small, subtle ways. Now, the family has finally come back together again, and Joseph now gives thanks to God.

> O my Lord! Thou hast indeed bestowed on me some power, and taught me something of the interpretation of dreams and events, O Thou Creator of the heavens and the earth! Thou art my Protector in this world and in the Hereafter. Take Thou my soul (at death) as one submitting to Thy will (as a Muslim), and unite me with the righteous. (Quran 12:101)

Joseph ends his story of oppression by proclaiming God as his protector in this world and the hereafter. Joseph asks for death—but this is not a death of despair. Instead, Joseph is asking that his exit from this world be a noble one, a death as a Muslim submitting to God's will. Why would a Prophet have to ask for this? Because Joseph is not assuming that he has arrived. Even after he's reached all this grace, Joseph is still asking God that he pass away as a Muslim.

Now that we've reached the family's reunion and understanding, the whole story is wrapped up. Its wisdom is underlined and sent to the prophet, so that he can take the lessons from it, as can we.

Inspiration for the Prophet, inspiration for us

Different parts of the prophets' stories appear in different places in the Quran, because the Quran was revealed over the course of twenty-three years, to strengthen the Prophet from within. The right verses appear at the right moment, just when the soul needs to be watered by them.

There isn't, for instance, a chapter called "Moses," with an A-Z history of everything about this prophet. Nor is there one for David or Jesus.

However, with the story of Joseph, the entire story comes all at once, soon after the Prophet is accused of not having a story to tell.

Joseph's story comes to tell Muhammad about what the prophets before him faced, and to give him inner peace, insight, and strength. It is the same for us: When we reflect on these stories, we can strengthen our emotional, mental, and spiritual muscles.

The Prophet didn't witness the story of all that happened to Joseph and his family. The Prophet, upon him peace and blessings, was illiterate, so he didn't read this story from books, nor did he hear it from others. It is a story that came as a revelation, from beginning to end, with such fluidity that no one would be able to refute its status as revelation.

God finished the story by reminding Muhammad to have realistic expectations of his mission.

> Yet no faith will the greater part of mankind have, however ardently thou dost desire it. (Quran 12:103)

Some people will accept the word of the Prophet, and yet many will reject it. This doesn't mean the Prophet shouldn't exert himself. But when we are exerting, it's not about results. We shouldn't distort our faith just to get more followers to join us. Instead, truth is spread through sacrifice and adherence to one's values.

God also reminds the Prophet that one might reach a level of extreme sadness, as Jacob did. We might lose hope in people, as Jacob did in his sons. But we should not fall into despair and lose faith in God.

This story also underlines the difference between how liars and truth-tellers are inspired.

Those who are inspired by God are trustworthy and honest people, while liars are inspired by their egos or Satan. And yet Joseph didn't condemn his brothers to always be liars. Just so, neither should we.

A story for those enduring oppression

One of the lessons from this story, God tells us, is about God's wrath toward oppressors.

All throughout our lives, we need to be mindful of oppressors, liars, and people who are not trustworthy. In the short run, they can harm others gravely. But ultimately, they also destroy themselves. Sometimes, it might seem as though their oppressive deeds will continue unabated. But just because God is forbearing doesn't mean punishment won't come. We can't provoke God to act, but when He wills, He will respond.

When we see oppressors in their full power, it's difficult to believe they will ever be punished. But if we look at their stories over time, we see that they do self-destruct.

We should always be afraid of the wrath of The Forbearing One, and we should never take God for granted just because The Forbearing One has not yet manifested His wrath. Those who believe they can get away with their oppression are deluded: If they are getting away with it, this only means their story has not yet ended.

Sometimes, when we look at history, there seem to be tyrants who were not served justice on earth. But justice is not always witnessed on earth. We need to remind ourselves that our stories do not end on earth, and justice is sometimes served in full in the hereafter.

The end is not always clear

> *(Respite will be granted) until, when the messengers give up hope (of their people) and (come to) think that they were treated as liars, there reaches them Our help, and those whom We will are delivered into safety. But never will be warded off our punishment from those who are in sin.* (Quran 12:110)

At this point in the Joseph story, we're reminded that the prophets, too, have been accused of being liars. The prophets were faced with tremendous trials and tribulations, and the prophets reached a point when they had used all means available and achieved no result. And yet what they lost hope in was in their capabilities, and in the means they were using, not in God.

Truth does not come quickly, and God's time is different from human time. Victory often comes after we have lost hope in ourselves and our means. In this way, it is clear that victory has come from God.

Liars can become deluded that they have won, as Joseph's brothers must've once thought they had triumphed over him. Yet the oppressor should have no hope in God. Sooner or later, they will meet the wrath of The Forbearing One.

The truth of the story

There is, in their stories, instruction for men endued with understanding. It is not a tale invented, but a confirmation of what went before it, a detailed exposition of all things, and a guide and a mercy to any such as believe. (Quran 12:111)

Joseph's story is not fiction. Instead, it is a revelation with lessons explained, faith clarified, and a series of truths unfolded. In it, God tells Muhammad what to tell the rest of us on Earth.

The story is aimed, first and foremost, at those who are experiencing some kind of oppression, and it reminds us we cannot demand a quick victory over our oppressors. The road to faith is steep, and there will be many hurtful moments that help nudge us toward God.

This, like other stories in the Quran, is a way of healing, a mercy that prevents us from falling into sin, and guidance for those who believe in God and in the hereafter.

SOLOMON AND DAVID: LESSONS ON GRATITUDE AND WISDOM

The relationship between leader and led is not always an oppressive one. The stories of Solomon and Bilqis show positive ways to exercise power.

What Is—and Isn't—Bravery?

> *The abuse of greatness is when it disjoins remorse from power. And, to speak truth of Caesar, I have not known when his affections swayed more than his reason. But 'tis a common proof that lowliness is young ambition's ladder, whereto the climber upward turns his face. But when he once attains the upmost round, he then unto the ladder turns his back, looks in the clouds, scorning the base degrees by which he did ascend.*
>
> —*Julius Caesar*, William Shakespeare

The David and Goliath story is used by people around the world as a structure and a storyline to help them understand their own actions. The story has a wide appeal: It's empowering for any of us to see ourselves as a small, unlikely "David" figure fighting against a behemoth of a "Goliath." After all, justice was on David's side, while Goliath had brute force and worldly power. And David won.

This story has been adapted to the purposes of people who sit at many places along the political and religious spectrum. Ultra-right-wing commentators have called themselves Davids against a Goliath entity of the mainstream media; ISIS fighters paint themselves as a David against the Goliath of the United States military might. There have been heroic David-figures as well. Nelson Mandela has been called a David against the South African apartheid regime's Goliath. Or a small whistleblower standing up to corporate corruption might also be called a David.

It's an easy story to fall back on. As important and appealing as it is, when read simply, the story can blind us to criticism, allowing us to see ourselves as a tiny hero against powerful aggressors.

But what was David's story, really?

David and Goliath in the Quran

King David's honor and import spans religious traditions. In Judaism, he is remembered as the legendary second King of Israel and ancestor of the coming messiah. In Christianity, he is known as the forefather of Jesus and the psalmist. In Islam, he is a king and a Prophet revered for his righteous wisdom and willingness to stand against oppression.

According to Islamic teachings, David was an honorable king who acted according to God's teachings. He was called upon to fight because part of faith is fighting against oppression, and he had to fight Goliath in order to end oppression. But this wasn't a simple matter of deciding that he was going to fight Goliath. First, David honed his self-discipline. In the time before battle, he and his followers were not indulging themselves: They were focused on doing what was right.

> When Talut (David) set forth with the armies, he said: "Allah will test you at the stream: if any drinks of its water, He goes not with my army: Only those who taste not of it go with me: A mere sip out of the hand is excused." but they all drank of it, except a few.
>
> Then when he had crossed it along with those who believed with him, they said: "This day We cannot cope with Goliath and his forces." But those who were convinced that they must meet Allah, said: "How oft, by Allah's will, Hath a small force vanquished a big one? Allah is with those who steadfastly persevere." (Quran 2:249)

Second, David was not looking to become a hero, and he didn't believe he was saving the world. Indeed, he was relying on God, and acting for God.

> By Allah's will they routed them; and David slew Goliath; and Allah gave him power and wisdom and taught him whatever (else) He willed. And did not Allah check one set of people by means of another, the earth would indeed be full of mischief: But Allah is full of bounty to all the worlds. These are the

Signs of Allah: we rehearse them to thee in truth: verily Thou [O Muhammad] art one of the messengers. (251-252)

This complicated story of perseverance and listening to God has been boiled down to tough, brave, little David standing up to big, powerful Goliath and bringing him down.

Am I David or a troll?

We're all called on to be brave and to stand up against oppression, but that is not a simple matter of targeting any powerful group and standing against them. We might feel like a "David" when we're acting like an internet troll just as much as we might feel like a "David" when we're confronting an unjust power.

How to tell the difference? It seems an easy thing, but the human ego is very treacherous, and it can whisper in our ears, encouraging us to tell stories in a way that builds us up and tears others down. This doesn't mean that, if we see ourselves acting in a self-aggrandizing way, we should hate ourselves or our stories! Instead, it means we should be mindful about how the human mind can rationalize. We should always be in a state of listening and investigating, and not divorce ourselves from the fact that we're always in a state of needing God's assistance.

Even when we're fighting nobly, we need to be careful not to hype up vulnerable and impressionable people, and always to listen, love, and be humble. That is real bravery. There are several questions to ask.

Are you being a listener? To truly follow the path of the brave, we must listen even to those who oppose us. The fight is never a fight of hatred, it's always a fight of love.

Brave people are not interested in silencing others. The way to falsehood is through silence. If a person who thinks they're following David's path is shouting down their opponents, then they need to stop immediately and reconsider. And listen.

Many people see themselves as tough, outsider renegades. Far-right commentators often praise themselves for "taking the heat" and "saying what needs to be said." And indeed, they might feel strongly criticized, and as though they're standing up to a giant power, even if they also have many followers and listeners.

When the TV host Trevor Noah had far-right radio host Tomi Lahren onto his show, he asked why the actions of Colin Kaepernick—

who knelt during the US national anthem in support of Black Lives Matter—bothered her so much. After all, wasn't he just kneeling in his own space, harming no one?

Here, Lahren didn't acknowledge Kaepernick's grievances, nor did she address his rights. She seemed to want only to silence her opposition. She wanted the right to speak, while she did not want to listen. This is not the path of David, who listened well.

If you have followers—or are a follower of a "David"—what sort of connection is there between followers and leader? Followers should be able to call their leaders on their bad behavior, and there should never be a herd mentality where followers all attack as a herd. Sometimes, to know a person, we need to look at their followers.

There is a story of Muhammad, upon him peace and blessings, and one of his close companions, Umar ibn al-Khattab. When Umar became Muslim, he was of such noble rank and influence that some stopped attacking the nascent Muslims immediately.

A man who had loaned money to Muhammad came to claim it from him, and he did so in an aggressive manner. Umar stepped in and roundly criticized the man, shooing him off. Muhammad chastised Umar and told him to repay the money-loaner extra for his sharp words.

Here, we can see that they didn't all attack an outsider, even if he approached them aggressively. Muhammad did what was just, and he addressed the man's tone later. This is important because of how the Prophet resolved conflicts and received criticism from those who came to claim their rights from him in an abusive manner. He addressed their rights first, before their abusive behavior.

When you win a battle, are you humble and loving? One of the great manifestations of a brave and real victory is that, when you win, there is no revenge. After all, we are fighting to remove oppression, not to be in power.

When a person tastes victory, as David did, the first thing they should feel is a sense of humility, because this victory didn't come from them alone. They should bow in gratitude, since God and many others made this possible.

When you are fighting others, your aim is not to destroy them, but to nurture them. The brave person fights not from hate, but from love.

Lessons from the "Let's Be Great Again" Syndrome

I have learned silence from the talkative, tolerance from the intolerant, and kindness from the unkind[.]

—Khalil Gibran

In any community, there are those who believe the solution to their problems is a rise to power. I'll call these the "let's be great again" voices: They're voices that hate being in the second chair, hate being a minority, and hate the sense of being out of control.

These voices might come from any community—a faith community or otherwise. In a faith community, they stem from a sense that faith is tied to a "result" and that this result is power. Yet that's not what faith is about.

Still, these voices can provide an excellent lesson, as any disease of the heart shows us something we need to avoid. If you see someone who's intolerant, it can give you a better idea of how intolerance manifests itself. It can also help us look inward: We may not be aware of the ways in which intolerance has sprouted seeds in our own hearts.

One guide who can show us how to avoid being "great again" is Salman al-Farisi, or Salman the Persian, who lived in the seventh century. He was born into a Magian family, and while he converted to Christianity, he didn't reject his family. He later came to the Prophet Muhammad, peace and blessings on him, yet he didn't reject Christianity, either. Al-Farisi didn't come to a position of power in faith, yet that was not what mattered to him.

This is the case for any of us who are trying to be people of truth, whatever community we're from. Walking toward truth is not about rejecting where we're from, but about embracing what we discover and supporting every part of ourselves. Just so, it's also not about clambering to get into power.

Salman al-Farisi followed his heart, and he sought the community that echoed the truth as he could see it, but he was not seeking power, nor was he granted power. He left a powerful community to become part of a minority, walking away from power toward truth.

His path can be a lesson: Just because Muslims are facing discrimination in the US and Europe, and face colonial practices elsewhere, that doesn't mean that we—as ISIS claims—should be looking for a previous power and glory.

It's clear that those on the "let's be great again" bandwagon, wherever they may be, are blind to those who they're persecuting. Once the dominating voice is "let's be great again," a person is no longer focused on following their principles and values. But, as al-Farisi showed us, that's the important thing. Maybe these values will bring you to a place of acclaim, money, and power. Maybe they won't.

Salman al-Farisi was treated very well by his family, and he particularly beloved by his father. But he'd walked into a church service, reflected on the teachings of Christianity, and accepted the religion into his heart. It's a lesson for all of us: When we accept something, we should focus on that. Al-Farisi wanted to be a good Christian, not to attack his father's faith.

I once met a woman who'd converted to Islam, and she called her parents kuffar, or infidels, and denied them to right to visit her children. But Islam shouldn't ever be used as a stick against someone, and coming to Islam is not like coming to a football team. Part of Islam is to honor your family and community, and another part is to engage in coexistence.

Al-Farisi shows us this path, as he didn't reject who he was. He didn't change his name to call himself "Salman the Arab." He was Persian. Just so, we can all be proud of our heritage.

The British scholar Abdul Hakim Murad, who is also known as Timothy Winter, once answered the question, "Is joining Islam a rejection of one's previous identity?" by saying, of his British identity, "In some sense every conversion entails that. But for many it also involves a reconnection with aspects of Britishness that have been lost to globalization."

Stumbling against corruption

Once he'd taken Christianity into his heart, al-Farisi devoted himself to being a good Christian, despite obstacles. Among these obstacles was a corrupt priest. But instead of being swayed from the teachings of Christianity by a corrupt priest, al-Farisi spoke out against him.

Indeed, al-Farisi wasn't looking for utopia, like many of those who want to hark back to an "idealized" era that occurred at some time in the past. He was looking to do the best he could in the real world.

Indeed, it was this corrupt priest who taught al-Farisi to recognize corruption. This is a very important skill! Anyone can be caught in a situation with a corrupt or abusive authority figure. But if we don't learn to understand from them what corruption is, then we are likely to run from an abusive parent to an abusive spouse, and then to another. What we need to do is to learn to see the abusive authority figure, just as al-Farisi saw the corrupt priest. To echo Gibran, al-Farisi learned from this how to be ethical. Attraction to narcissists is also a disease of the heart, and we must be able to look inward and pluck it out.

Al-Farisi's next teacher was a good man, and he continued with this teacher until the man passed away. After that, al-Farisi went looking for the coming Prophet, who the teacher had told him would arrive among men.

How to see the corrupt and abusive for what they are

Al-Farisi was raised in a loving home, and that may be one of the reasons why he was able to see the corrupt priest for what he was. For others, it can be harder.

But one of the things shared by the corrupt is their insistent desire for power and glory. They cannot be inferior. They cannot be happy in a position of deference. They must be constantly in the limelight, and a sense of greatness is very important to them. This craving for greatness is one of the diseases of the heart, and it's very different from wanting power just to serve others. The corrupt must be in power, and if they must violate their values to get in power, then they will do that.

A person with a healthy heart, however, is going to follow their values. If their values don't bring them to power, then they accept this, just as a person of faith accepts there's a divine plan at work.

I have told women before: If you want to test a man's mettle, pretend to be weak. When Moses, for instance, came across two women whose father was ill and who were having a hard time watching their flock, he didn't use this as an opportunity to lord over them or be their savior or protector. He didn't take advantage of their vulnerability. Instead, he gave them quiet and straightforward assistance. He did not act the part of the "great" man, but instead was the man following his values.

Certainly, those who fall into this pattern aren't bad people. But they act in ways that make them a magnet for corruption. Until the disease is removed, they will continue to go from one abuser to the next.

The promise of a utopia is another thing that should make us wary. One of the ways that ISIS attracts young people is by enticing them with the glories of past Muslims, who, in the ISIS ideology, were perfect beings who never did anything wrong. These, apparently, were infallible

Muslims who lived in a perfect land. But that's not reality. That's an illusion.

This doesn't mean we can't ever be great

Not aiming ourselves primarily toward power doesn't mean that we don't work hard in everything we do: building a positive community, leading others. It's not defeatist or fatalist. It is instead a recognition that the idea that "let's be great again," or of ascending to power on the backs of others, will bring harm to you or to others.

Acting based on our principles will sometimes bring us to power. Some excellent teachers, writers, and public speakers rise to fame and acclaim. But some others, whose YouTube videos have only a handful of views, are also excellent teachers who are living out their values. What's important is not the fame, but living in accordance to one's principles.

We should always put work and thought into our teachings, or whatever we do. Two scholars might put in the same amount of work. One might get a million YouTube views while the other gets 100. The important thing is not the number of viewers, but to be sincere in one's values. The idea is not to be great "again." It's to be true to your principles, your faith, and your sense of integrity.

Making greatness great again

Perhaps the loudest political slogan of 2016 called on people to "Make America Great Again."

But what sort of "greatness" are we aiming at? It is easy for people to become obsessed with greatness—or prominence, or power—for its own sake. But this sort of empty greatness can often erode our integrity. This is not the greatness of Solomon or Bilqis, but is instead a greatness that's divorced from empathy, compassion, and who we really are as humans.

A nation-state like America can become obsessed with greatness for greatness' sake. This can lead us to look down on the "non-great" with scorn, as some Europeans look at refugees, even though their parents or grandparents might have sought refuge from war. Or as some Israelis look at Palestinians.

Individuals, too, can be obsessed with greatness. But is it so important to be great?

Sometimes, "greatness" is used as a way of ridiculing contemporary Muslim believers, asking: What do Muslims do that's GREAT? These onlookers indicate that, since there aren't many Nobel Prize winners this year from Muslim-majority countries, it means that the region or religion must be "backwards."

One way that people answer these charges is by scuttling around, collecting names of Muslims who are and have been "great": from tenth-century philosophers, to scientists, to young Malala Yousafzai, the youngest-ever winner of the Nobel Prize. But another way is to question this idea of "greatness," and what it means.

Too often, greatness is associated with being a star. By this understanding, popularity or fame itself is enough to make someone "great." The central force in the slogan "Make America Great Again," Donald Trump, is an excellent example of this false sense of self, building up a gigantic exterior around a diseased heart. For instance, Trump frequently mocked politician Anthony Weiner for his sexual indiscretions without considering his own sexual assaults on women.

But it isn't just Trump. For many, the road to greatness itself defines our self-worth or truth. We resist stopping to ask: Where am I going? In this journey to greatness, we can easily lose sight of important dimensions of our humanity.

Faith is not about being perfect, nor is it about being great. Faith includes all of our failures, faults, and shortcomings. In the words of Dr. Abdul Lateef Krauss Abdullah, a counselor in social work and peace studies:

> [W]e are here to experience, and it is okay to fall down, it is okay to trip, it is okay to mess up (whatever 'messing up' means) and it is okay to get back up again. Get down. Get back up, a custom course work. Everything that is happening at every moment is the next lesson, like the next 'flash card.' Every person that walks in the door is the next flash card for you, your lessons. Everything that you feel is the next flash card for the next lesson. Everything that you see, everything that you taste, everything that you smell, everything that you hear and all of your realizations are part of the next lesson. Now 'faith' is starting to become something real and personally engaging.

But I get up again

Sometimes, we see greatness only as standing—motionless—at the top of a pinnacle. In Shaykh Qays' words, "Some people see the call to virtue as a denial of the reality of the human being or the human condition."

But we all have different strengths and weaknesses, and that's where our concerns should be. We can only compare ourselves with where we were yesterday.

As for those who are public figures, they are held to a double accountability, and their responsibilities are even greater. Someone who's aspiring to greatness should not be preoccupied with the image of greatness, but with responsibilities and accountabilities.

If you're aiming at real greatness, then your thoughts should be similarly aimed at how to help the most vulnerable. Not about the next book-signing or in mocking the weak and vulnerable. What should preoccupy those who wish to be great is questions such as: Are the most vulnerable taken care of? Are their needs being met? What issues do I need to resolve? And how can I improve my skills to better serve society?

A greatness that's divorced from remorse and responsibility is a hollow greatness.

There have been people throughout time who have reminded us what greatness really is, as Socrates reminded and challenged the Athenians.

Some say that the Muslims and the Islamic Empire once were great—during the Golden Age of Islamic science—and then ask where these "great things" have gone now. But such is life: You go up, you go down. One day you might be in power, one day not. If you're attached to this false sense of greatness, then you only come to a religion that's at the center of power, during the summer of its year.

Summer is when all the labor is done and the fruits are here. The rest of the seasons are when the hard work is done: planting, digging, fixing, watering, and, perhaps most of all, showing patience.

Greatness and weakness, greatness and strength

Sometimes, a leader—like Pharaoh, like Donald Trump—might fear expressing vulnerability or remorse, as that might seem like weakness. And yet the ability to express true remorse, as Adam did in conversation with God, is surely a stronger and truer position.

Some people's idea of greatness is all roar and no responsibility. But if you can't express remorse, how strong are you? Strength comes from being able to repent, be accountable, repair harm, and change.

No one can go through life without making a mistake. Sometimes I have an argument. The next morning, I wake up and realize that I was the one in the wrong. I want to be accountable and repair the harm, because that's what my strength is about.

When we see a public figure exposed, as Trump was about his sexual assaults, this is a time for accountability, but not for bashing. Sometimes there's a lynch-mob mentality against the offender, as if we don't need to look at this issue personally. We need to look, instead, at the impact of what the person has done, as Michelle Obama did in a beautiful speech in New Hampshire, which was not mocking or ridiculing, but held those who commit sexual assaults to account and set the record straight. Indeed, when she called Trump to account for himself, it was a sign of mercy.

This is very different from responding with mockery, as mockery often masks vulnerability. Mockery can be a mask that's something like a small animal's defense mechanism, making it look bigger than it is.

Where, then, are you going?

Throughout history, humans have sought greatness. In the Quran chapter at-Takwir, there is a beautiful question that is posed to those who go blindly in search of greatness: "Where then are you going?"

This is our reminder that death is everyone's final destination. Hopefully, this reminder can help us walk humbly on the earth, grounded in reality, open to accountability and repentance. And this is the road to greatness.

Solomon and Bilqis: Healthy Power

If any do seek for glory and power, to God belong all glory and power.

—Quran (35:10)

Recently, I began a conversation with Shaykh Qays Arthur, reflecting on the importance of being true in one's journey to God. Here, we reflect on a courageous meeting between two people, both given power and glory by God. One belongs to the world of faith, while the other was born into a society of no faith. What happens when the world of "faith" and "no faith" collide? In this journey, we will explore the engagement of two powerful people who are true to themselves, their values, and their people.

My first question requires an introduction. The representative from the world of faith is the beautiful Prophet Solomon, upon him peace. He was given power and glory by God that no other human being will possess.

In my research into human psychology, I found a wonderful essay on narcissists and "little voices," which I believe forms the bedrock of every oppression we face. It was the underlying reality of the oppression faced by Moses, upon him peace, at the hands of Pharaoh. It is the spiritual reality of oppression of women who face oppression at the hands of a male partner. To fight any oppression, we need to have a thorough understanding of the psychological dimension of the narcissists and the "little voices."

This is one reason why I worry about obligating the "little voices" to serve society. As we see in domestic-abuse situations, or in dysfunctional families, the call to serve can become an emotionally abusive demand for the little voice to serve the narcissist in order to be valued and accepted in a family or society. As I note elsewhere in this book, how a person deals with those who are small, unprotected, and misunderstood tells us a lot about them.

In the Quran, we see a meeting between Solomon (upon him peace) and ants in a low valley. I'd like us to reflect on the inner reality of Prophet Solomon (upon him peace) and his response to the fear of the ants from his power.

> Until, when they came upon the valley of the ants, an ant said, "O ants, enter your dwellings that you not be crushed by Solomon and his soldiers while they perceive not." So [Solomon] smiled, amused at her speech, and said, "My Lord, enable me to be grateful for Your favor which You have bestowed upon me and upon my parents and to do righteousness of which You approve. And admit me by Your mercy into [the ranks of] Your righteous servants." (Quran 27:18-19)

What does this verse tell us about Solomon's inner reality despite the tremendous power given to him, in comparison to Pharaoh?

Shaykh Qays: "In the name of God, the Merciful, the Compassionate. Peace and blessings upon Prophet Solomon. What we see from Prophet Solomon (upon him peace) is an unflinching focus on God. He is constantly directed to God, as opposed to being directed to the self (or ego) when one has blessings of worldly nature. Prophet Solomon (upon him peace) is given the ability to hear the animal kingdom—this is one of many different abilities given to him. Many forces were subjugated to Solomon as blessings from God. Such abilities and marvels were signs of high station, power, and reputation—all things that people aspire to. Even the ants are aware of him, and in awe of him. His response to all these blessings is to turn to God in gratitude and to seek refuge in God from losing the way and to seek the Divine pleasure. That is faith. The fact that he is directed to God in everything and not to others or his ego in every turn of his life is a sign of his true faith."

The world of "no faith"

And from the world of "no faith," we have the Queen of Sheba, a woman who reigned over her people with wisdom. Many times, people think that just because someone spoke against a tyrant that they are brave. But in reality, there are people who are psychologically oppositional and defiant by nature. To be oppositional simply for the sake of being oppositional is a disease. It has a name: oppositional defiant disorder. One clear symptom of this disorder is a "hostility directed toward authority figures." In other words, a hatred of authority or people in power, no matter whether they are doing good or evil.

The difference between brave people and oppositional people is that the former hates oppression and seeks the betterment of society, while the latter hates authority and seeks to be in power. There is a difference between being strong willed and being oppositional and defiant. I do not advocate people diagnosing others with this disorder; rather, we should reflect on our own behavior whenever we oppose something.

In any case, I want to draw your attention to a verse about the Queen and her response to the letter from Prophet Solomon, upon him peace. Also, she comments on the behavior of kings, when they enter a country or town, and sheds light on the fact that she is not in denial. Sometimes, during conflict, people say such things as "make love not war." In a sense, this is a form of escapism from difficult and complex situations. By contrast, the Queen's intelligent analysis of power shows her intellectual, political, and emotional competence. She did not go around fearmongering or hate-mongering, even though she had under her power men who were "endowed with strength, and given to vehement war." Rather, she consulted her chiefs. The Queen's people respected her to make a decision, illustrating she was not a narcissist and was capable of listening to "little voices."

> She said, "Ye chiefs! here is delivered to me, a letter worthy of respect. Indeed, it is from Solomon, and indeed, it reads: 'In the name of Allah, the Entirely Merciful, the Especially Merciful, Be not haughty with me but come to me in submission [as Muslims].'" She said, "O eminent ones, advise me in my affair. I would not decide a matter until you witness [for] me." They said, "We are men of strength and of great military might, but the command is yours, so see what you will command." She said, "Indeed kings, when they enter a city, they ruin it and render the honored of its people humbled. And thus do they do. But indeed, I will send to them a gift and see with what (answer) return (my) ambassadors." (Quran 27:29-35)

Can you comment on these verses? What is the difference between the Queen's internal reality and that of Pharaoh?

Shaykh Qays: "Well, it is certainly evident that she is not of this oppositional profile, which isn't surprising given that she is herself a figure of authority. However, she is far from a typical authority figure. Much of what the verses mention show that she is a wise and fair leader who knows politics, knows how Kings are, and consults with her court. This shows political competence as well as lofty character. Like Solomon, she, may be contrasted with Egypt's Pharaoh who became deluded with his power. We see a woman who is aware of her circumstance, consults with her court, and seeks out wisdom. Wise people do not presume they are wise. They seek out wisdom as was said when we discussed Salman al-Farisi.

"She is also genuine and astute. She is neither a cowardly ruler nor a tyrant. It is expected that she is not oppositional because she has power and seeks wisdom sincerely. Because she was not arrogant, she was able to recognize Prophet Solomon. She deals with her own court in a way that makes her own people amicable to Prophet Solomon. Indeed her many virtues, despite her faith idols, are examples of God's enabling grace.

"She was not yet a believer but possessed a sincere heart. Everyone's destiny and final outcome is known to God. I have a ruling, you have a ruling, and the Christian lady next door and atheist down the street have a ruling with God in terms of our final outcome. God is not waiting to find out anything. So Queen Bilqis or Sheba is a believer in God's knowledge even if it was not yet manifest to anyone including herself. However, her heart was the place that was fertile for faith and faith grew because she was a person of sincerity, wisdom, and true virtue. That virtue is what stands out to me."

Before I continue, let me clarify something. There is a difference in the understanding and view of the Prophets in the Quran and the Bible. According to Islamic teachings, the prophets are sinless, and the negative attributes and actions associated to them are not accepted as true. The Quran tells their stories, so Muslims can learn from them how to be true and follow in their footsteps as the Prophets are the light and the way to God.

Whenever we seek to learn anything, we always study or seek out the experts. From math, sports or to cooking, we seek out the best in the field if our aim is to be the best in that field. Likewise, in faith. Studying and reflecting on what extremists do, does not help one to understand Islam. To understand faith the conversations must engage in depth on the journeys and inter realities of the prophets, truth seekers and those brought near to God. Hence, let us continue with the conversation.

Arriving with a gift

The Queen of Sheba, whose name is Bilqis, goes to meet Prophet Solomon, upon him peace, bearing a gift. In this next verse that I'll quote, Prophet Solomon was not moved by the "abundance in wealth." Throughout history and today, narcissists wage wars to steal the resources of towns or countries. The internal reality of both Bilqis and Solomon, upon him peace, was that they were seeking to benefit the other, and not to enslave or abuse the other. He is not, like typical kings, thinking of how he can take over and make the noblest the weakest. How do you understand his response?

> Now when (the embassy) came to Solomon, he said: "Will ye give me abundance in wealth? But that which God has given me is better than that which He has given you! Nay it is ye who rejoice in your gift!" (Quran 27:36)

Shaykh Qays: "Some of it has to do with diplomatic protocol of the time. When monarchs engaged with each other they sent/brought gifts to solidify their intent since the default position was war. If a nation was not fighting it was preparing itself for the next fight. That was the historical and political reality. Lavish gifts were often goodwill gestures, peace offerings or not-so-subtle indicators of the wealth and power of the sender. Such offerings were either accepted or rejected according to the party's perceived intent and how the relationship was developing.

"Sometimes corrupt rulers would kill the emissary and seize the gift. Whatever the response the sending party would know what kind of rulers they were dealing with. Solomon, upon him peace, rejected the wealth and indicated his intent to march and conquer in God's way. He would not be appeased by what he saw as a pompous show of wealth to which he was unattached being a prophet and a man of deep spirituality.

"The important point here, again, is his directedness to God. The abundance of wealth was meant to impress him, but it did not impress him or sway him. Queen Bilqis had an apprehension regarding what kind of King he was from his peculiar letter with a clearly religious intent. Much of what she did was to test him. Likewise, he was testing her."

To be made small

In the ninth chapter of the Quran, on a battlefield, Muslims were ordered to subdue their enemy to the rule of law. When we reflect on the description of the political reality of oppression, we must listen to this quote from Bilqis: "Kings, when they enter a country, despoil it, and make the noblest of its people its lowest thus do they behave."

When those who are true of faith are given power, they can bring the worst of people to follow the rule of law. When Islamophobes argue that Islam seeks domination, they often use the word "saghiroon," or to make small. Here, Prophet Solomon, upon him peace, uses that same word.

Based on Bilqis's description of kings, one can see that many rulers at the time were corrupt, acting without a sense of accountability to anyone. These people are oppositional in nature and attached to power. Prophet Solomon, upon him peace, was also dealing with people who were aggressive and defiant in nature, such that they had to be put in a humbled state in order to bring law and order and subdue their aggressive nature.

Go back to them, and be sure we shall come to them with such hosts as they will never be able to meet: We shall expel them from there in disgrace, and they will feel humbled (saghiroon). (Quran 27:37)

Do you agree?

Shaykh Qays: "Well, rulers of the past didn't have the instruments of state that are available after several industrial and technological revolutions. Modern instruments of state that rely on quantum leaps in technological advancement facilitate an unprecedented level of control that obviate, for the most part, the use of trauma, humiliation, and fear to establish rule and control. In the past, conquerors had to establish rule by force to bring law and order. There was no UN or nation-states or, might I add corporations, as we know today. The rule of a ruler, whether just or otherwise, was only enacted after subjugation of those he conquered. That subjugation could come by way of consensus because the people are organized, and they have a leader and the leaders submit or through more traumatic means. Queen Bilqis's people were organized having had a court and a leader.

"But often there were only loose tribal structures where any political change or disruptions quickly lead to chaos. War not only destroys physical structures but social ones as well. Today, we see it now for example in Libya. Libya was not a firmly established state by modern standards. Qaddafi had his own Arab, pseudo-socialist system in place. The institutions were not as well organized and structured as other modern states. So when he was removed pandemonium quickly spread. Past rulers generally operated in a similar manner, so to prevent chaos and anarchy after conflict it was necessary to exert sheer power to subdue everyone to order.

"So 'saghiroon' may be said to refer to a post-modern form of rule of law but the context needs to be understood. The Quran is giving guidance concerning the political reality of war and chaos in pre-modern conflict and warfare and that does still often apply today. The term 'rule of law' is a loaded term with distinctly modern implications, and there may be some misunderstanding if saghiroon is applied to it without properly unpacking and contextualizing the discussion.

"So for someone to take such verses and say they indicate that Muslims seek to subjugate people, is simply not fair. If the Quran said nothing about such matters, then we would be without needed guidance addressing the reality of conflict and war and people would not know the limits. Through the exchange between the Queen of Sheba and Solomon (and through many other incidents and verses) the Quran expounds on how nations fight, as opposed to how they ought to fight and win and establish rule. The difference is that the believers are directed to God like Prophet Solomon, upon him be peace, and are told to observe the limits of God. The limits of God are the higher rules of war, peace, and everything in between."

How Solomon tests the Queen

We've discussed how the Queen was testing Solomon, but Solomon was also testing the Queen. He asked for his forces to bring her throne in order to test her, and this was a beautiful test. Solomon did not test Bilqis to see if she had ever said a wrong word or done a wrong deed. He did not test her to see if she was like him, and thought like him, and was willing to assimilate to his culture.

Instead, it was a beautiful test. Solomon hid the image of her throne: its beauty, its grandeur, and its honor. Here, she was being tested to see if she was true to her people or was instead seeking power and glory. He also put her throne in front of the palace, demonstrating that he was not seeking to dethrone her. True faith neither fears a woman in power nor a person of no faith in power. The antagonism of true faith is directed toward people who are oppressors, as faith has a responsibility to repair the social harm done by narcissists to belittle people.

Bilqis's response shows that she was also testing King Solomon, upon him peace, to see if he was interested in elevating her and her people, or if he was seeking power over them and their resources. When she found her throne, it spoke volumes to her. She realized that he was not seeking to make the noblest of her people into the little people, and hence she embraced Islam. Let's reflect on the following verses:

> Said one who had knowledge of the Book: "I will bring it to thee within the twinkling of an eye!" Then when (Solomon) saw it placed firmly before him, he said: "This is by the Grace of my Lord! to test me whether I am grateful or ungrateful! and if any is grateful, truly his gratitude is (again) for his own soul; but if any is ungrateful, truly my Lord is Free of all Needs, Supreme in Honor!" He said: "Transform her throne out of all recognition by her: let us see whether she is guided (to the truth) or is one of those who receive no guidance." So

when she arrived, she was asked, "Is this thy throne?" She said, "It was just like this; and knowledge was bestowed on us in advance of this, and we have submitted to God (in Islam)." (Quran 27:40-42)

Shaykh Qays: "He was testing her character and she was doing likewise as Imam Baghwi and others mentioned in our books of Tafsir. Both parties were sincere and genuine and by that point they were both directed to God. Queen Bilqis's empire was symbolized in her beautiful throne. She was not attached to her throne and recognized it despite the change to its appearance. Furthermore, she was not moved by its presence where it was not supposed to be. She was somewhat casual yet cautious in her response, saying 'it seems/is like it,' which the scholars of Tafsir mention showed the strength of her intellect as well as non-attachment to the world since she stopped short of expressing certainty when what was apparent didn't indicate certainty.

"With regards to the second verse, we find a reference to knowledge in Solomon's court and in the court of the Queen of Sheba. The Queen's testing Prophet Solomon was like Salman al-Farisi when he came to Medina with foreknowledge to test Prophet Muhammad, upon him peace and blessings. He was given knowledge of what to look for from the Christian priest. Similarly, she was given knowledge of how to test him from her spiritual advisers. We do not know what it was in its entirety but Imam Razi and other mention that signs and the conduct of Solomon himself were taken into account, but it was to test his sincerity, genuine and truthfulness and by the time the Queen reached Solomon and beheld her own thrown she was already convinced of the truthfulness of his claim of prophethood. Everything that she knew and was advised to look for was there, so she did what a sincere person of integrity does: When the writing is on the wall, you submit to it.

"That is a journey of faith. It is not acting on a lust for power, oppositional or defiant tendencies or a desire to retain power. Someone like Pharaoh would have denied the whole thing even though his advisers gave him sincere advice on what to look for. He was advised and saw the writing on the wall, but he rejected it. His was a severe, twisted egoism. The Quran calls it arrogance. Arrogance needs props to reinforce the self and promote the ego. That is why power is sought and the more the ego gets, the more it craves. Then after excess upon excess and persistent immortality the spirit and the heart dies and the truth becomes meaningless to it.

"In contrast to Pharaoh and his power, Prophet Solomon was not attached to the power he was given. In contrast to Pharaoh and his arrogance, when Queen Sheba saw the truth she submitted."

The inner reality of gratitude

If we take another look at the same verse, we can reflect on Prophet Solomon's inner reality: gratitude. The argument of "no faith" in a nutshell is that one can rely on the self, whereas the argument of faith in a nutshell is: rely on God. Prophet Solomon was himself tested with his own power, which was given to him by God.

> This is by the Grace of my Lord! to test me whether I am grateful or ungrateful! and if any is grateful, truly his gratitude is (again) for his own soul; but if any is ungrateful, truly my Lord is Free of all Needs, Supreme in Honor! (Quran 27:40)

Can you comment on his response?

Shaykh Qays: "Often in the Quran, gratitude is associated with faith and is contrasted with lack of faith which is associated with ingratitude. What we see in the verses you mentioned is power and knowledge joined with faith and gratitude, not delusion and ingratitude. We see in the actions and states of Solomon that the limits of God are heeded.

"Anyone who learns anything has to be on guard regarding arrogance, since knowledge enables power, as we mentioned earlier with regard to the ego. What we learn from Solomon is only by being sincere, by constantly remembering God, being directed to Him and being grateful that guidance will come from the gaining of knowledge and the exercise of power.

"This discussion is important to emphasize the importance of integrity in faith. Muslims need to have integrity and be people of true virtue when tested with the glitter of this world if our claim to faith is to be proven true as individuals and collectively.

"When rituals and rites are practiced as they ought to be, with a directedness to God, and the decisions that we take in life—shall we consume interest or not, shall we cheat a little here and there or not, shall we break our contracts or simply ignore them or not—also have that directedness and when we repent for our moral failings and move on from them. We need to follow the footsteps of righteous people like Queen Bilqis and Prophet Solomon.

"Faith requires such integrity and perpetuates it, first at the individual level and then at the collective level. What perpetuates integrity isn't merely reason, but rather it comes when the human being can act outside of himself and his immediate self-interests and gaze at the Eternal. Solomon said, 'O my Lord! So make me that I may be grateful for Thy favors.' When the human can smash idols of self, tribe, power, wealth or anything which, like he or she, is created and return instead to God with gratitude, hope, and longing, then that is Religion.

"So the Islamic testimony of faith, 'There is no deity but God' is about that kind of human integrity. It is a declaration that there is no ultimate goal, entity, or ego that I will turn myself to internally and externally apart from God, who is entirely unlike His creatures. It calls us beyond ourselves and the frustrating, stress-inducing transience of this world to the Perfect, the Divine who we are created to recognize as the Queen of Sheba recognized. For she was a person of integrity who knew, and acted like she knew, that life is about much more than the 'stuff' we see around us, like her throne.

"And we ask God for guidance, success, and bliss eternal."

Experiencing Humility and Power: In the Footsteps of David and Solomon

And We had certainly given to David and Solomon knowledge, and they said, "Praise [is due] to Allah, who has favored us over many of His believing servants." (Quran 27:15)

When the prophets heard the words of God, they would often prostrate themselves in tears. These heartfelt prostrations came because they felt God's words not just in their heads, but because they were fully living a complete experience of God.

It's just like when a flavor or song lyric triggers a memory, bringing along a flood of emotions. For those who live close to God, as the prophets did, the word of God can do the same. Every word brings floods of memories and experiences.

But this holistic attachment to God's word didn't come from a life of ease. This feeling, of inviting God fully into their lives, came through hardships. We certainly never ask to be tried, just as the prophets did not. But if we never experience hardships, we can never feel the dire need of God. And if we never experience humility, then we can't learn about ourselves. And without knowing ourselves, we can't know God. In hard times, God brings us close to Him through humility, through patience, and through dire need of Him.

The Prophet Joseph had a hard life, with many knocks, before he received rank and recognition. By the time Joseph was elevated, his experiences had taught him not to knock others down, particularly because he had embraced his humility: Joseph understood what it's like to be powerless at the bottom of a well, waiting on your fate, or to be falsely accused by someone in power.

We all start in this world by being helpless infants. Every time, throughout our lives, when we experience helplessness, it keeps us humble.

It's hardships that bring us face-to-face with humility. And only through humility can we reach a holistic form of worship, as Joseph did, that encompasses our emotions, thoughts, memories, and physical being, so that they're interconnected, layer upon layer.

As scholar Shaykh al-Jilani has said: I looked at all doors and paths to God and found most of them very crowded. Then I looked at the path of humility, and I found it wide open. If a person can take this path, then they can reach God in a short distance.

What is humility?

The stories of the prophets tell us that humility is not about word or performance. It's about pushing back your ego in ways that can be uncomfortable.

The prophets didn't walk around bragging about their humility. Just so, a humble person doesn't walk around saying, "Hey, look at me, I'm humble!" The prophets did realize the value of humility, and they were perpetually seeking help from God to keep them humble. But humility isn't a finished state. It's instead a process of seeking.

We can know the prophets were humble because they attributed anything good that they did to God, and they also perpetually and continuously repented.

As we see from Moses and the stories of the other prophets, those who are humble are those who easily repent. They're not just saying the words, "I repent," but facing their present, past, and future without making excuses for their behavior.

Humility is not self-hate

When the prophets express humility and ask forgiveness, it is not by exclaiming they are bad people. Indeed, the focus is not on their badness, or even on any particular sin. In repenting with humility, you focus not on yourself, but on the greatness of God.

All of us want to be seen and heard by others, as that's a natural human need. But humility is being aware of another set of eyes—God's eyes. The prophets felt these eyes upon them, and so they felt a sense of shyness before God. Since God was important to them, and since they had a good opinion of God, they wanted to do their best in His presence, which was everywhere.

Indeed, those who feel they're bad people often find it very hard to repent. They're more likely to curl up inside themselves in fear and dread. Moses wasn't thinking that he was bad when he repented, but about the greatness of God.

The wonderful aspect of trials and tribulations—experienced by all prophets, and also by all of us—is that we need to be constantly asking for and experiencing forgiveness. If we experience repentance as a continuous process, then we can lift our gaze away from our sins and focus on God's presence, because God will be constantly turning to us in compassion and mercy.

Keeping the ego low

Repentance is very hard for people who are arrogant. You can know you're walking the path of humility when you find it easy to repent, even in your ordinary relationships, but also with God.

Walking the path of humility, as Shaykh al-Jilani tells us, is about walking that uncrowded path of keeping your ego low, as our egos can become intoxicated with praise. At first, walking the path of humility can mean a fight with your ego, because your ego will fight back!

After all, the ego loves to be seen and heard. But this fight is not about crushing your ego; it's about trying to transcend it. The prophets were divinely protected from sin, and they lived as examples for each other and for us. We, on the other hand, can fail. But it doesn't matter whether we reach a state of truthfulness or die trying. What matters is not whether we've achieved results, but that we keep on trying.

We know from the stories of the Quran that pious people slip up, sin, and often need to repent. Being humble isn't about being infallible.

It's about continually striving to be truthful with oneself and, thus, with God.

The desire to be known, the desire to do good

As al-Jilani says, we should never be moved by praise.

But being humble doesn't have to mean being unknown. When we think about the blessings and the dangers of being famous, we should think about Solomon, who asked God for power so that he could do good.

Solomon didn't desire fame so that he could be praised, and he knew how easily power corrupts. So he asked God to give him power, but also to give him sincere advisers and help. And Solomon was right to ask for power, because we needed good leaders back then, just as we need them now.

We do need good influential people.

But we must be, like Solomon, intentional in whatever we seek.

If we get the blessing of influence, then we have to be careful with everything, just as David and Solomon were.

The Prophet David, upon him peace, married King Talut's daughter, after the king had said: Whoever defeats Goliath shall marry my daughter. And here comes young David, a shepherd with barely any power. He was so small and slight that he wasn't even able to put on his armor. But David wanted to defeat Goliath not for his own fame, but to do good for others. And when he approached the battle, he went full of faith and the presence of God.

A stone thrown with faith in God, and in the presence of God, is different from a stone thrown alone.

So David married the king's daughter. His new father-in-law was not a bad man, but this old king became jealous. After all, David had a lot of blessings: He had wisdom, he had a beautiful voice, and he caught people's attention.

Power and influence is like all blessings: It can stir jealousy. Indeed, power and influence has perhaps the most power to stir negative feelings in people. Just so, as we remember, it stirred negative feelings in Satan when Adam was given power and influence.

How did David protect himself against all those who were jealous, including his own father-in-law? The Prophet David constantly remembered and felt himself in the presence of God. As the stories tell us, David loved to remember God so much that he would sing with the birds. And God subjected the birds to David's will, so that they would sing with him, and the mountains would echo with their beautiful music. Singing, for David, was a way to remember God.

David also constantly fasted, and he constantly did other acts that kept him in touch with God and with his gratitude for all his gifts.

David was so in touch with his gratitude, the Quran tells us, that he told God: Every time I thank You, I realize I have to thank You for thanking You, because that, too, is a blessing.

This is an important story to keep in mind when we are seeking power in order to help others, because the higher you get up any social ladder, the more dangerous and narcissistic people you are likely to find around you. In this, we have to be very careful, keeping in mind how easy it is to go from being the oppressed to being the oppressor.

MOSES: LESSONS ON POWER AND OPPRESSION

And We did certainly confer favor upon Moses and Aaron. And We saved them and their people from the great affliction, And We supported them so it was they who overcame. And We gave them the explicit Scripture, And We guided them on the straight path. And We left for them [favorable mention] among later generations: "Peace upon Moses and Aaron." Indeed, We thus reward the doers of good. Indeed, they were of Our believing servants. (Quran 37:114-122)

Muslims and the Elephant in the Room

God! There is no deity but He! To Him belong the most Beautiful Names. Has the story of Moses reached thee? (Quran 20:8-9)

Sometimes, people ask why we should focus on the lives of other prophets, rather than solely on Prophet Muhammad, upon them all peace and blessings. Prophet Muhammad was nurtured by the stories of those who came before him, so it's natural that these stories should nurture us as well. But there is also so much noise around the words "Prophet Muhammad" by now—positive, negative, and just confusing—that it becomes almost impossible to hear oneself think.

So it's better for us to get to a quieter space. The area around Moses is one of those.

One of other things that makes it hard to listen to new stories is having an "elephant in the room." This elephant is supposed to be an obvious, gigantic truth that no one is allowed to talk about. But these obvious truths are often not so truthful after all.

As Omar Ghabra wrote in *The National*, "In the hours following a shooting that left a Canadian soldier dead, [TV commentator Bill] Maher had this to say: 'Turns out the attacker was Islamic—what are the odds, huh? It's almost like there's an elephant in the room.'"

It is like there's an elephant—although we might see that elephant in a somewhat different way, as a creature built out of prejudice and assumptions. These elephants can come to be when we discuss the oppressed without listening to their stories. This makes it hard to listen to any other truths outside of the "obvious" elephantine one that stands at the center of the room.

What we need to do is crack the windows of these rooms, opening them up so that we can hear the voices of those outside. The Prophet Muhammad was one of these voices from outside the rooms of the powerful, and so too was the voice of Moses.

It's important, as we listen to these stories outside the room, to recognize that there is not just one story for us to hear. The elephant tells a single story. But, as novelist Chimamanda Adichie argued in her powerful and popular TED talk, our lives, and our cultures, are composed of many overlapping stories. Listening to just one definitive story—one story about Muslims, about the Prophet Muhammad, about Moses—risks a critical misunderstanding.

Adichie quoted the Palestinian poet and memoirist Mourid Barghouti, who writes in I Saw Ramallah that, if you want to dispossess a people, the simplest way to do it is to start their story with, "secondly." Start the story with the arrows of the Native Americans, and not with the arrival of the British, and you have an entirely different "definitive" story, one that creates an unassailable elephant in the room.

Open the windows! Let in the light, and the giant shadow of the elephant—made up of prejudices and biases—will begin to disappear.

The conversations that happen outside the windows don't seek out the crowd. Rather, they seek out small groups of people who, within their circles of influence and power, can take the conversation forward, creating a ripple to other circles of influence. This is the style used by the Prophet Muhammad, upon him peace and blessings, and, in this way, he tore down psychological and social constructs that prevented the light from entering the rooms at the center of power.

I was recently in Saudi Arabia for hajj, or pilgrimage. A group of us climbed the mountain of Hira and saw the cave where Prophet Muhammad used to spend time to reflect. When he received revelations, he started out alone with a few supporters and, slowly, he invited others to listen. He was offered power, money, and material gifts to give up his mission, but he continued to build a community of people who enjoined the good and forbid the wrong. In this way, he let in the light.

The Prophet Muhammad's journey was not about staging a coup, taking over the space inside the room, and pushing other people outside. Instead, it was about inviting all of us to leave the room and listen to the stories outside.

After the Charlie Hebdo tragedy in January 2015, when 12 people were killed by a pair of Muslim gunmen, many powerful voices built up an elephant in the loud, dark room of power. At the University of Minnesota, an event supporting free speech was organized without any Muslim speaker. Here, people were interrogated, psychoanalyzed, and judged, but didn't listen to or engage others as human beings.

The word for oppression in Arabic is dhulm, which means darkness. By contrast, one of God's names is an-Nur, or The Light. Hence, one understanding of dhulm is a disconnect from God, The Light.

Once we let the light into the room, we are compelled to reflect and investigate the many different truths and stories that exist outside the centers of power.

Opening the Windows to the Stories of Moses

God! There is no deity but He! To Him belong the most Beautiful Names. Has the story of Moses reached thee? (Quran 20:8-9)

Among the stories that can help us let in the light are those stories of the Prophet Moses, upon him peace. He is one of the five resolute prophets, those who are given a tremendous number of trials and stand firm after all of them. Moses is mentioned more times in the Quran than any other Prophet and, importantly, Moses is also present in Judaism and Christianity. In all three traditions, Moses is someone who is guided by God, a law-giver, and a person who struggled against Pharaoh and helped alleviate the suffering of an oppressed people.

But there is not one single story to be told about Moses. Sometimes, Moses is shrunk down to one story about good vs. evil, Jews vs. Pharaoh's regime. But the stories of Moses are large and diverse, and they have many stories nested within them. Also, there are not just the good and the evil. Instead, there is a diversity of people on both the side of the oppressed and the side of the oppressors.

The stories of Moses, upon him peace, are stories about power and oppression. However, these are not simple stories. Amongst those in power, there are many shades, from those who oppress to those who support the call to truth. Amongst the weak, there are also people who support the oppression of their own people. There are also a few righteous believers.

The elephant is an "us vs. them" story where people are changeless and locked into a single group identity. But the many stories outside the room show that truth is many-faceted and has many shades.

From the Quran, we learn that, under the watchful gaze of God, Moses, upon him peace, was raised in the home of Pharaoh. The beauty of this story is that God tells us that He cast His love into Moses in the home of Pharaoh. Here, Pharaoh's wife, Asiya, developed a fond love of Moses, upon him peace. She wanted to keep him as a son, hence protecting him in a climate of deep-seated oppression:

> Throw (the child) into the chest, and throw (the chest) into the river: the river will cast him up on the bank, and he will be taken up by one who is an enemy to Me and an enemy to him': But I cast (the garment of) love over thee from Me: and (this) in order that thou mayest be reared under Mine eye. (Quran 20:39)

So it was that Moses was reared, like all prophets, by God Himself. From their birth, they are connected to the light of God, as they are to be the light and the way to God.

The stories of Moses are beautiful stories of power and oppression, and it's time to open the windows and let in the light from these stories, so they can show that the elephant is not at all what we'd thought.

How Do You Know You're Really Fighting Oppression?

Oppression is real. And in any oppressive social setting, there is more than just pain, humiliation, and hatred. There is a general disrespect for life, and a lack of compassion for how destructive oppressive acts and settings can be on a victim's soul. These settings impact all of us, oppressor, oppressed, and bystander, although some more than others.

In fighting oppression, there are lessons we can learn from the stories of how the prophets fought for a more just society. I have often wondered how the prophets would approach the conflicts of our times. Would their response always be war? Or would they talk and talk and talk, trying to change the framework of the argument?

These are questions I ask myself when I read the Quran.

Moses knew a great deal about oppression. Under Asiya's protection, Moses grew up like a prince in a world of privilege. Yet he knew about the daily sufferings of his fellow Israelites. Because of his interventions, the sufferings of the Israelites were reduced. Yet they were still slaves in Egypt: scorned and mistreated.

Despite his lavish surroundings, Moses grew up with faith, and he was very much conscious of what his people endured. He tried to reduce their pain and suffering, but there was only so much he could do: It was a bit like dispensing a Tylenol or Advil to treat a severe, chronic infection.

Two beautiful names of God are particularly important to know in understanding this part of Moses's story. The first is al-Hakim, The Wise, and the second is al-Khabir, The All-Aware.

"Al-Hakim" means God is endlessly wise in His knowledge and in His deeds, while "al-Khabir" means God knows the hidden inner lives of everything. He is the one whose knowledge reaches the deepest, darkest, and the most hidden corners of His kingdom, where neither human intelligence nor His angels can penetrate. Even things that have not yet happened—but are in a state of formation or being planned and hidden, like secrets within secrets—are manifest to Him. None can escape His attention.

Moses had a chance to know both of these aspects of God when, upon reaching adulthood, he faced an event that threw him out of his life of privilege and drove him out of Egypt.

One day, at a time when the streets were empty and marketplaces were closed, Moses entered the city. He found two people fighting: a fellow Israelite and an Egyptian. The Israelite was being maltreated, and he called out to Moses for help. After all, Moses had a high position, which he had used to protect the Israelites. He was upset and rushed over.

What he witnessed was his fellow Israelite being harassed by soldiers. It was, as we might say now, police brutality. And it was endemic in the system.

As they argued, Moses accidentally struck the Egyptian and killed him. Immediately, Moses said:

> "This is of Satan's doing. Indeed, he is a clear, misleading enemy! My Lord, indeed I have wronged myself, so forgive me!" and He forgave him. Indeed, He is Forgiving, the Merciful. He said, "My Lord, because of the favor You have

bestowed upon me, never will I be a supporter of criminals!" And he became, within the city, fearful and anticipating the spread of the news. (Quran 28:15-18)

It's important to reflect on Moses's deep remorse, which was instant. Within a split second of the man's death, Moses felt it. This remorse was a private and intimate communication between him and God.

Indeed, no one else knew of what had happened—only Moses and his fellow Israelite. At this point, Moses had already committed himself to severing his privileged ties with Pharaoh and Pharaoh's tyrannical regime, which was engaging in divide-and-conquer policies inside Egypt, as well as brutally restricting the freedoms of the Israelites. Moses was willing to give up his privilege and high rank to do what was right. But now he had been hyped up by someone, a fellow Israelite, and he'd been driven to kill a man. What would happen next?

The following day, the Quran continues the story:

So he saw the morning in the city, looking about, in a state of fear, when behold, the man who had, the day before, sought his help called aloud for his help (again). Moses said to him: "Thou art truly, it is clear, a quarrelsome fellow!" Then, when he decided to lay hold of the man who was an enemy to both of them, that man (Israelite) said: "O Moses! Is it thy intention to slay me as thou slewest a man yesterday? Thy intention is none other than to become a powerful violent man in the land, and not to be one who sets things right!" (Quran 28: 18-19)

The Israelite who called for help in this way in beating back his oppressor, twice, wrongly assumed that Moses was going to get hold of him. When the man feared for his life, he immediately told people what had happened the day before, and thereby put Moses' life in danger.

This is a good place to pause and reflect.

This Israelite was indeed facing cruel oppression, like the rest of his people. But instead of acting thoughtfully, he used his position to whip up anger and worsen the violence. He screamed against oppression, screamed for others to come to his aid, as though what he really wanted wasn't an end to oppression, but revenge and power.

Moses, on the other hand, was resisting not for himself, but for his fellow Israelite. In doing so, Moses put his rank and privilege on the line. Of the two of them, only Moses felt remorse at the loss of life, a feeling that remained with him the following day such that it made him full of anxiety.

That Israelite had a pattern of getting himself in trouble and crying out for help. He was not just a troublemaker, but he was also acting from selfish motives. First, it's evident that he didn't care about the loss of life he'd caused. If he had, he would have felt so much remorse that it would've left an impact on him the following day. It would've prevented him from being in trouble yet again. And upon seeing Moses again in the city, he wouldn't have called out to him for help.

But the very next day, this unnamed Israelite was in trouble again, and he was again yelling for help. Yet his loyalty to Moses was very thin. When he assumed his life was in danger, he wasn't concerned for anyone but himself. He forgot the protection that Moses offered him the day before, and he disclosed what had happened, thereby putting Moses' life in danger. He then projected his internal reality onto Moses, accusing him of seeking "to become a powerful violent man in the land, and not to be one who sets things right!"

The test

According to Islamic teachings, prophets and Messengers are divinely protected from sin. In this way, Moses's trial is understood not as a failure, but as a test. There is wisdom in the mistake that Moses made, and it helps us understand how we can face our own trials.

What does Moses do? Now that he's been ratted out by his fellow Israelite, who he'd wanted to protect, his life is in danger. He could have used his privilege and power to claim that the other Israelite hyped him up—and thus had the man arrested. He could have hit the other Israelite for dragging him into a fight in which he'd had no intention of engaging, then leaving him to suffer the consequences. That is not what he did. God, the Wise and the All-Aware, guided him to leave.

> And there came a man, running, from the furthest end of the City. He said: "O Moses! the Chiefs are taking counsel together about thee, to slay thee: so get thee away, for I do give thee sincere advice." He therefore got away therefrom, looking about, in a state of fear. He prayed "O my Lord! save me from people given to wrong-doing." Then, when he

turned his face towards (the land of) Midian, he said: "I do hope that my Lord will show me the smooth and straight Path." (Quran 28:20-22)

True reformers are people who have the capacity to feel remorse. They value life—all life. They are people of sacrifice and, when their lives are in danger, they turn to God and seek guidance on the best way to respond. At times, God inspires you to put the babe in the basket. At times, He inspires you to raise that child as your own. At times, He inspires you to leave, as He has other plans for you.

Nurture Thyself

> *God! There is no deity but He! To Him belong the most Beautiful Names. Has the story of Moses reached thee?* (Quran 20:8-9)

In those early days, when he lived in Egypt, Moses was impatient. He needed a greater strength to stand up and deal with a cruel tyrant. He had to be strengthened from within. This was one of the gifts of his time in exile.

Oppressive societies don't allow a person to grow, and it is very difficult to nurture oneself under a tyrant. There is only a certain amount that a person can grow, as though trying to grow tall under a very low ceiling, and Moses had reached that ceiling. There was no room for him to grow any further.

And so it was not a bad thing that Moses, upon him peace, went from living like a prince and pursuing a life of privilege and prestige, to being a fugitive who was running away from a tyrant out to slay him, to the land of Midian.

> He prayed "O my Lord! save me from people given to wrong-doing." Then, when he turned his face towards (the land of) Midian, he said: "I do hope that my Lord will show me the smooth and straight Path." (Quran 28:22)

The land of Midian was inhabited by Arabs. Some commentators say that the Arab prophet Shuaib was in the town, while others say it was the esteemed believer, known in the English-language Bible as Jethro, or as Yathra in Arabic. Although Midian was not a utopia—as no place is— it was a place where Moses could live in relative freedom.

But it took Moses some time to reach this freedom. When Moses arrived in Midian, he had been traveling for eight days, driving himself to the very limits of exhaustion. He'd reached a point of starvation, with his feet bleeding from walking tirelessly without water or food except what he could find on the trees. He came near a well and fell underneath the shade of trees for shelter. He had absolutely nothing with him, and he had fully exhausted himself—to the very depths of his body and soul—in pursuit of survival.

It was not an easy experience. In that state, what does he do?

Some would commit suicide. Others might go on shooting rampage, or otherwise try to numb their feelings and escape from the pain and fear of this difficult new reality. Moses, on the other hand, experienced and accepted the event. He surrendered to his new reality, since this was where God had brought him.

Then, in a state of dire need and exhaustion, he saw two women who were also needy. Instead of being absorbed with his own near-starvation and exhaustion, Moses got up and approached them, asked a clarifying question, and then addressed their need. He asked them for nothing in return. He made no assumptions or ugly accusations about how they were standing with their flock instead of allowing a male relative to do the job.

> And when he arrived at the water of Midian he found there a group of men watering their flocks, and beside them he found two women who were keeping back their flocks. He said, "What is the matter with you?" They said, "We cannot water (our flocks) until the shepherds take their flocks. And our father is a very old man." Therefore, he watered their flocks for them, and then he turned back to shade, and said, "My Lord! Truly, I am in need of whatever good that You bestow on me!" (Quran 28:23-24)

Here, I would like to reflect on the following names of God: Al-Wahhab, which means a donor who gives without expecting return, and al-Muhaymin, or The Protector and Guardian.

Moses hoped for anything to help him survive, as he was near starvation, and yet he did this good deed for the two women without expecting anything in return. God rewarded Moses's unconditional generosity, giving him shelter, food, job, and a family. There is something to notice here: A true leader cannot have a deep-seated prejudice toward women. He can neither see them as objects nor exploit them.

A leader or reformer does not violate the boundaries of another human being, does not manipulate, does not hype others up, does not overpower others for selfish motives, and is open to embracing and receiving wisdom and knowledge from others. He does not look down on other cultures or embrace xenophobia or bigotry. He does not fear learning from a "Western education" and encourages Western societies not to fear "Eastern education."

> O humankind! We have created you from a male and a female, and made you into nations and tribes, that you may know one another. (Quran 49:13)

Like Prophet Muhammad, Moses, upon them peace and blessings, was not a tribal leader who promoted tribalism or racism. He was able to live amongst Arabs in Midian, to embrace other cultures, and to appreciate them.

Another important point to note is that one of the women hinted to her father about her desire to marry Moses. The relationship between father and daughter was deep and loving. He did not pressure his daughter to marry Moses, but merely facilitated the process.

> Then there came to him one of the two women, walking shyly. She said, "Verily, my father calls you that he may reward you for having watered our flocks for us." So when he came to him and narrated the story, he said, "Fear you not. You have escaped from the people who are wrong-doers." And said one of them (the two women): "O my father! Hire him! Verily, the best of men for you to hire is the strong, the trustworthy." He said, "I intend to wed one of these two daughters of mine to you, on condition that you serve me for eight years, but if you complete ten years, it will be a favor from you. But I intend not to place you under a difficulty. If Allah wills, you will find me one of the righteous." He (Moses) said, "That is settled between me and you whichever of the two terms I fulfil, there will be no injustice to me, and Allah is Surety over what we say." (Quran 28:25-28)

Like all reformers, Moses was given the gift of insight and awareness. First, he was made to observe and witness the negatives and ugly consequences of what Pharaoh and his soldiers were doing. Later, he surrendered to God's will and accepted the way things are, and was nurtured by his new family of faith, knowing that there was a higher wisdom that was yet outside his grasp.

Moses married the woman, named Zopparah, and spent the next ten years working with her father (either the Prophet Shuaib or Jethro) and raising his own family. He went from a life of privilege, where he'd learned about leadership, politics, and government, to the solitary life of a shepherd. Instead of watching his people suffering and humiliated, he was made to ponder the wonders of God and the universe. Here, he had time to feel the kind of awe that penetrates one's soul when one looks at stars in the midst of darkness.

During his time in Midian, Moses was a shepherd, like many of the prophets. Some argue that people are like sheep, and, in order to guide people and nurture them, the prophets were trained by attending to sheep. So it may be. But if you talk to a shepherd, this is not an easy job! Like humans, sheep are animals that require constant care and attention. A shepherd must be constantly on alert, attending to the animals' safety and wellbeing. The whole flock must be watched over, and the shepherd must guide them back if they stray. Moses's new profession increased his knowledge, wisdom, and insight. One might also speculate that it allowed him to heal.

After the ten years of service, Moses gathered his family together and made the long journey back to Egypt, but he got lost and was looking for guidance and how to find his way.

> Then, when Moses had fulfilled the term, and was traveling with his family, he saw a fire in the direction of Mount Tur. He said to his family, "Wait, I have seen a fire; perhaps I may bring to you from there some news, or a burning fire-brand that you may warm yourselves." (Quran 28:29)

Moses walked towards the fire, and as he did, he heard a voice.

> Blessed is whosoever is in the fire, and whosoever is round about it! And far removed is God from every imperfection, the Lord of all that exists. "O Moses! Verily! It is I, God, the All-Mighty, and the All-Wise." (Quran 27:8-9)

Throughout his whole stay in Midian, Moses was under the watchful eyes of God, being nurtured and prepared for prophethood.

Now that he was trained and nurtured, he was ready to change the oppression he'd witnessed and to liberate the Israelites. Now that he had nurtured himself, his next task was to train and nurture his people so that he could liberate them.

What does this mean for us?

As Moses is called to the fire, so is he called to prophethood. Again, we read:

> Blessed is whosoever is in the fire, and whosoever is round about it! And far removed is God from every imperfection, the Lord of all that exists. "O Moses! Verily! It is I, God, the All-Mighty, and the All-Wise." (Quran 27:8-9)

Moses, upon him peace, was a strong military leader, but he did not wage war against Pharaoh. The scholar Reza Aslan has noted that people are less inclined to hurt the people they know. By this measure, the solution to Islamophobia is relationships. This is both true and false, but first we must ask: What type of relationships? After all, people do hurt people they know. Most cases of rape are between people who know one another, and domestic violence is one of the leading causes of injury to women in the United States and beyond.

Oppression cannot be fought by simply having dinner and being kind to your neighbors, who are sometimes also your oppressors. A case in point is the Chapel Hill shootings, where three youths were shot dead execution-style by their neighbor, who apparently knew them and yet still hated them, apparently for their religion. He knew them, yet the father of two of the victims said that the killer had brought a gun to their house before and threatened them with it. Healthy boundaries within relationships are necessary for coexistence and harmony. There was not a healthy boundary to protect the three young people from their neighbor.

This lesson can also be found in the story of Pharaoh, who kills his wife Asiya. According to Islamic teachings, Asiya is a role model for all women. Yet Pharaoh believed he was the deity, and that everyone should look up to him. He saw others as objects to exploit and enslave, acted like judge, jury and executioner, and did whatever it took to maintain power. There was no one to call him to account for his cruelty or slaughter of others. He acted with impunity, with no accountability to any rule or power.

He knew his wife very well, but this didn't stop him from killing her, since he believed he had the right to do it. Perhaps he even believed he was "defending" himself.

The oppressed, like the Jews during Moses's time, find they must resist abusive power to liberate themselves. Repeatedly throughout history, religion has been used as a justification and a tool when fighting wars. Some of these have been wars of liberation, while others have been a distortion of religious teachings. So it is now, when some Muslims distort and twist Islamic teachings to promote themselves as "reformers" while harming others in the process.

One cannot trivialize or discount the valid grievances that many Muslims have toward powerful countries today. An article by Nafeez Ahmed called "Unworthy Victims" states that Western wars have killed four million Muslims since 1990. Much of this is the result of unchecked power. But there are other powers that are corrupt and unchecked, among them many Arab and Muslim leaders in many areas in the Middle East.

It is ludicrous to blame everything on the West, just as it is ludicrous to blame everything on Islam. The clash between the West and Islam is really all in our minds: It is a way to avoid looking at the real issues. These are: Who has power, what sort of power, and what is it being used for?

These issues cannot be wished away by getting to know each other. Many influential US columnists travel to Arab and Muslim lands, engage, share meals, and discuss issues. Yet what type of relationships do they establish with the residents? As a case in point, Nicholas Kristof, who has traveled to many Arab- and Muslim-majority areas, participated in cheerleading and shutting down public debate on the Iraq war, a war that contributed to the rise of ISIS.

Chris Hedges describes these false friends well in his article on Truthdig, "The Treason of the Intellectuals." Hedges' argument shows that the relationships these people created were not healthy, equal ones, where each knew and appreciated the other, but relationships that enabled and supported unchecked abusive power while silencing the voices of the oppressed.

Likewise, CJ Werleman elsewhere equates the language and arguments of Christian crusaders and 21st-century US and UK neo-conservatism. How many conversations, discussions, and relationships have these commentators had with Muslims and Arabs? What sorts of relationships are they? Indeed, when one acts like a cheerleader for war and shouts down critical thinking, these are actions of a Pharaoh.

Moses, upon him peace, went through many tests in order to show us the inner reality of his struggles, helping us to reflect on our own inner selves. His were difficult and severe trials, through which he surrendered to God's will, allowing God to be his teacher.

The test of the Midian was a particularly beautiful test, and many of us face a similar one when we immigrate to another land and need to establish wholly new relationships. We can look at the relationships Moses established and ask what's in our own heart. Did we run from Pharaoh physically, yet does he still lurk in our heart and soul? When God places another human being who is weak and unprotected before us, do we fulfill their needs without asking for anything in return, or do we exploit them? Do we justify their oppression and persecution because we were once persecuted?

When some Muslims and Arabs fled persecution from various Muslim and Arab countries, how did they treat women, minorities, those who are weak and unprotected? When some early European-Americans fled persecution from Europe, what happened to the earlier residents of this land? When Jews fled persecution from Europe to Palestine, what happened to the residents there?

Moses's lessons and trials teach us to look inward and ask ourselves, first and foremost: Who lurks in our heart and soul? The first medicine that faith offers to the oppressed is not to rise up in arms and put oneself in power. Instead, it is to remove Pharaoh from one's own soul. Don't be a Pharaoh to others.

As with Prophet Muhammad, upon him peace and blessings, one of the first things prescribed for Moses and his followers was prayer.

> But when he came to the fire, a voice was heard: "O Moses! Verily I am thy Lord! therefore (in My presence) put off thy shoes: thou art in the sacred valley Tuwa. Verily, I am God: There is no deity but I: So serve thou Me (only), and establish regular prayer for celebrating My praise. Verily the Hour is coming. My design is to keep it hidden, for every soul to receive its reward by the measure of its Endeavor. Therefore let not such as believe not therein but follow their own lusts, divert thee therefrom, lest thou perish!" (Quran 20:11-16)

God does not benefit from our prayers or our remembrance of Him. The prayers benefit us and our hearts: They allow the light of faith to increase and thus protect us from allowing Pharaoh to enter. Here, I would like to reflect on two names of God. The first is "as-Sami," The All-Hearing, who hears all that comes from the lips, passes through the minds, or is felt by the hearts. According to Shaykh Tosun Bayrak al-Jerrahi al-Halveti, as-Sami hears "the rustling of leaves in the wind, the footsteps of the ants and the atoms' moving through the void." The other name is "al-Basir," The All-Seeing, who sees all that has passed, all there is, and all there will be.

The oppressed are often silenced by the cheerleaders of war and abusive power, and they may have a strong desire for a witness to hear their pain and suffering. Malcolm X said that power respects power, and indeed healthy power respects everyone. However, abusive power only respects power that will hold it in check. For this reason, when one finds themselves weak, and those in power are abusive, and their leaders are corrupt, one must connect to The All-Seeing and The All-Hearing to seek His guidance.

God spoke directly to Moses, and Moses was told the wisdom behind everything that had happened to him. All of this was in preparation for his mission in life as Prophet and messenger of God.

This was the first sign for Pharaoh:

> "And throw your stick!" But when he saw it moving as if it were a snake, he turned in flight and looked not back. (It was said): "O Moses! Draw near, and fear not. Verily, you are of those who are secure." (Quran 28:31)

Another sign for Pharaoh:

> "Move thy hand into thy bosom, and it will come forth white without stain (or harm), and draw thy hand close to thy side (to guard) against fear. Those are the two credentials from thy Lord to Pharaoh and his Chiefs: for truly they are a people rebellious and wicked." (32)

The staff that Moses used as a shepherd is turned into a snake to illustrate to Moses that God is not limited, and that one should use these means while relying on God. Although Moses was very strong on the outside, what we see through this dialogue with God is his humility, his humanity, and his vulnerability. A healthy person does not see themselves as a deity who can take on the world, but is instead in touch with their weaknesses and vulnerability. It also shows us that when Moses, upon him peace, faced Pharaoh, he faced him not by relying on himself, or the means in his hand (a staff). Instead, he relied on God, commanded by Him and protected by Him as he went to speak to Pharaoh.

The key is Moses's humility and vulnerability. And indeed, Moses never forgot the man he accidentally slew in error.

> He said: "O my Lord! I have slain a man among them, and I fear lest they slay me." (Quran 28:33)

Moses, upon him peace, had an inner life that shows he was aware of his weaknesses and was a deeply humble person. He even argued that perhaps he was not the most qualified person for the job. But God had selected him and would also protect him.

> "And my brother Aaron. He is more eloquent in speech than I: so send him with me as a helper, to confirm (and strengthen) me: for I fear that they may accuse me of falsehood." [Allah] said: "We will certainly strengthen thy arm through thy brother, and invest you both with authority, so they shall not be able to touch you: with Our Sign shall ye triumph, you two as well as those who follow you." (28:34-35)

God directed Moses to go to Pharaoh.

> Go, both of you, to Pharaoh, for he has indeed transgressed all bounds; But speak to him mildly; perchance he may take warning or fear (God). (Quran 20:43-44)

To varying degrees, we all have a Pharaoh and a Moses within us. The dominant voice within is based on our relationships with those in power and those who are unprotected. If we obsess only over our security, and are cheerleaders for those in power, then we are Pharaoh or Pharaoh's yes-men. If we seek power and are obsessed with our own pain and suffering only, then we are the Israelite who fought for selfish motives, a Pharaoh wannabe.

If we, however, align ourselves with those in power and hold them in check and align with those who are oppressed and support the oppressed, then the dominant voice within us is Moses.

Growing the Moses Within

God! There is no deity but He! To Him belong the most Beautiful Names. Has the story of Moses reached thee? (Quran 20:8-9)

Oppression works in many ways. One way is by convincing people that they're bad: that they're thugs, savages, or terrorists. A people can be controlled psychologically when an oppressor makes them feel as though they can't overcome a mistake they've made or defines them by their worst moment. This is also true if an oppressor defines an entire group by the worst actions of the fringe amongst them.

In doing this, an oppressor thus doesn't allow a people to grow. To oppress another, you have to dehumanize them in your eyes first and then, later, in the eyes of others. An oppressor takes a group's worst acts and worst moments and keeps people hostage to those acts or moments.

Sometimes, we react to this by trying to show only our best moments. In contemporary America, this creates a cycle of showing good Muslim/bad Muslim, good Muslim/bad Muslim, and it doesn't advance the discussion. A case in point is 9/11 or the Paris attacks, when many in the Muslim community reacted to being demonized by working to prove that Muslims are model citizens.

Even though it doesn't seem so, it is counter-productive for Muslim-Americans to present everything that Muslims do as good. It feeds into the psychological construct of oppression by not allowing Muslims to admit error and grow. We cannot "prove" that Muslims are perfect, because there are also bad and ugly aspects of Muslim communities, as there are everywhere. Our argument should be, "We are human," and then we should turn the mirror around and say, "Like you."

Craig Hicks, who assassinated three young people in Chapel Hill, counted himself an atheist. Of course, this hardly proves all atheists would act in this way! But it does tell prominent atheists, some of whom are also prominent bigots, that the people in their group are human, too.

But we can't just condemn bigots. We also need to give opportunities for growth and repentance, because God is a perpetual forgiver.

Going to Pharaoh

Last we saw Moses, God was directing him to go to Pharaoh.

Go, both of you, to Pharaoh, for he has indeed transgressed all bounds; But speak to him mildly; perchance he may take warning or fear (God). (Quran 20:43-44)

But before we go with Moses to Pharaoh, it is important to understand that Moses had also been affected by the toxic environment of oppression—his entire group was defined by the oppressor. For that reason, he had to remove himself from that environment, to detoxify the mind and the spirit.

Later on, we see the use of oppressive tactics in the communication between Moses and Pharaoh, particularly the use of magicians to play with his mind, and the use of fear, obligation, and guilt.

But Moses didn't run from his oppressor. Owning up to the reality of the tyrant is being true to oneself. We see this in Moses's response to God. Although Moses, upon him peace, was strong and powerful, when he went to see Pharaoh, he went relying on God, and not on himself.

> They said, "Our Lord! Verily! We fear lest he should hasten to punish us or lest he should transgress all bounds against us." (20:45)

Moses definitely did not want to go see Pharaoh. Moses felt Pharaoh would "transgress all bounds," and Moses approached Pharaoh with fear. But God told him to go, and Moses let himself be prepared by God for this visit, to speak to Pharaoh not with angry tones, but "mildly."

Moses's immediate repentance at his accidental murder of an Egyptian soldier, and his repentance again when meeting with Pharaoh, shows his true internal state. Moses knew that a person has to call themselves out before they call others out. Moses repented and, when God told him to go, he accepted criticism. Part of fighting tyranny is not saying that, "I'm all good and you're all evil." It's to be open, to express remorse, and to be willing to accept criticism. Pharaoh reminded Moses of the life of privilege he'd lived and how he killed a man. He accused Moses of being ungrateful.

> Moses said, "I did it then, when I was an ignorant (as regards my Lord and His Message). So I fled from you when I feared you. But my Lord has granted me religious knowledge, and Prophethood, and appointed me as one of the Messengers. And this is the past favor with which you reproach me, and that you have enslaved the children of Israel." (Quran 26:20-22)

The beauty of this passage is in the abundant gifts that genuine repentance brings. In a prophetic narration, it is said that God loves those who repent. Why? Besides manifesting God's mercy and perpetual forgiveness, repentance empties the person of their ego and opens them to receive gifts from God, gifts that will not allow them to betray their soul. The reality of love is to give of oneself, and God loves to give to His creations. But to receive, like Moses, you must empty yourself of the social ills around you and allow God to fill you with His gifts.

It is a message to the oppressed: We should neither rationalize injustice nor an answering vengeance. It's also a message that those who make mistakes should seek forgiveness.

Speaking Truth to Power

There is an Arab proverb that says, "What made you, O Pharaoh?" Pharaoh replied: "I didn't find anyone to tell me stop."

Indeed: Silence and sycophancy are the building blocks of tyranny.

In every field, we use benchmarks to measure our work, to check our performance and the results produced. Likewise, God tells us the stories of the prophets to compare our work, performance, deeds, thoughts, and feelings with the prophets to measure ourselves against them. Faith is about making choices and not about following blindly. At each of these many junctions, we have to make a decision: one path calls to faith and another calls away from God.

One such junction point is when we need to decide whether and how to speak out against injustice.

Speaking out against injustice doesn't mean just helping the oppressed. Prophet Muhammad, upon him peace and blessings, said to help your brother if he is either the oppressor or the oppressed. People responded: We know how to help him if he is oppressed, but how do we help him if he is the oppressor? "You can restrain him from committing oppression. That will be your help to him."

This hadith illustrates how Islam gives light and elevation to all, the oppressor and the oppressed, regardless of other considerations. Prophet Musa, upon him peace, oversaw the destruction of Pharaoh and the destruction of those who instigated and approved of calf-worship. The children of Israel were underdogs, but that didn't stop them from oppressing themselves.

If you are an officer of the law, for example, you can use your power to restrain others from committing oppressive acts. If, contrarily, you are alone in the face of tyranny, you must use your voice. But this doesn't mean name-calling or ridicule, it means creating a way for the oppressor to save face and to become a better person, just as Moses attempted with Pharaoh.

Part of speaking truth to power is reminding the tyrant that there is someone who can hold them to account, someone who has more power than they do. Tyrants act in the belief that no one will call them to account, and that belief needs to be punctured and deflated. The prophets reminded those in power of God's presence and power. This reminder was to wake them up so they might see their vulnerability and the vulnerability of others, not to oppress them. Tyrants have a hatred of weakness, be it in themselves or others.

Prophet Abraham, upon him peace, reminded Nimrod of this by telling him that he could not make the sun rise:

> Abraham said: 'Lo! God causes the sun to rise in the east, so you cause it to come up from the west.' Thus was the disbeliever absolutely defeated. And God guides not wrongdoing folk. (Quran 2:258)

In this way Moses, upon him peace, also speaks truth to power.

He does not allow Pharaoh to rationalize oppression. In this dialogue, Pharaoh questions God's power and justice, overlooking his own reality: that he's enslaving others. Moses, upon him peace, directs Pharaoh to focus on the diversity of God's creations and how each is nurtured. Open your eyes to the present moment, Moses says.

What is interesting about this advice is that many healers likewise encourage their patients to go into nature and look at the diversity of plants and creations, and to observe them. There is a healing effect in just looking at stars and sky and the present moment.

Moses then brings their conversation to the people, because tyrants hate transparency.

> (When this message was delivered), (Pharaoh) said: "Who, then, O Moses, is the Lord of you two?" (Quran 20:49)
>
> He said: "Our Lord is He Who gave to each (created) thing its form and nature, and further, gave (it) guidance." (50)
>
> (Pharaoh) said: "What then is the condition of previous generations?" (51)

He replied: "The knowledge of that is with my Lord, duly recorded: my Lord never errs, nor forgets." (52)

[It is He] who has made for you the earth as a bed [spread out] and inserted therein for you roadways and sent down from the sky, rain and produced thereby categories of various plants. Eat [therefrom] and pasture your livestock. Indeed, in that are signs for those of intelligence. From the earth We created you, and into it We will return you, and from it We will extract you another time. And We certainly showed Pharaoh Our signs, all of them, but he denied and refused. (53-56)

He said: "Hast thou come to drive us out of our land with thy magic, O Moses? But we can surely produce magic to match thine! So make a tryst between us and thee, which we shall not fail to keep, neither we nor thou, in a place where both shall have even chances." (57-58)

Moses said: "Your tryst is the Day of the Festival, and let the people be assembled when the sun is well up." (59)

So Pharaoh withdrew: He concerted his plan, and then came (back). (60)

Moses said to him, "Woe to you! Forge not ye a lie against Allah, lest He destroy you (at once) utterly by chastisement: the forger must suffer frustration!" (61)

So they disputed, one with another, over their affair, but they kept their talk secret. (62)

They said: "These two are certainly (expert) magicians: their object is to drive you out from your land with their magic, and to do away with your most cherished institutions. Therefore concert your plan, and then assemble in (serried) ranks: He wins (all along) today who gains the upper hand." (63-64)

They said: "O Moses! whether wilt thou that thou throw (first) or that we be the first to throw?" (65)

He said, "Nay, throw ye first!" Then behold their ropes and their rods, so it seemed to him on account of their magic, began to be in lively motion! So Moses conceived in his mind a (sort of) fear. (66-67)

We said: "Fear not! for thou hast indeed the upper hand: Throw that which is in thy right hand: Quickly will it swallow up that which they have faked what they have faked

> is but a magician's trick: and the magician thrives not, (no matter) where he goes." (68-69)
> So the magicians were thrown down to prostration: they said, "We believe in the Lord of Aaron and Moses." (70)
> (Pharaoh) said: "Believe ye in Him before I give you permission? Surely this must be your leader, who has taught you magic! be sure I will cut off your hands and feet on opposite sides, and I will have you crucified on trunks of palm-trees: so shall ye know for certain, which of us can give the more severe and the more lasting punishment!" (71)

Here, we stop and ask ourselves to reflect on the following questions: Who used the language of projection and prejudice, and who called for listening? Who hyped the crowd, and who educated the crowd? Who operated in the shadows, and who called to the light?

Two Names of God: The Patient and the Just

> *God! There is no deity but He! To Him belong the most Beautiful Names. Has the story of Moses reached you?* (Quran 20:8-9)

Sometimes, it takes time before God's justice will manifest. Oppressors are sometimes given many chances. God opened a door of repentance, and, in the case of the magicians, they saw the truth and told Pharaoh:

> So the magicians were thrown down to prostration: they said, "We believe in the Lord of Aaron and Moses."

Pharaoh was more and more alone in his oppression, particularly after the chief magicians bore witness that Moses was not a sorcerer or a liar.

> (Pharaoh) said: "Believe ye in Him before I give you permission? Surely this must be your leader, who has taught you magic! be sure I will cut off your hands and feet on opposite sides, and I will have you crucified on trunks of palm-trees: so shall ye know for certain, which of us can give the more severe and the more lasting punishment!"(20:71)
> But the magicians were willing to sacrifice themselves for the truth.

> They said: "Never shall we regard thee as more than the Clear Signs that have come to us, or than Him Who created us! so decree whatever thou desirest to decree: for thou canst only decree (touching) the life of this world. For us, we have believed in our Lord: may He forgive us our faults, and the magic to which thou didst compel us: for Allah is Best and Most Abiding." (72-73)

Initially, the magicians had been fraudulent sycophants, seeking only to please and profit from Pharaoh. Yet, after they witnessed the truth, they repented their wrongdoing. This is an important lesson: Despite how corrupt some people are, the reformer doesn't come to destroy them. Instead, the reformer comes to nurture them and to open the door to repentance. If the door isn't open, many will lose hope and continue doing evil. You cannot fight tyranny if people aren't given a door out, and a path to transformation.

God is The Oft-Forgiving and Most Merciful, and He will forgive those who sincerely seek His forgiveness.

After witnessing the truth, the magicians transformed into witnesses to truth and died as witnesses. Just so, the people around Pharaoh now witnessed that he was a liar. But instead of humbling himself, Pharaoh grew even more enraged and insisted on proving Moses a "fake news" liar. He wanted to join forces with anyone among the Israelites who would side with him in exchange for fame and riches. There was one, Hamam, who he asked to build him a tower, and to whom he granted great privileges.

> Pharaoh said: "O Haman! Build me a lofty palace, that I may attain the ways and means. The ways and means of (reaching) the heavens, and that I may mount up to the god of Moses: But as far as I am concerned, I think (Moses) is a liar!" Thus was made alluring, in Pharaoh's eyes, the evil of his deeds, and he was hindered from the Path; and the plot of Pharaoh led to nothing but perdition (for him). (40:36-37)

After the magicians left him, Pharaoh felt livid, humiliated, and betrayed. His kingdom had been built by oppressing the people and holding their hearts and minds captive. But his grip on them was crumbling, and this caused rumors to spread. People began to say that he wasn't as powerful as he claimed. People started to question their fear of their ruler.

Yet Pharaoh refused to look at himself or his actions. Instead, he started to spread rumors. When he should have become humble, he grew in arrogance. The power infrastructure was beginning to fall apart, so he doubled down on his brainwashing of the people.

Fake news

When a tyrant is caught, often he starts to spread rumors. Much like when Donald Trump thought he was going to lose the 2016 election, he suggested it had been rigged, Pharaoh spread news that Moses and some magicians had secretly organized for Moses to win over the magicians. In reality, it was Pharaoh who had plotted in secret.

Yet he projected his own plotting onto Moses, accusing Moses of "rigging" the challenge to justify his loss.

So that people wouldn't lose their fear of him, Pharaoh had the magicians killed and hung in public places. However, even though the magicians stood by the truth, not everyone was willing or able. Some of the oppressed blamed Moses for the ill-treatment they'd received and feared what Pharaoh would do now that Moses had returned. They, too, saw the truth. But, unlike the magicians, they were still in the grip of fear.

Pharaoh increased his oppression, and many blamed Moses.

Oppressors moved through the city like a furious wind, committing evil after evil. Yet Moses could do nothing about it but wait on God. Some of the Israelites began to turn against Moses, and some of them refused to stand with him.

Hamam was one of Moses's relatives who stood with Pharaoh against him, and so was Qarun. Both called Moses a sorcerer and a liar, and both joined openly in attacking him.

In exchange for standing with Pharaoh, Qarun was granted both wealth and status, while all around him people were destitute. Moses called Qarun to pay a "poor tax," but Qarun refused, and he joined with Pharaoh in spreading rumors about Moses.

Moses was given laws to nurture the community, and one of those laws was similar to zakat—a tax on the wealthy to aid the poor. Qarun wouldn't pay, and he even accused his cousin Moses of using the tax to enrich himself. After he spread these rumors, God punished Qarun by opening the earth and letting it swallow him as though he'd never existed.

Qarun was doubtless, of the people of Moses; but he acted insolently towards them: such were the treasures We had bestowed on him that their very keys would have been a burden to a body of strong men, behold, his people said to him: "Exult not, for Allah loveth not those who exult (in riches). But seek, with the (wealth) which Allah has bestowed on thee, the Home of the Hereafter, nor forget thy portion in this world: but do thou good, as Allah has been good to thee, and seek not (occasions for) mischief in the land: for Allah loves not those who do mischief." (Quran 28:76-77)

The story mentions Qarun and Hamam because it's important to realize there are opportunists among the oppressed. It was never that all Egyptians were evil and all Israelites innocent. There were opportunists among the oppressed who would sell their people, and there were good people among the Egyptians. In every underdog community, there are people who will sell out their own community for gain.

If we understand these stories, we can come to expect people to sell out their communities. Thus, just because someone comes from a community doesn't mean they can fully represent it. We should expect opportunists and fully investigate their arguments. If their arguments are smoke, mirrors, and fearmongering, then they should recall to us Qarun and Hamam.

Haman and Qarun stood with Pharaoh against their own people, for selfish gain. After Qarun was punished by an earthquake swallowing him up, then slowly people began to listen to Moses, and this infuriated Pharaoh, who summoned Moses to the palace.

Yet, just as Moses had close relatives who worked with Pharaoh, Pharaoh had close relatives siding with Moses. Moses never asked for Qarun to be killed. But Pharaoh had the relatives who stood against him killed, or he plotted to kill them.

There was one government official whose name is possibly Hazqil or Habib, who kept his faith secret and argued on behalf of Moses. He was not just an advisor to Pharaoh, but also a relative, his cousin.

A believer, a man from among the people of Pharaoh, who had concealed his faith, said: "Will ye slay a man because he says, 'My Lord is Allah'? when he has indeed come to you with Clear (Signs) from your Lord? and if he be a liar, on him is (the sin of) his lie: but, if he is telling the Truth, then will fall on you something of the (calamity) of which he warns you: Truly Allah guides not one who transgresses and lies!" (Quran 40:28)

The secret advisor eloquently defended Moses, a powerful man speaking to power.

Then Allah saved him from (every) ill that they plotted (against him), but the burnt of the Penalty encompassed on all sides the People of Pharaoh. (40:45)

At this point, God commanded Moses to give stern warnings to Pharaoh and those in power. They must let the children of Israel go, or they would suffer a severe punishment.

Moses, where is your power?

Pharaoh began to fear losing his power, and he called all the people in his lands to a huge gathering. He claimed to be their Lord, pointing out that Moses was no more than a lowly slave with no power. He even mocked his speech impediment.

Despite all the signs, many people still obeyed Pharaoh. Falsehood doesn't always listen to evidence or reason, but rather to power.

It was then that God's wrath descended.

God brought a drought. Pharaoh appealed to Moses, the drought eased, and Moses gave Pharaoh a deadline to let the Israelites go. But Pharaoh went back on their agreement. So they began again.

This, too, is part of the story of power and oppression. There are often repeated violations of treaties, as well as false negotiating followed by false peace-making.

People don't always wake up after seeing a truth, particularly when fear has built a nest in their hearts. Many continued to believe in Pharaoh's power, not realizing it was they who gave him that power, and that only God's power is true.

Next, God sent a massive flood, and the false peace-making began again.

False peace

Every time the penalty fell on them, they said: "O Moses! on your behalf call on thy Lord in virtue of his promise to thee: If thou wilt remove the penalty from us, we shall truly believe in thee, and we shall send away the Children of Israel with thee." (Quran 7:134)

After this false truce was declared, Moses appealed to God, and the land returned to normal. But again, Pharaoh refused to fulfill his promise and he continued to oppress the children of Israel.

The cycle continued, and, next, God sent a plague of locusts. People begged Moses for help, and the door to repentance swung open. Yet as soon as the locusts departed, they went back on the terms of the treaty.

The punishments—and the chances—continued. Next was a plague of lice, then a plague of frogs. Next, God caused the Nile to turn to blood. Only for the children of Israel did the water remain pure. Yet again, the same cycle of false peace-making went on.

> But every time We removed the penalty from them according to a fixed term which they had to fulfil. Behold! they broke their word! So We exacted retribution from them: We drowned them in the sea, because they rejected Our Signs and failed to take warning from them. And We made a people, considered weak (and of no account), inheritors of lands in both east and west, lands whereon We sent down Our blessings. The fair promise of thy Lord was fulfilled for the Children of Israel, because they had patience and constancy, and We levelled to the ground the great works and fine buildings which Pharaoh and his people erected (with such pride). (Quran 7:135-136)

Next, God ordered Moses to move his people out of Egypt.

Tyranny benefits from the labor of the oppressed. The United States could not have been built without the labor of enslaved people. Likewise, Egypt's beautiful buildings and great works were the handiwork of the oppressed Israelites. The loss of this labor would destroy the empire. Word reached Pharaoh that Moses was working to lead the Israelites out of Egypt, so Pharaoh gathered his military forces and pursued them.

The soldiers had all types of weaponry and fast horses, and thus they were able to catch up with the Israelites just as they reached the Red Sea. The Israelites had the dust from the soldiers' horses behind them, and in front of them the Red Sea.

They felt trapped, powerless, and helpless. What could they do now? The image of a massacre must have appeared in the minds of many.

Some began to blame Moses. Panic spread as they watched the approaching army grow closer and closer. Instead of comforting and supporting each other and their leader, many complained and blamed Moses. Some still had a love-hate relationship with Pharaoh, and wanted to be Qarun and Haman.

And so they were: the enemy behind, the Red Sea in front.

Moses marched to the front and stood before the Red Sea. Some narrators said that Joshua questioned Moses and said, "The sea is before us, and the enemy is behind us; surely death cannot be avoided!" But Moses trusted God. He stood with his brother Harun, or Aaron, and waited for God to guide him.

Just then, God inspired Moses to strike the sea with his stick. And, before their eyes, the Red Sea parted, creating a safe passage to pass.

Moses waited at the back for the last person to pass before he followed his people. They all reached the other side, but were still filled with panic, as the army was close behind and had entered the seabed.

This, finally, was the appointed time of justice.

> We took the Children of Israel across the sea: Pharaoh and his hosts followed them in insolence and spite. At length, when overwhelmed with the flood, he said: "I believe that there is no god except Him Whom the Children of Israel believe in: I am of those who submit (to Allah in Islam)." (It was said to him): "Ah now! But a little while before, wast thou in rebellion! and thou didst mischief (and violence)! This day shall We save thee in the body, that thou mayest be a sign to those who come after thee! but verily, many among mankind are heedless of Our Signs!" (Quran 10:90-92)

After patience, then justice

God sent many people to nurture the hearts of the oppressors. Warnings came to shake him up, but that didn't make Pharaoh take heed.

Even at the very end, Pharaoh didn't have to enter the seabed. But he deluded himself, believing he was all-powerful. Intoxicated by his own self-deception, he thought he, too, could part the sea.

But the sea folded back, and Pharaoh and his soldiers drowned.

Sometimes, it seems as though a cruel tyrant will live forever. No matter what evils they do, and how many stand bravely against them, it seems they will never fall. But in the end, God's justice comes.

When Pharaoh saw his death before his eyes, he cried out to "the God of Moses," still too arrogant to call God his own Lord. Even in this moment, Pharaoh wasn't truly remorseful.

Several of the names of God are echoed by this story. The first is al-Adl, or The Just. The other is as-Sabur or The Patient One. Both were seen in their own time.

New World, Old Habits

> *God! There is no deity but He! To Him belong the most Beautiful Names. Has the story of Moses reached thee?* (Quran 20:8-9)

Trauma and oppression impact our souls. If there is no faith alive in our souls, then we absorb the darkness of the oppressor and, sooner or later, we become one. To avoid this, we must repel oppression with faith. Only faith and turning to God can repel the spirit of an oppressive regime.

Even though Moses saved his people, and took them across the Red Sea, many didn't cultivate faith in their hearts. Thus even when they were physically free, many couldn't free themselves from turning their hearts toward their old lives under Pharaoh.

> We took the Children of Israel (with safety) across the sea. They came upon a people devoted entirely to some idols they had. They said: "O Moses! fashion for us a god like unto the gods they have." He said: "Surely ye are a people without knowledge." (Quran 7: 138)

Moments after they had crossed the sea, they were already turning back toward their life under Pharaoh. Instead of showing the joy and happiness—the exclamations of gratitude—that would demonstrate their faith, they wanted their old lives back. They were like people who had left one narcissist abuser only to run into the arms of another. They lacked faith, and thus did not value themselves.

We want this, and we want that

Many of Moses's people, for lack of faith, were in a continual state of craving. They wanted protection from the sun, so Moses appealed to God, who sent clouds to protect them from the scorching sun. They wanted various types of food, so God sent them what was healthiest and best for them. But they wanted even more.

> He said: "Will ye exchange the better for the worse? Go ye down to any town, and ye shall find what ye want!" (Quran 2:61).

They were more worried about the pleasures of food than with gratitude or eating what was good for them. Their souls should have connected with the invisible world, but they were still connected with the material world. Instead of being grateful to God, the attitude of many was, "Serve me, do this for me."

In this, they were still connected to the world of oppression. They weren't willing to disconnect from it, or to disengage. They experienced a great trauma, and now they had to disengage, disconnect, and get to know themselves away from this old world. They even had to detach from the emotional engagement with these former foods.

This part of the story shows us one of the ways that faith deteriorates.

Instead of embracing faith, and what was best, they wanted what they had known. Instead of being concerned with their great purpose, they were obsessed with the material world.

They didn't show gratitude. And, in the end, faith is about gratitude, which means recognizing that all blessings come from God. Not only does gratitude humble us—because whatever blessings we have come from God—but we also don't also look down at those who are deprived, because we are all equal. Instead, what we see is an opportunity to reach out and help them.

Without gratitude, we don't raise up others, but instead blame them for having less. Without gratitude, we enter the cycle of oppression all over again.

Several generations of humiliation and oppression had left many of Moses's people with deep-seated trauma. They came across a people worshipping idols, and their materialism-filled hearts longed for idols as well. They completely forgot that they experienced and witnessed, and they abused and insulted Moses and forgot their worship of God.

Next, they were asked to stand up to their old oppressors. This, too, they refused to do.

> Remember Moses said to his people: "O my people! Call in remembrance the favor of Allah unto you, when He produced prophets among you, made you kings, and gave you what He had not given to any other among the peoples. O my people! Enter the holy land which Allah hath assigned unto you, and turn not back ignominiously, for then will ye be overthrown, to your own ruin." They said: "O Moses! In this land are a people of exceeding strength: Never shall we enter it until they leave it: if (once) they leave, then shall we enter." (Quran 5:20-22)

Next, they came to a land of people who had oppressed them, and they were asked to walk in Moses's footsteps, and to speak truth to these oppressors. It is important not to allow trauma to live on inside us: We need to take a stand and find the strength to face our oppressors.

Here, "overthrow" doesn't mean violence. It means there is a responsibility to face the perpetrator of oppression, and to push them back within their boundaries. Yet despite all that they had seen, Moses' people refused to even walk into this city and face their old oppressors. This large group could have entered as Muhammad, upon him peace and blessings, entered Mecca. They could have said: We're coming in, and we're going to grant you amnesty.

But they didn't. Even after all they'd seen, the majority wanted Moses to face oppressors for them.

Why? They were still afraid, and they didn't want to make any sacrifices. They weren't connected to the spiritual world, and they hadn't cultivated faith in their hearts. Their faith was not a spiritual faith, but one of affiliation.

What the story tells us is that this isn't really faith.

The only way we can repel tyrants is through real faith, and for this, we need to be connected to the spiritual world. We need to allow the light of God to come through us in order to bring down tyranny and open doors for the oppressed. If that spiritual reality doesn't exist within us, then our words won't have an impact.

Moses' people are, instead of cultivating a better world, putting themselves in a vulnerable position. They will be sitting ducks for another oppressor.

Moses out of sight

Moses had to leave his people and return to Mt. Sinai, where he fasted for forty nights.

God gave Moses two stone tablets, which were revelations sent down to aid him and his people on their journey: the famous Ten Commandments. These commandments were the foundation upon which the Judaic Law was built, and they are also recognized by Christians and Muslims.

But as Moses fasted, his people were complaining the whole time.

It is here that another character appears: as-Samiri, whose heart was inclined toward evil.

With Moses out of sight, he took the opportunity to collect peoples' jewelry and build from it a Golden Calf for them to worship, like the idols that had been worshiped back in Pharaoh's land. As-Samiri acted like the magicians back in Pharaoh's land, before those magicians had turned to God.

During the casting of the calf, he threw in a handful of dust to impress the foolish. As-Samiri had been raised by the Angel Gabriel, and he took a handful of dust trod on by Gabriel to lead others astray. As-Samiri was thus an educated corrupter. He took something that had been truth, and he used it to distort and lead people astray.

Prophet Aaron, Moses' brother, spoke against this, but he was of a gentle and mild nature, and he was overcome by the threats of the bullies. When Moses returned, he was hurt to see his people returning to how they'd been under Pharaoh.

> So Moses returned to his people in a state of indignation and sorrow. He said: "O my people! Did not your Lord make a handsome promise to you? Did then the promise seem to you long (in coming)? Or did ye desire that Wrath should descend from your Lord on you, and so ye broke your promise to me?" (Quran 20:86)

Moses came back to a group of loud bullies who had nearly killed Aaron, and who had also threatened the pious minority.

The hearts of many were still with Pharaoh and with everything he was doing. Here, not only did they disregard God's message, but they weren't connected to each other. There wasn't love and solidarity among them.

In the end, this wasn't an issue of gullibility, but of arrogance.

The Golden Calf represents materialism, but also heedlessness and a lack of responsibility. What you worship is a reflection of what you're seeking. They weren't seeking to grow, to heal, or to gain knowledge. And when they were confronted with their wrongdoing, they didn't learn or ask to be guided. They made excuses and tried to cover up what they knew was wrong.

Confronting as-Samiri

Moses punished as-Samiri—who used the truth to mislead his people—by exiling him.

> (Moses) said: "Get thee gone! But thy (punishment) in this life will be that thou wilt say, 'touch me not'; and moreover (for a future penalty) thou hast a promise that will not fail: Now look at thy god, of whom thou hast become a devoted worshipper: We will certainly (melt) it in a blazing fire and scatter it broadcast in the sea! But the god of you all is the One God: there is no god but He: all things He comprehends in His knowledge." (Quran 20:97-98)

As-Samiri had betrayed his people. A Pharaoh is not someone who does not know the truth. Instead, it's someone who knows the truth, but has a desire for greatness will twist and distort it for material wealth and to gain power over others.

Fighting the Pharaoh Inside Us

And [mention, O Muhammad], when Moses said to his people, "O my people, why do you harm me while you certainly know that I am the messenger of Allah to you?" And when they deviated, Allah caused their hearts to deviate. And Allah does not guide the defiantly disobedient people. (Quran 61:5)

Very few among us have the power of a Pharaoh. But, as we read the Quran, it's important for us to reflect on what we do with the power we have. Sometimes, our leaders are a reflection of us. Part of the story of what happens to Moses' followers helps us reflect on how it's possible to enable bad governance, oppressive systems, and how we can make someone like Pharaoh more powerful than they really are—because we don't tell them to stop.

Moses and Aaron were virtually alone when they stood up to a brutal, cruel, and powerful leader. Moses was willing to accept exile, and he never placed obligations or demands on God.

Moses' followers had seen what Pharaoh had done with them. They had seen how Moses and Aaron stood up for them, and they knew they were children of prophets. They had all that knowledge, and yet they were more impressed with the material world.

So it was that Moses received the command to take care of Pharaohs who were among his people. And so Moses, after his people wronged themselves by rebuilding systems that they'd had under Pharaoh, called on them to surrender to God with humility.

Moses chose 70 elders from among them to seek repentance and appeal for mercy, and he took them to Mount Tur. There, these 70 elders shocked Moses by demanding to see God with their own eyes before they would seek forgiveness.

Before this, Moses had asked to see God out of love. When God had said this wasn't possible, Moses accepted it. But when these elders asked, they were trying to force God, to obligate their Creator. They were saying, unless we see you, we're not going to believe.

This had been a test for the 70 elders, who had a responsibility to stand up to the bullies in their community. Instead, they'd acted treasonously. They were like those who fill the vacuum of power when a tyrant falls, coming in and creating chaos. So God caused them to die.

Just as God had dealt with Pharaoh, so He dealt with these men.

Moses was astounded, and he turned to God, appealing for mercy. Although they had done wrong, he didn't divorce himself from his people, nor say he was above punishment. Instead, he asked for mercy and forgiveness, and for protection from punishment for his people:

> "Thou art our Protector: so forgive us and give us Thy mercy; for Thou art the best of those who forgive. And ordain for us that which is good, in this life and in the Hereafter: for we have turned unto Thee." He said: "With My punishment I visit whom I will; but My mercy extendeth to all things. That (mercy) I shall ordain for those who do right, and practice regular charity, and those who believe in Our signs." (Quran 7:155-156)

And God returned the 70 men to life, and Moses continued to travel with his people.

There are many lessons for us here. The 70 elders had a responsibility to speak up. They had never spoken out under Pharaoh, and they didn't speak up against the bullies within their own community. Thus, the bullies easily gained power.

Sometimes, you can bring down a tyrant—such as Saddam Hussein—and another darkness can spring up. When we take down tyrants, we must do so while reflecting how to make our community better, and not while falling into old patterns. We must unite people against abuse and oppression, and speak out against bullying everywhere, inside and outside the community.

It's important for us to see who the bullies are, and who the Aarons and Moseses are among us.

If you bring down the tyrant, and your community is not united, then the worst of the community might gain power. So, when one is fighting oppression, the first lessons are in what not to do. Don't reflect the behavior of the oppressor—the oppressor is teaching you what not to do, and those are important lessons.

Moses' people didn't take in those lessons. As soon as he was gone, they were trying to restore things to how they'd been under Pharaoh. They still had Pharaoh inside them. Instead of allowing truth to emerge, they preferred to keep creating false perceptions.

Deep down, they were afraid for the truth to come out because they were attached to their old lives. When you start to run away from the emergence of truth, instead of running toward it, this means that, deep down, your heart is tarnished by a love of material things. Someone could be very rich but keep the money in their hands, not in their heart, using it to help and nurture people. Others could be poor, but materialist and entitled.

The Promised Land

After what happened on Mount Tur, Moses stayed with his people.

After years of wandering, Prophet Aaron died, and Moses lost his greatest spiritual supporter. Like Aaron, Moses died without reaching the Promised Land. He was surrounded by his people, who were still not open to receiving God's mercy, and thus couldn't enter the Promised Land.

Moses and his people never made it to the Promised Land. The older generation had to die out, and a new generation had to be nurtured before they were able to leave the state of wandering. Their hearts had been too polluted by the love-hate relationship with Pharaoh.

Passing the torch to Joshua

Often, when we think of success, we think of people who have taken on high stations, such as the presidency, or else those who have lived to see the results of their work. This overlooks the hard labor, challenges, and attacks faced by those who made sacrifices to pave the way for others, working with neither appreciation nor results in sight; working out of pure faith.

When we think about success, we can all benefit from and feel inspired by the story of Moses, upon him peace, as well as the stories of all the prophets.

Moses and his brother Aaron, upon them peace, never made it to the promised land. It was Prophet Joshua, upon him peace, who made it there. However, Moses, upon him peace, was one of the five resolute prophets and one of those most-often mentioned in the Quran.

Joshua, or Yusha ibn Nun, is not mentioned by name in the Quran. However, in many narrations by Prophet Muhammad, upon him peace and blessings, Joshua is the "companion" of Moses mentioned in the Quran, in chapter 18:60-65.

Moses, upon him peace, opened the door for the next generation, and he nurtured Joshua as a righteous student to take the torch forward. Moses focused on his principles and values, and the outcome might not have been results in his lifetime, but it was righteous students who brought the next generation to the promised land, while the older generation, who were stuck in their ways, died out in the desert.

Sometimes, we plant seeds so that our grandchildren or future generations can benefit from them, as these seeds require fertile soil, new generations—as well as years to sprout.

To Always Be in a Humble State

And they found a servant from among Our servants to whom we had given mercy from us and had taught him from Us a [certain] knowledge. Moses said to him, "May I follow you on [the condition] that you teach me from what you have been taught of sound judgment?" He said, "Indeed, with me you will never be able to have patience." (Quran 18:65-67)

During the years that Moses was wandering in the desert, he asked, or was asked, if there was anyone on earth more learned than him. In either case, Moses didn't answer arrogantly. Instead, he answered this question as truthfully as he could: I am the most learned, he said, thanks to the knowledge and wisdom given me by God.

God responded, telling Moses he was wrong. There was someone more learned than him. Part of the Quran's teachings is to always be in a humble state and to strive to increase one's knowledge. And so Moses—being a humble man, and having a healthy curiosity—wanted to meet this person who knew more than he.

Moses was always interested in being corrected, and in hearing from those who knew more than him. After all, he knew that the person who cannot be corrected cannot learn.

Certainly the message of Moses' story is not that we shouldn't question God. There are those who argue and ask questions, like al-Mujadila. But when she argued with Muhammad, she did so with a clean heart, and he called her to patience until God sent him a revelation.

We should never think: If we question, God is going to strike us with a lightning bolt. We are encouraged to seek understanding or question in humility, but to do so in an open, true way, where we are looking for truth.

Where the two seas meet

Because Moses wanted to meet this person more knowledgeable than him, God directed Moses to take a live fish in a container. When that fish disappeared, God said, that was where Moses would find the man more knowledgeable than him.

It's important for us to know that it was God who directed Moses to this man, named al-Khidr. This person didn't approach Moses and claim superior, secret knowledge. It was God who put Moses on al-Khidr's path.

Moses set out with Joshua on a journey to find this man.

After a long trek, they reached the place "where the two seas meet," which alludes to two kinds of knowledge: knowledge of the seen, and knowledge of the unseen. The knowledge that we humans can access—even including prophets like Moses—is the seen. This is the knowledge of evidence, rules, and laws. But there is another type of knowledge, beyond our capacity to grasp.

Where the seas met, Moses and Joseph slept, and that night the fish swam into the sea. Joshua noticed it, but he forgot to tell Moses. Later in the journey, Joshua suddenly remembered, and he turned and told Moses. Although they now had to retrace their steps, which made the journey even longer, Moses was determined to find al-Khidr. So they turned and walked back to the place where they'd slept, where the fish had escaped into the sea.

This story, which is mentioned in the eighteenth chapter of the Quran, is not meant to make us seek out charlatans or frauds who claim to have secret knowledge. Al-Khidr, after all, is nothing like as-Samari, who had a small amount of knowledge from the Angel Gabriel and used this knowledge of the unseen to play with the minds of others. Al-Khidr is not like the psychologists, teachers, or mentors who abuse their knowledge.

Al-Khidr didn't try to create a god-like authority or abuse the knowledge he had.

Indeed, when Moses wanted to follow al-Khidr, he discouraged it. He had a greater knowledge than Moses, but, out of mercy, he didn't want to share something that Moses couldn't comprehend or verify with his senses. He didn't act as a charlatan would've.

We're not exactly sure when Moses met al-Khidr, but we believe it was before Moses came in contact with as-Samari. In that way, Moses could better understand unseen knowledge and understand how it could be used unethically, to deceive.

Yet there is another important lesson here: Our ignorance is much greater than what we know. We should beware those who come, seeking us out, telling us they have great knowledge of the unseen. Yet we should also realize there is a lot out there we don't know.

Al-Khidr discouraged Moses, telling him he wouldn't be patient enough for this sort of knowledge. Moses humbly asked that al-Khidr give him a chance to learn. Al-Khidr agreed, but then he asked Moses to not ask questions.

In the first instance, Al-Khidr made a man's ship unusable, and Moses couldn't stop himself from asking why he'd done such a thing. In the second, al-Khidr killed a small boy. Again, Moses couldn't be patient, and he had to know how such a thing could be permitted. In the third instance, townspeople refused hospitality to al-Khidr and Moses, and al-Khidr went to find a wall that was falling down, and he set it right. Now, again, Moses was confused: Why hadn't al-Khidr asked to be paid for his labor?

At this point, they had to separate, although they did so with goodwill, and after al-Khidr explained his actions, which were God's will and command. Al-Khidr explained:

> As for the boat, it belonged to certain men in dire want: they plied on the water: I but wished to render it unserviceable, for there was after them a certain king who seized on every boat by force. As for the youth, his parents were people of Faith, and we feared that he would grieve them by obstinate rebellion and ingratitude (to Allah and man). So we desired that their Lord would give them in exchange (a son) better in purity (of conduct) and closer in affection. As for the wall, it belonged to two youths, orphans, in the Town; there was, beneath it, a buried treasure, to which they were entitled: their father had been a righteous man: So thy Lord desired that they should attain their age of full strength and get out their treasure, a mercy (and favor) from thy Lord. I did it not of my own accord. Such is the interpretation of (those things) over which thou wast unable to hold patience. (Quran 18:79-82)

At this point, Moses understood and accepted that there were things in this world he could not grasp with his human mind. And so it is for us: There are things beyond our capacity for understanding.

And yet there are no laws that allow us to act, judge, prosecute, or penalize based on these unseen realities. The aim of the story, instead, is to help us understand that when bad or disturbing events happen, there is often a higher wisdom behind it.

Some scholars have suggested that al-Khidr was an angel, since he operates outside the laws of human beings. Scholars are not in agreement about what he is, and yet indeed, he works in a world beyond the laws of humans. And, out of mercy for us, he does not try to share that knowledge.

What's important for us to remember is that these—Moses, Aaron, Pharaoh, as-Samiri—are archetypes that exist within the sphere of power and oppression.

Two of the names of God

There are two of God's 99 names that are important in this story: ar-Rahim and al-Alim.

Rahim is the idea of constant repetition and the giving of a generous reward to those who deserve and seek it. Ar-Rahim indicates that which is extremely and continuously loving and merciful, the dispenser of grace and love as a result of our deeds and supplications, and a special type of mercy for those who are very intentional.

Al-Alim is the One who comprehends everything, who is intuitively aware of all things, even before they happen, as we humans are not. Al-Alim is The One Who Knows with certainty, whose knowledge of past, present, and future is deeply rooted and complete in all respects.

JESUS AND MARY: LESSONS ON HUMILITY

[And mention] when the angels said, "O Mary, indeed Allah gives you good tidings of a word from Him, whose name will be the Messiah, Jesus, the son of Mary, distinguished in this world and the Hereafter and among those brought near [to Allah]." (Quran 3:45)

A faith community can be talking about God and the law in a very correct manner, and yet tarnish prophets like Mary and Jesus because humility is absent in their faith. What does humility mean for us? How can we live it?

Jesus in the Bible, Jesus in the Quran

Jesus appears differently in Christianity and in Islam. Yet between the two, Jesus is a point of connectivity: His teachings and his life story are important in both the Bible and the Quran.

For me, as a Muslim, the teachings of Jesus remind me of the central importance of vulnerability. Jesus was born into a marginalized community during the rule of the powerful, patriarchal Roman Empire. He had no father to protect him. And it wasn't just the agents of the Roman Empire who opposed Jesus's works. His own community was often against him. So Jesus faced many forces that wanted to silence him.

Against all these forces, we're told, young Jesus had only his mother Mary to defend him.

Prophet Muhammad, peace and blessings upon him, underlined the link between himself and Jesus: "Both in this world and in the Hereafter, I am the nearest of all the people to Jesus, the son of Mary, peace and blessings upon him. The prophets are paternal brothers; their mothers are different, but their religion is one."

According to the Quran, all prophets faced rejection and opposition. But Jesus, who is known as one of the resolute prophets, had a particularly hard time. He was stuck between the corrupt leaders of his own community and the corrupt rulers of the Roman Empire. Within his own community, he suffered from the harsh, legalistic, and material way faith was misapplied.

A vulnerable voice for the oppressed

Jesus, like the other prophets, spoke out against oppression.

When Jesus was born, local leaders by and large didn't support members of their own oppressed community. Instead, the leaders of his faith were obsessed with power, material goods, and making deals with the Roman Empire. This sort of deal-making repeats throughout history. It's not unlike the leaders of many of today's marginalized nations, who make deals with world powers at the expense of their own people.

When Jesus arrived, he came as a representation of steadfast vulnerable humility, and also of peace. Young Jesus lived a very modest life. Still, whenever he tried to preach, there was always someone plotting to distort what he said, or else calling him out as an enemy of the Roman Empire.

Some who speak out about oppression are just manipulating the vulnerable. They validate the fears of the oppressed, and then turn things to their own end. But Jesus himself was one of the vulnerable. Far from benefiting, he helped guide the oppressed to God. He stood up to the misapplication of faith that benefited only the rich, spoke out against materialism, and was a model of humility. He reached out to the condemned in society and connected with them.

Jesus in the Quran

Like Christians, Muslims believe in the virgin birth of Jesus, upon him be peace, and in his miracles. Jesus' life and mission are mentioned in eleven chapters of the Quran. A few of the chapters are: Maryam (Mary the Mother of Jesus); Imran (Noble Family of Jesus), and Ma'ida (the Last Supper). Jesus, upon him peace, is glorified in the Quran and is referred to as "the Messiah," "a Word of God," and "a Sign of God."

Muslims regard Jesus as one of the mightiest messengers of God. He and his supporter, John the Baptist, and John's father, Zakariya, are two other prophets of God. They are of an unbroken noble lineage that goes back to the father of monotheism, Abraham. Peace and blessings upon them all.

We're told that Jesus's maternal grandmother Hanna was barren. She prayed for a child to devote to God's service, and God answered that prayer by giving her Mary. The Quran calls Mary "the most honored woman among all nations."

When Mary, upon her be peace, was just a teenager, Archangel Gabriel came to her and said: "O Mary! God giveth thee glad tidings of a Word from Him. His name will be Christ Jesus, the son of Mary, held in honor in this world and the Hereafter, and of (the company of) those nearest to God."

Being a virgin, Mary could not understand this news.

Gabriel comforted her by explaining that, when God wished to create anything, He said, "Be," and it was. Muslims find similarities between Jesus' birth and that of Adam, peace and blessings upon them. Both were created without father or mother. Both births were a miracle.

Like every woman, Mary, upon her be peace, suffered during childbirth. But Mary's suffering was compounded by fears about how she would explain her pregnancy to her noble family. Muslims believe that Jesus performed his first miracle in the cradle by speaking up to defend his beloved mother.

Muslims do not believe in original sin or that Jesus died to atone for our sins. Rather, Muslims believe Jesus's mission was to repair the misapplication of faith and abuse of the Divine Law. Religion had become harsh and legalistic, and Jesus came to leaven those teachings with humility and spirituality.

A religion for the poor

When Jesus was born, many laws were applied exclusively to punish the poor. It was, in some ways, not unlike today: If you were poor and broke the law, the powerful came down on you in the harshest manner possible. If you were wealthy, then you could escape punishment.

Yet the Laws of God were never meant to help the powerful dominate the weak. Instead, they were meant to protect the weak from the exploitation of the strong: During Jesus's time, the laws of God had become divorced from the spirit of God's love. The Laws became an end in themselves, when they were supposed to be a means to nurture hearts and aid humanity in their worship of God.

Jesus's message was a powerful agent of change. Still, he realized that not all people could be reached with words. In the Quran, Jesus says: "God has given me the power to give life to the dead, sight to the blind, sound to the deaf; but He did not give me the power to heal the fool of his foolishness."

Muslims believe that, after plots were made to kill Jesus, he was not crucified. Instead, he was raised to the Heavens. Muslims await the second coming of Jesus, when he will come back again as a just ruler, like Moses and Muhammad, peace and blessings upon them.

Although there are differences between the Muslim and Christian views of Jesus, the Quran repeatedly guides Muslims not to dispute with other monotheists, except in the best manner, over matters of doctrine. Instead, Jesus should be a point of connectivity between the billions in the world who follow Christianity and Islam.

Seeking God al-Wahhab, and Seeking God ar-Razzaq

Indeed, it is Allah who is the [continual] Provider, the firm possessor of strength. (Quran 51:58)

Or have they the treasures of the mercy of thy Lord, the Exalted in Power, the Grantor of Bounties without measure? (Quran 38:9)

"Al-Wahhab" and "ar-Razzaq" are two of the Most Beautiful Names of God. These names, and the people who embody them, can teach us about how to ask God for what we need.

The stories around Moses, peace and blessings upon him, tell us a lot about oppression. Many of the people who surrounded Moses—particularly Pharaoh—are the very archetypes of oppression. The stories around Jesus (Eesa) and Mary (Maryam) are different. Here, we learn from the faithful, and we find many archetypes of faith.

Reaching out to God al-Wahhab

The story of Jesus begins with his grandmother, who is known as Hannah in the Quran and as St. Anne in the Christian tradition. Hannah and her husband had long prayed to God to have a child. But she grew old and lost hope of a baby.

Yet when the doors to our hopes seem sealed shut, God al-Fattah, or The Opener, can unlock them. Hannah was old when God sent a bird to her, and the sight of this bird feeding its young renewed her desire for a child. Hannah prayed to God that, if He granted her a child, she would dedicate this child to God's service.

With this prayer, Hannah was reaching out to God al-Wahhab: "the donor of all, without conditions, without limits[.]" Sometimes, in life, there are unsurpassable barriers in front of us. For Hannah, it was her age. She was no longer young enough—or so the laws of nature said—to have a child.

For us, other doors may be sealed shut in front of us. We might be an ex-felon, and it might be nigh-on impossible to get a decent job. Or we might be a refugee who's fled to a new country where our credentials and work history aren't recognized. In this situation, we can't rely on our own hard work and efforts. We've run into closed doors and closed windows, extreme prejudice and persecution, or perhaps other insurmountable hurdles.

At this point, we can reach out to God al-Wahhab, the Giver of Gifts without Limits. When we do this, we continue to live up to our commitments and our values. When we pray to God al-Wahhab, He will test us, as He tested Moses. When Moses was a refugee, and had nothing, he was faced with two vulnerable women. Moses could have taken advantage of these women. But instead he lived up to his values and helped them.

Hannah, too, was tested when she prayed to God al-Wahhab for a child, and God answered her prayers. Yet although she had prayed for a child who could serve God in the temple, Hannah gave birth to a girl: Maryam. When Hannah was pregnant, we believe, her husband passed away. Yet despite her circumstances, and despite the child being a girl, Hannah kept her promise and dedicated her daughter to God, with the help of the Prophet Zakariya, upon him peace.

Hannah's sister had married the Prophet Zakariya. So, when Maryam was young, Hannah turned to her brother-in-law to help her nurture Maryam to be a woman of faith. Today, some scholars consider Maryam a prophet, and she is certainly the most honored among women.

From a very early age, Maryam's life was dedicated to God:

> Right graciously did her Lord accept her: He made her grow in purity and beauty: To the care of Zakariya was she assigned. Every time that he entered (Her) chamber to see her, He found her supplied with sustenance. He said: "O Mary! Whence (comes) this to you?" She said: "From God:

for God provides sustenance to whom He pleases without measure." (Quran 3:37)

Just as the birds nudged Hannah, renewing her hopes such that she turned to God al-Wahhab, so Maryam's goodness nudged Zakariya into praying to God for a child.

> There did Zakariya pray to his Lord, saying: "O my Lord! Grant unto me from Thee a progeny that is pure: for Thou art He that heareth prayer!" (Quran 3:38)

Like Hannah, Zakariya and his wife were old. Scholars say that Zakariya was already in his 90s. But when doors are closed, we can turn to God al-Fattah, the Opener, and God al-Wahhab, the Giver of Gifts without Limits.

At this point, God tested Zakariya. Maryam was near him, under his protection, and she was a young and appealing woman. He could have married her and fulfilled his desire for a child. But instead he stayed with his wife, who was barren, and he lived up to his promise to nurture Maryam spiritually. At the same time, he continued to pray to God al-Wahhab.

Zakariya was told that his prayers would be answered, and he asked: How will I know? God told Zakariya that he would know his wife had conceived by the fact that Zakariya would no longer be able to do what comes normally to him. When Zakariya suddenly found himself unable to speak, he knew his wife had conceived.

But as with Hannah, the gift did not come entirely as expected. Hannah had a girl to dedicate to the service of God, instead of a boy. Zakariya was told to name his son John, or Yahya, a name that means "life." This way, Zakariya understood that his son would be martyred young, and that he would remain alive with God.

> And do not say about those who are killed in the way of God, "They are dead." Rather, they are alive, but you perceive [it] not. (Quran 2:154)

Sometimes, when God al-Wahhab answers our prayers, it is not exactly in the way we expected. God granted Zakariya a loving, obedient son who was a Prophet (John the Baptist), upon him peace, but who was also a son he would lose early.

[God] said, "O John, take the Scripture with determination." And We gave him wisdom [while yet] a boy; And affection from Us and purity, and he was fearing of God; And dutiful to his parents, and he was not a disobedient tyrant. And peace be upon him the day he was born and the day he dies and the day he is raised alive. (Quran 19:12-15)

These stories should both comfort us and humble our expectations.

Gifts and givers

Hannah received a great gift from God al-Wahhab. She, in turn, dedicated that child to God. Zakariya watched Maryam grow in purity and beauty, but instead of taking, he continued to give of himself. Maryam also gave of herself. She didn't attempt to marry Zakariya and become the wife of a prophet. She chose God, and she gave herself to God.

Part of receiving gifts from God al-Wahhab is protecting and nurturing others. When we ask for gifts from God al-Wahhab, we do so while also giving of ourselves without asking anything in return.

Hannah's wish for a boy to serve in the temple did eventually come true, when Jesus was born. And Prophet Zakariya, too, was granted a child. Even though he was martyred, he is alive.

Praying to God ar-Razzaq

God ar-Razzaq is The Sustainer, the source of nourishment and sustenance, who rewards us for our hard work. If we want to find God ar-Razzaq, then we work hard at everything we do and take responsibility for our actions. If we want clean air, we don't just pray to God al-Wahhab, we also work hard on environmental policy.

As always, this is an individual relationship between us and God. It is not up to others to determine whether we approach God al-Wahhab or God ar-Razzaq. The name "ar-Razzaq" should never be used as a stick to abuse the poor, telling them to work harder if they want doors to open. The only one who knows our hearts completely is God.

But if we have the means, then we should work hard. If God has facilitated the world of means for us, then we must honor that. We shouldn't give up at the first difficulty. If, for instance, a man can't conceive, that doesn't mean he should throw up his hands and say all doors are shut before him. Nor should he violate his values and marry woman after woman, looking for someone who can conceive a child with him. This man can help to raise another child, as Zakariya helped raise Maryam. He should work hard to the extent he's capable and honor his values and the people around him.

We pray to God ar-Razzaq when opportunities are open. We get up, get working, and God ar-Razzaq will come and reward us.

> On those who believe and work deeds of righteousness, will (God) Most Gracious bestow love. (Quran 19:96)

The poor and the rich, not The Poor vs. The Rich

Who should you pray to? God al-Wahhab or God ar-Razzaq? This depends on your circumstances. Certainly, we should all pray to God ar-Razzaq when we can. We should work hard, try hard, educate ourselves, and live up to our highest values. We shouldn't immediately turn to God al-Wahhab and ask for all doors to swing open before we've even tried the handle.

It's also important not to separate the people around us into an "us" vs. a "them." God is the protector of both the rich and the poor, the haves and the have-nots, and all of those struggling in between. Some people are born with advantages much greater than our own. Envying them is a waste of our effort. The question before all of us is: What can we do with what we have?

But we should never use the name of God ar-Razzaq to justify mistreatment of the disadvantaged, or to justify blaming someone for their poverty. We don't know what another person has tried, or what difficulties they might have faced. The point is not to judge others. It's that we should—all of us—turn to God.

Mary, Hagar, and the Importance of Independence

> *He is the First and the Last, the Manifest and the Hidden, and He is the Knower of all things.* (Quran 57:3)

Every chapter of the Quran begins with a reminder that God is most merciful and most compassionate. By opening each chapter this way, God shows us the way He wants to be known to His creation. God doesn't remind us of His power, but rather of His compassion. And indeed, God is always there to support us and bear us up, even in subtle ways we might not immediately see.

Because God created humanity, He has an intimate knowledge of our nature, and He knows our vulnerability and our weaknesses. He knew our trials on Earth would be difficult for us. But although we need to work hard in this life, he never intended to deprive us of his mercy.

One of God's names is "al-Batin," which means that God knows and sees our hidden realities, and yet does not expose people to hurt or shame. Other humans may shame and blame us, but God comforts and gently nurtures us.

We humans begin life as weak creatures, in need of compassion, loving kindness, and support, particularly in the face of others' judgment. God knows that we will face major difficulties, and He is ready to offer us comfort. But it's not our responsibility only to be comforted. It's also up to us to offer comfort to others.

Finding *fitra*: What do we do if we see others facing a trial?

All around the world, our fellow humans face enormous trials. Earthquakes, wars, mass migration, starvation, hurricanes, and other hardships face individuals and communities.

In one recent video, after a building collapse, a group of devastated men were digging in the rubble. Instead of sinking into the ground with grief, this group of men tried to excavate around the collapsed building. As they dug, they found, suddenly, a small child alive underneath the chunks of concrete. In this trial, sadness and God's joy are twined together. If you watch the video, it's almost as though the men have rescued themselves and are reconnecting to their childlike souls.

If you are tested with a trial, and you reach out and save the child, then that's God's grace coming out to meet you.

"Fitra" is a word that represents our pure desire to worship God. We often, during a difficult trial, find our *fitra*, which brings us closer to God. *Fitra* pushes us to worship in a pure, instinctual way. Knowledge is then necessary to help us to use that inclination to come closer to God.

As we live our daily lives, we often absorb the world around us without knowledge, without verifying what we've learned. This includes absorbing all the social ills around us. Trials and tribulations come to shake us up and to scrape back the layers of all the ills we've absorbed, so we can come closer to God and call on Him with our innate *fitra*.

Major trials force us to look beyond what is immediately around us and to connect with God. During a trial, we must look beyond the tribe, beyond what we've been taught by our parents, beyond our immediate life. The trial shakes us, and the soul finds comfort with God.

During trials and tribulations, we often praise and worship God because we feel our vulnerability. Then, during good times, we may become arrogant again, claiming we earned everything we have by our own effort.

It's not only our own trials that help us experience *fitra*. Other people's trials can elevate us and help us deal with social ills happening around the world. When people rush to aid each other, that, too, is *fitra*.

Judging Others in a Trial

> *But when He tries him and restricts his provision, he says, "My Lord has humiliated me." (Quran 89:16)*

It's important to remember that we cannot judge others who are undergoing a difficult period. God could be elevating a person to nurture them and give them wisdom. There are many reasons for human suffering.

If a trial is happening to us, then we should reflect on our life. Is this something we called down on ourselves? Did we help those who are suffering and sick? If we find a lack in ourselves, then we should address it.

But when others suffer, we should go to help them. As Muhammad, peace and blessings on him, said, "God is with you while you help your brother."

The Prophet also said: "God aids His servant as long as His servant aids others."

God brings a trial and shows us our true reality. But, when we know about the trials of others, God is also helping us grow.

After the catastrophic earthquake in Haiti in 2010, many in the United States and around the world gave money to Haitians to rebuild. What the Haitians then gave in return was even more important. They showed us, by example, the inspirational reality of gratitude, submission, and humility before God.

It may feel as though we are giving to those in need. But, in reality, we are the ones on the receiving end, as we're getting a much-needed lesson in how to embrace the reality of our existence.

This 2010 earthquake in Haiti was, to me, a wakeup call. It was a call to remember that, regardless how much we empower ourselves, that empowerment is all an illusion.

In reality, we are weak, and solutions to our problems must be embedded in an embrace of our mortality, vulnerability and humility before God.

As we look at any major tragedy, we must act on our own faith, values, and convictions, and we must respond to the calls for support. We can do it in the spirit of giving, or we can recognize that, in reality, we are the ones receiving a gift. And it is just as important to turn to God when witnessing others being tried as it is to turn to God during our own trials.

It's important to ask ourselves: When we are spectators watching others in the trial, do we reach out and help them? Do we come to their aid, or do we pass a homeless person and say they deserve it? In each instance, we're being tested to see what we do.

Connecting through our vulnerability and our independence

When we disconnect from our own vulnerability, it's hard to connect to others. Feeling our vulnerability is the root of our compassion with others.

Yet being vulnerable, and turning to God, doesn't mean we throw everything in God's lap and do nothing on our own.

Like Hagar and Mary, we need to exert ourselves to the utmost. In the desert, Hagar established her independence and worked hard to find water for her infant. Mary, during childbirth, was asked to shake a palm tree to help herself.

God doesn't want us to become dependent on anyone other than Him. However, being dependent on Him—in the sense that we acknowledge our neediness to Him—requires that we obey Him by worship, God-Consciousness, diligence, and actions that are pleasing to Him. This way, we become independent of others. We should never be waiting around for a savior or a superhero, just as Hagar didn't wait around for a savior, for her husband, or for anyone else.

Hagar relied on herself and on God. She had hope and trust in God, but she also exerted herself to the fullest. Then, after she discovered water and people came to her with food, they didn't come as saviors. Instead, they came as part of a mutually interdependent community.

She had water, and they had food, and they developed a relationship of respect and mutual benefit.

Vulnerability doesn't mean dependency or putting out a signal that you're waiting for a knight in shining armor. Often, if a "knight" does arrive, it's an abuser.

Yes, we need to be vulnerable, but that vulnerability should be kept in safe spaces. When we share our vulnerability, the question we need to ask ourselves is: Are we waiting for a savior? If the answer is yes, then we need to keep our vulnerability for God.

The next question we need to ask ourselves is: Are we exerting ourselves to the fullest, as Hagar did in the desert? Or are we waiting for someone to come take care of us? If you're not exerting yourself, then you may not recognize true help when it comes along.

We must, like Hagar and Mary, exert and develop the mental, social, and emotional muscle of independence. Indeed, God the Merciful wants to give us the gift of independence so that other humans cannot exert control over us.

What about saving others who are undergoing a trial?

When you see others undergoing a trial, certainly your first thought should be: Let me reach out and help this individual. Yet we also need to protect ourselves from individuals who are stuck in a bad pattern. Just as we want ourselves to be independent, it's important to help others from a place of mutual interdependence. It's important to remember that we're not a knight in shining armor, nor are we going to "fix" other people.

We certainly want to help others, but we need to do so in a partnership that maintains the independence and dignity of all. When we offer assistance, it's a choice. Just as it's freely given, it can be freely accepted or refused.

Having Conversations Across Differences

A bird does not sing because it has an answer. It sings because it has a song.

—Chinese Proverb

Having a conversation across differences can be exceptionally difficult. Much of the time, we protect ourselves against these conversations. On social media as elsewhere, we often stay inside groups where people echo the same opinions.

As pleasant as this is, this isn't a conversation. Speakers and listeners are enjoying each other's attention and having a nice get-together. It only darkens when someone speaks from outside the group's norms. Often, this person—whose voice sounds discordant in the otherwise harmonious group—is labeled a hater and ignored.

To have a conversation, there must be a level of openness. I can't control the other speakers or listeners. But I can enter the conversation feeling open to other ideas, rather than entering with the swagger that I'm 100% correct and going to prove it to you. This can happen with someone who's very different or with someone who appears much the same. I could be with somebody who's Palestinian from the same block, but if this person is not open, we are never going to have a conversation.

It works best when we approach a conversation holding our beliefs in a looser grip. I say to myself: This is what I believe is beneficial, but I am open to listening to what you have to say to me.

To do this, I focus on the differences between critical thinking and projection. It's not just about having the facts—it's easy to use facts to imply a false reality, if your mind isn't open and if you insist on generalizing about other groups.

Entering into a conversation isn't just about rationalizing and justifying your own beliefs. If it's a good conversation, you can say to yourself at the end: Hey, I grew.

Starting a conversation

The most important questions are not the ones you ask of others. They are the questions you ask yourself. If you're not open to understanding yourself, and the reality of who you are, then it's going to be very difficult to have a conversation where you understand another human being.

Questions to ask include: What do I believe in? What am I trying to defend? Why do I insist that this person or group is bad?

It's also important to check yourself. Are you just trying to control the other person's perspective? Or are you both sharing your views?

First, you need to set boundaries in any conversation. If everybody speaks at once, then you create chaos. We also can't allow personal attacks and hate speech. Boundaries can help us move from a chaotic place, where everybody speaking and only the powerful have a platform, to a place where equals are having a conversation driven by intelligence, critical thinking, understanding, and empathy. Where, most importantly, we can arrive at something new.

But sometimes, even when there are boundaries, people can't hear each other. Often, when there are conversations across differences, the communications channels grow clogged. The same accusations and questions are made and asked, over and over. For instance, since September 2001, Muslims have been asked, again and again, why they didn't condemn the attacks. For as many times as Muslims—ordinary people, leaders, writers, teachers—have condemned terror, it isn't being heard. This channel has become clogged.

How to unclog it?

A few years back, I was in a restorative-justice training session. Angry words were being thrown out by those who supported Israel, saying "Hamas," and "terrorist," and many things that were indeed facts. But these things weren't being shared with a sense of openness. Instead, the speakers seemed to want to knock any other voices down and prove that they were evil.

It's always good to let those voices get their day first.

After that, conversations can sometimes be unclogged by interrupting them. With these interruptions, we can answer not in the way that's expected, but by reaching out to people and asking them to look at themselves. Passover was coming up, and I asked how the logic of killing and imprisoning Palestinians to make Israel secure was different from Pharaoh's logic of killing Jewish male children for security.

At this point, a Jewish man stood up and changed the course of the conversation. At this point, it was no longer a conversation between two camps. We broke the "us vs. them" chain, which helped to unclog the channels. Ultimately, reflection has to come from within, because people have to know themselves. This Jewish man helped the group have a reflective, internal conversation.

Being changed by conversation

But having a successful conversation isn't just about changing someone else: I also have entered conversations and come out a different person. At one point, I belonged to a social-media group for Palestinians. I felt very passionate when I saw something that was posted there.

Immediately, one of the other members called me out and said that it was anti-Jewish. I couldn't listen to him right then, and I reflexively answered that it was not anti-Jewish. We got into an argument, and it wasn't resolved. But then once the heat of the argument had worn off, and I had thought about it, I was able to be open to his statements. I thought about the points he was making and reflected on why I had made my arguments. I realized that I was the one in the wrong, and I returned and apologized to him.

One of the things that helped was that he didn't say I was evil. I was challenged, and then I was given the space to confront myself and to learn something from the exchange.

When I was a high-school student, I was challenged in a conversation about Salman Rushdie. I didn't know much about the author of Midnight's Children and The Satanic Verses at the time—I just followed whatever local Muslims were saying. So I was antagonistic to Rushdie. I was challenged by a teacher, in a reflective way, which led me in turn to challenge myself. After that, I could see why censuring Rushdie didn't promote truth. I was challenged, and I grew out of that challenge.

What makes a healthy challenge?

Not every challenge is a healthy challenge. In a healthy challenge, the individual speaks directly to you, face to face, or they call you out by name. They don't go in the shadows. This is the way Moses approached Pharaoh to challenge someone is to approach them plainly. Speak to them, not about them.

Also, a healthy challenge isn't made just to get the upper hand. A healthy challenge also has to include a platform where the other person is allowed to speak. Moses, for instance, said to Pharaoh: Let's have this discussion, but let's have it openly for everyone to see. A healthy challenge has to be open. It has to be transparent.

Bullies are all about control, and they act in the shadows. A healthy challenge is made in the light.

That said, let us challenge each other to reach across the divide between us and work toward a greater understanding.

MUHAMMAD: BEAUTIFUL PROPHET, BEAUTIFUL MESSENGER

Allah and His angels send blessings on the Prophet: O ye that believe! Send ye blessings on him, and salute him with all respect. (Quran 33:56)

His Birth

The consensus is that Prophet Muhammad, upon him peace and blessings, was born on a Monday in the month of Rabi al-Awwal. On the 12th night, according to the strongest position, before Fajr or dawn. The majority of the scholars say that he, upon him peace and blessings, was born in the Year of the Elephant, after its occurrence by 50 days, around 570 AD.

Our prophet is Muhammad Bin Abdullah bin Abdul Muttalib bin Hashim bin Abdi-Manaf bin Qusayy bin Hakim bin Murrah bin Ka'b bin Luayy bin Ghalib bin Fihr bin Malik bin al-Nadr bin Kinanah bin Khuzaymah bin Mudrikah bin Ilyas bin Mudar bin Nizar bin Ma'add bin Adnan.

His mother is Aminah bint Wahb bin Abdi-Manaf bin Zuhrah bin Hakim.

He is from the tribe of Quraysh and the descendants of Hashim. He had 11 uncles, and among them were al-Hamzah, al-'Abbas, and Abu Talib. He was born in Mecca, and, while he was still in his mother's womb, his father died in Yathrib.

These tribes were chosen because of their nobility.

In the sixth year after his birth, his mother took him to Medina, and, during her return, she died at al-Abwa. Upon them peace and blessings.

In the eighth year after his birth, upon him peace and blessings, his grandfather, Abdul Muttalib, died. His uncle Abu Talib took over his care.

Abdullah met a Jew who had knowledge of the revealed books, and, in those books, there are details mentioned about the Prophet. This Jewish man told Abdul Muttalib that now was the time, and that the parents of the final Messenger would marry. Abdul Muttalib was not married at that time; either he was divorced or widowed. The Jewish man asked him whether he was married, and he said no. Abdul Muttalib had a great personality. The Jewish man told him to marry from among the Bani Zuhra, because the Messenger's mother was to come from that tribe, and he thus might be the father of that Messenger.

Abdul Muttalib was the best man of Quraysh, according to the Jewish man. And it was in their books that the best man from this tribe would marry a woman from the tribe of Bani Zuhra. Abdul Muttalib loved Abdullah the most of all his 10 children, and so he summoned him and said: Let us go to Bani Zuhra and get married, both of us. He had a plan that one of them might end up being the father of that Messenger.

On the way there, a woman stopped Abdullah and told him she wanted to marry him. She offered him 100 camels. Abdullah refused, because he was being obedient to his father and wanted to follow him. But the woman saw a light in his face and wanted to marry him, because she wanted to be the mother of this Messenger.

The Prophet, upon him peace and blessings, had a wondrous lineage. Whenever a branch split, his light would pass to the best of the two branches.

After his marriage was consummated, Abdullah saw the woman of 100 camels once again, and she had no interest in him at all. He asked her why her feelings changed. She said that the previous night, when he'd passed her, there was a light in his face. Now, it had left him. Scholars say that the light passed from him to Aminah. In that lineage, every time a son was born, there was light in him until he got married, and that light would travel to the woman until she gave birth, and so on until the Prophet was born. That light stayed with her for nine months until he was born.

The blessed pregnancy

Aminah said that, in all her life, she had never carried anything that was lighter. It was not like normal pregnancies that women spoke of. The Messenger did not cause any such problems to his mother. The only thing that made her realize she was pregnant was that she stopped menstruating. She also saw many visions while she was pregnant.

Sent to all mankind

The Messenger was sent to all mankind as the seal of the prophets, and he is honored to be the seal.

Every Prophet told his people of his coming. Prophet Muhammad, upon him peace and blessings, said that if Prophet Moses, upon him peace, appeared in his time, he would obey him. He was the Messenger even of prophets themselves, upon them peace and blessings.

There is a hadith that says: The first to be created was the light of your Prophet. Some say the hadith is weak or fabricated. God knows, but it is too weak to base knowledge on it. Yet there are authentic hadiths with similar meanings. Muhammad was asked: When were you made Prophet? He said, I was a prophet before Adam was created.

The point is to remember that all the scholars agree that the Prophet Muhammad is the greatest Prophet, and the slave of God. No one worshipped God better than he did. That was an honor that was given to him by God, upon him peace and blessings.

Abdullah died and was buried in Medina. Aminah was waiting for him, as she was still in the honeymoon phase of their marriage, which lasted only six months. She was sad, but the pregnancy consoled her. She loved him so much that she composed beautiful poetry, and she did not marry after him. It was willed that the parents of the Prophet did not marry anyone before their marriage, nor did they marry after him. People wanted to marry her after Abdallah's death, but she refused.

During Aminah's pregnancy, she saw many visions, and, when she gave birth to the Prophet, it was a Monday. She had no pain whatsoever when giving birth. Instead, she saw a vision of light coming out of her that reached all the way to Basra, which was the farthest they could imagine. This meant that her son's light would reach to the ends of the earth. She heard a voice tell her that she had given birth to the greatest boy in the world, and that she should call him Muhammad.

The perfect baby

The midwife was surprised when Muhammad was born, as he did not cry, nor was there any filth or blood on him. He was spotlessly clean, and his body was fragrant. She did not need to perfume him, as his natural smell was better. Indeed, she had never smelled such a smell. Also, he was already circumcised, and the umbilical cord was cut. All she did was wrap him up and give him to his mother.

Then, when Muhammad was born, the first thing he did was prostrate. Babies cannot prostrate, and yet his face was turned downward. He prostrated, and then he looked up at the sky. After that, he grabbed a handful of dirt. This shows his great station, as Prophet Muhammad was expressing his position by prostrating himself before God.

This was how he began his life, and this was how he ended it. He looked up at the sky, and this showed his great resolve and how he was attached to the heights with great expectations and great ambitions.

The dirt in his hand meant that the entire earth was in his grip. There would come a time, it meant, that Islam would spread all across the earth. His first word was Allah, or God, and his first sentence was, "la ilaha illallah," or that there is no god but God.

In the Quran, God calls Muhammad by his station or title. But on the Day of Judgment, Muhammad will be in prostration, and God will tell him: O Muhammad, raise your head and you will be given. Other prophets made their prayers during their lives, but Muhammad has saved his. He was so selfless that he wanted to protect his ummah, or his people, on the Day of Judgment.

Baby Muhammad was very attached to the sky, and he was always looking at it. It was the habit of his people to cover babies with a pot. But they found the pot split in half, and Muhammad looking at the sky. He was always looking at the heavens, as if in supplication.

The nursing story

The Arabs used to send their newborns to the desert to protect them from illness, as, when pilgrims came to Mecca, it was possible for the babies to get sick and die. Mecca was a place of plagues. Even today, visitors must vaccinate themselves against a range of diseases. In those times, if children picked up the visiting viruses, they would die. They were also sent to the desert to learn better Arabic, as Arabic was spoken more eloquently in the desert than in the cities, where there was a mishmash of different languages and dialects.

Babies were also taken from their young mothers so that the mother could relax and enjoy life as a young married woman. So how did grieving Aminah manage without the Prophet, upon him peace and blessings?

The Importance of Listening

The first duty of love is to listen.

—Paul Tillich

Muhammad isn't just one among the prophets; he connects the stories of all the other prophets together. We are told that, as part of his journey, Muhammad traveled to Jerusalem, where all the prophets joined him in prayer. All the prophets' stories help guide us in our lives, but Muhammad's story is the thread that brings all the others together. He brings together the stories of Moses, David, Jesus, and all of those who shone out to help us steer our own lives.

One of the key things we can learn from Muhammad's life is to listen. We learn that, when we really love someone, we make the effort to listen to what they have to say. The same goes for loving one's community and the wider world.

One of the signs of Muhammad's great love was that he listened to everyone around him before judging their situation. He listened so much that he was mocked for his listening skills.

> Among them are men who abuse the Prophet and say, "He is (all) ear." Say, "He listens to what is best for you: he believes in Allah, has faith in the Believers, and is a Mercy to those of you who believe." But those who abuse the Messenger will have a grievous penalty. (Quran 9:61)

Muhammad was called "all ear," because he was always listening to everyone, including the poor, the low status, and those considered of no account. Although his detractors saw this as a negative, it pointed to his loving and accepting nature. When he was in power, he continued to listen to the orphans, the sick, and the powerless.

Indeed, listening to stories about Muhammad is what brings Islam alive for many.

One shaykh, said that, from the beginning, "one thing that truly attracted me to the Prophet, upon him peace and blessings, was stories that would be read to me by my paternal grandmother who used to live with us and by my own mother and that I would hear from my maternal grandfather."

Indeed, many people have been brought to Prophet Muhammad through stories from parents and teachers.

"If you think of the Prophet, you can't help yourself but to stop and say, Wow, that's amazing," this shaykh said.

Did I hear you wrong?

I came to Muhammad in a different way. I heard the stories and teachings of Muhammad in my childhood, but the stories I heard were misaligned or misapplied. These stories made the Prophet out as a leader who was not only sexist, but anti-woman, and that was troubling to me. I didn't want to take the rejectionist approach of throwing it all out, but instead I wanted to do my own research and study. I wanted to do a better job of listening.

When I finally delved into the story of Muhammad for myself, what I saw was totally different from what I'd been told as a girl. One thing that particularly struck me was Muhammad's marriage to Khadijah, his first wife. When they married, he was her twenty-five-year-old employee, and she was a forty-year-old woman: a respected, powerful businesswoman.

Khadijah was not a vulnerable elderly woman, as some stories have her. She was at the height of her career: powerful, wise, and successful. As a wealthy widow, she had been proposed to by people of high social rank, but she wasn't interested in marrying any of them. She was also reputed to be very generous. She gave money to her kin and to others in need.

Muhammad was also not a vulnerable young man. When Khadijah hired him, she recognized his worth, and she paid him double the wages of her other employees.

Moreover, Khadijah was not like al-Aziz's wife in Prophet Joseph's story. She fully respected Muhammad's autonomy, and she treated him as a human being, respecting his full rights. She found him to be a man of good character, truthful and trustworthy. Her income from trade increased after she hired him.

When she wanted to marry him, she didn't approach him or abuse her power over him. She neither tried to guilt nor obligate him. Instead, she proposed through her cousin.

Khadijah's cousin asked Muhammad why he wasn't married at twenty-five, and whether he would be interested in Khadijah. At first, Muhammad said that he couldn't afford a wife. When asked if he would be open to the idea if Khadijah freed him from his financial responsibilities, he responded: "Would she accept?"

Here, Muhammad shows that had been caught by surprise, which is indication of his honesty. He wasn't preying on her as a wealthy widow. There are no games, and he doesn't take advantage of her financial situation. These are two noble people who find each other, and they listen to one another.

In "What is Love?" Dr. Abdul Lateef Krauss Abdullah describes how, "through mutual surrender to Allah," Khadijah and Muhammad were "able to give and receive love without the hang-ups and psychological blockages that might otherwise not allow us to do so."

That is what drew me to Prophet Muhammad, upon him peace and blessings. I listened to and studied his character, and I saw how he interacted with women.

What we can (and can't) learn from the marriage of Khadijah and Muhammad

There are many great and beautiful lessons to be learned from the relationship between Khadijah and the prophet Muhammad, peace and blessings on him, and Muhammad's relationships to other women. However, there are also ways in which this story has been manipulated, often to pressure women into entering a relationship.

First: Who were Khadijah and Muhammad?

As I said above, Khadijah was a wealthy, influential woman in her community who had been previously married. She was a business owner who was exceptionally intelligent and was known to be honest and trustworthy. Much has been written about Khadijah, but for our purposes, it's important to know that she wasn't shopping around for a spouse or looking for someone to save her. She knew herself and knew what she wanted, and she had many proposals and opportunities. She was also capable of identifying good character traits in others, and what she found in Muhammad pleased her.

Muhammad had never been married. He was fifteen years younger than Khadijah, and he was financially poor but spiritually rich. He'd been orphaned at a young age, and he was known by his community as someone who was trustworthy and honest.

At this point, once Khadijah had identified Muhammad as a person who would be a good spiritual partner, what did she do? She didn't pressure him, hang around, or play mind games. She sent someone to check into Muhammad's opinion of the idea of marrying her.

At first, Muhammad said he couldn't afford marriage. After all, he wasn't looking for a wealthy woman. His response was: "Who am I? Who is Khadijah?"

From this response, we can see that he wasn't hinting, trying to be noticed, or trying to impress her. He hadn't been angling for a proposal. But when he thought about it, he found, in his heart, an interest in Khadijah. At that point, he said: "If she accepts, then I will accept." Women in particular can appreciate the spiritual richness of this response. He is looking for her consent in marriage first: this is modesty manifested in action.

When Muhammad was twenty-five years old, he married his first wife: Khadijah bint Khuwaylid, who bore all his children, with the exception of Ibrahim. Their children's names were Al-Qasim, Zainab, Ruqaiyah, Umm Kulthum, Fatimah, and Abdullah, who was called Taiyib and Tahir.

Muhammad received the call to Prophethood while he was married to her, and she was his comforter during his mission. She sacrificed her life, time, and money for his mission.

He witnessed her death at a very difficult moment in his life.

He witnessed the death of all his children, save Fatimah.

All his sons died in childhood.

Fatimah died six months after her father.

The fallacy of "Deen over Dunya"

Sometimes, we forget that faith is not about pushing things out onto the world, but about actively receiving a gift from God. The prophet received the love and affection of his spouses as gifts from God, and we can see the appreciation he had for them.

When people are pressured to marry another person, sometimes they are told that they should want "deen over dunya," or religion over the material world. Often recent converts are pressured to marry without knowing their rights, and the story of Muhammad and Khadijah is brought out to illustrate that wealthy women should marry poor men.

However, this is a willful misinterpretation. Khadijah wasn't searching for a handsome poor man to marry, nor was Muhammad looking for a benefactor.

Another misinterpretation or misapplication of this phrase is the argument that, "you're beautiful, so it's your fault I'm interested in you." Like the Prophet Joseph, Muhammad was known for his good looks. Indeed, it was even said that Joseph had only half the beauty of the Prophet Muhammad.

Yet even if Khadijah was interested in Muhammad for his looks, she acted responsibly. She didn't try to force herself on Muhammad, nor did she pester or manipulate him. She checked to see if he was interested in her first. She communicated responsibly. She never suggested that her feelings were more important than his. She said: Please go find out if he's interested. And neither did Muhammad. He said, "If she accepts, then I accept."

These are two souls, very alike in character and spiritual excellence, who are both primarily interested in the feelings of others. When you love someone, you are more interested in receiving—not in the sense of receiving material gifts, but in receiving their love for you. Instead of forcing ourselves on another person—mentally, socially, spiritually, or emotionally—love means accepting the other person's feelings come first. It means saying, "If you accept, then I accept."

Sometimes, people push others into relationships that are one-sided or unequal, and they use the story of Khadijah and Prophet Muhammad to help do it. But in doing so, they overlook the core message of this story. Although Muhammad and Khadijah were of different ages and financial statuses, they were very alike in the essential ways. Moreover, neither of them rushed in or pressured the other: They both checked, first and foremost, to see whether the other person was interested.

In many cases, "deen over dunya"—or spirituality over materiality—is a good way to be. But we shouldn't use it as a means to pressure people into relationships they don't want.

Trust and Trustworthiness

Here comes al-Amin.

—People who knew Prophet Muhammad

Muhammad, the trustworthy one

One of the Prophet's beautiful names, even before he was given prophethood at the age of forty, is al-Amin, or The Trustworthy One. This is due to his honest behavior with people in peacemaking, and especially in business, and his truthfulness when speaking of God. Studying his life can help a person know what to look for to identify and recognize trustworthy people.

A case in point is that, during the time of Prophet Muhammad, upon him peace and blessings, there was an attempt to fix the Ka'aba, as it has become old and needed repairs. Before he was a prophet, in the thirty-fifth year after his birth, a fire weakened the structure of the Ka'aba, and the Quraysh people decided to rebuild it. After the repairs were complete, the time came for the *Hajar al-Aswad*, the Black Stone, to be put back in its place. Each family from among the prominent tribes in Mecca felt they deserved the honor of putting the Black Stone in its place.

As we see in families and communities, the event led to a significant disagreement, which spilled over into a lot of fighting. Which family would get the unique honor of placing the black stone in its place?

Finally, someone had a suggestion.

He suggested that they wait for the following morning, see who entered the house of worship, and ask him to decide.

The following morning, as people waited anxiously, Prophet Muhammad, upon him peace and blessings, came. Everyone was happy to see him, and they shouted: "Here comes al-Amin." He was well respected throughout the community.

He smiled upon hearing this, and that's when he learned of the fight taking place over the Black Stone. He took his robe and put it on the ground, took the sacred Black Stone and put it in the center of the robe, and then asked a leader from each of the families to take one corner of the robe and lift it together. In so doing, he gave each the honor of placing the sacred Black Stone back in its place.

Prophet Muhammad, upon him peace and blessings, was chosen by all parties in the fight to handle this dispute. He tried to resolve the dispute by respecting the people's rights and desiring honor for all parties. Moreover, he was chosen by God to unite the parties who were fighting and to bring their hearts together. He did not push himself on them: unwelcome, meddling, or adding fuel to the fire. Often, when we try to solve problems or fighting, we engage in meddling instead of making peace.

The first duty of peace-making is that all parties must agree on the peacemaker. They must all respect the person who is making peace, and they must all trust this individual. Across the globe, we are witness to fighting that continues due to people's meddling, attempting to make peace without the right to do it and without the agreement of all parties in the dispute. Before taking it upon yourself to make peace between people, ask yourself: Am I seen as someone trustworthy by all parties?

It's particularly important for the underdogs of our world—people who've been bullied, abused, or oppressed—to recognize the difference between a person who is trustworthy and one who's a "trust-me" type.

The Quran doesn't ask us to trust blindly. Indeed, Satan is the archetype of the one who cannot be trusted. He approaches Adam in order to "whisper suggestions," promising that he's a "sincere adviser."

> Then began Satan to whisper suggestions to them, bringing openly before their minds all their shame that was hidden from them (before): he said: "Your Lord only forbade you this tree, lest ye should become angels or such beings as live forever." And he swore [by Allah] to them, "Indeed, I am to you from among the sincere advisors." (Quran 7:20-21)

Trust is an important human characteristic, and it is deeply important that we trust one another. Yet at times we put our trust in those "sincere advisers" who, like Satan, intend to take advantage of us and manipulate us for their own gain.

When a "trust-me" type appears, they can be excessively nice: doing things for us, listening, validating, and helping. Yet there's a hidden agenda. They work to create a relationship and gain our trust, but after that comes the hidden demand.

Once the demand comes, a person is often trapped. Now the abuser controls them. This could be a business deal, where someone is out to steal money or sell something that's just not there, or it could be something even more dangerous.

If this happens, it's important to accept responsibility for our part in this—we trusted someone who was untrustworthy—and to file a report with the relevant authorities. We must both take responsibility for our actions and protect others.

People who are the "trust-me" types often, like Satan, create a secret relationship. They often add a level of urgency to their demands, such that a person feels they can't investigate what they're being asked to do. In this situation, if a person hesitates, they will often be told: "Trust me." If the person inside the trap says "no" to a request, then guilt and obligation often follow.

When Satan approached Adam, he claimed he could be trusted. Although he made big promises, he had a hidden agenda, which was to harm Adam. He came and sold him an idea in a very deceptive way. But Adam also did wrong, because he had already been warned about Satan, and he didn't check up on Satan's story. Adam also could have said, "Hmm, let me first ask God." Or he even could've said, "Let me think about this."

After being tricked as Adam was, it was pointless to blame Satan or anyone else. What was most important was to do as Adam did, upon him peace. That is: to become knowledgeable and strong so we are not misled by others like this again. Instead of blaming others, Adam cried out:

> Our Lord! We have wronged ourselves. If You do not forgive us and do not have mercy on us, we shall surely be among the losers. (Quran 7:23)

Moses and trustworthiness

A trustworthy person is different. Someone who's trustworthy doesn't obsess over winning over people's trust. Instead, they act according to their values.

But the key is that, with a trustworthy person, there is no secrecy around the relationship, whether it's between a teacher and a student, between business partners, or between a doctor and a patient. A trustworthy person doesn't create a sense of urgency or secrecy, compel you to act without asking other people for advice, or force you to stay in the relationship. A trustworthy person allows you to verify what they have suggested and discuss it with family, friends, and experts.

Moses was just such a person. After he had left the company of Pharaoh, he came across two women standing near a well, waiting for their turn to water their sheep. Moses didn't make assumptions, but instead he came up and asked them what was going on, and why they were standing among all the men. The women explained that their father was an old man, and Moses helped them without any strings attached, then went on his way.

A "trust-me" type would obligate the women to do something to benefit him. Yet he does not. He doesn't suggest that they need his protection. He simply helps them and doesn't use his kindness as a bargaining chip.

Moses did not tell the women to hide their relationship with him. Indeed, he went willingly to meet with their father, which was when one of them said to their father: This is a trustworthy man.

Why did she say this? She had probably experienced many men at the well who were the "trust-me" type, and Moses's behavior likely stood out from the rest of the men. He didn't try to take advantage.

This was also true of Bilqis, who dealt with untrustworthy kings and then recognized Solomon, upon him peace.

It was also true of Khadijah, who recognized and remarked on the trustworthiness of the Prophet Muhammad, upon him peace and blessings, before she proposed to him.

Trustworthy people, like Moses, can face witnesses. They don't isolate you from others, and there is no trickery or manipulation. Moses married one of the daughters, but this man who had so recently lived as a prince, also was able to take on the very hard job of working as a shepherd.

No obligation in trust

Just as we shouldn't blindly trust anyone, no one should blindly trust us, either. We shouldn't feel bad if we don't trust someone else, and we should allow people not to instantly trust us, too. At an individual level, no one should feel slighted if someone says, "I don't trust you." For whatever reason, we are not what they need at that moment.

There are also varying degrees of trust: Trusting someone to be a teacher doesn't mean we have to trust them to be a bus driver. We might trust someone to be a good communicator, but not with secrets.

We need to know where to trust, and not be guilted

As philosopher Onora O'Neill said in a powerful TED talk, "More trust is not an intelligent aim in this life. Intelligently placed and intelligently refused trust is the proper aim."

As O'Neill said, we should place trustworthiness before trust. Adam knew Satan wasn't trustworthy, and yet he placed his trust in him. Trust should be a response. Before we give it to anyone, we must test the trustworthiness of that person. Are they honest? They might have the right skills, but are they ethical?

Where are you?

When we are trying to determine the trustworthiness of another person, we also have to think about what we're thinking and feeling. Sometimes, if a person is in dire need—really looking for that too-good-to-be-true business deal or relationship—they might be particularly vulnerable to a "trust-me" type of person.

Often, it's not enough to judge another person's trustworthiness. It's also necessary to judge oneself. In the case of Adam, he was seeking something too good to be true, and Satan took control of him by that. It made him overlook the fact that Satan was untrustworthy.

Moses, on the other hand, communicated his trustworthiness through his actions. And the women who agreed to his help were self-reliant even before he came along.

If someone makes themselves vulnerable to another party, that's good evidence that they are—or are becoming—trustworthy. Moses, for instance, made himself vulnerable by presenting himself and his story to the women's father. There, he opened himself up to questions and judgment.

This is particularly important in relationships with people who are in the position of the underdog, who must be particularly careful about protecting themselves, as those women surely were. Underdogs need to make sure the person they're placing their trust in is vulnerable before judgment. It's important for the underdog to listen to their gut, and that they aren't made to judge alone.

And if trust has been broken? It's important to remember that we can't simply rebuild trust between people. Instead, we need to focus on rebuilding the foundation of trust: trustworthiness.

The First Revelation

And he does not speak out of his own desire, no, it truly is nothing besides a Divine Revelation that is being revealed. (Quran 53:3-4)

Prophet Muhammad, upon him peace and blessings, was chosen by God, and he received the first revelation at age forty, while he was at Mount Hira.

Renowned compilers of the authentic traditions of Islam agree on the following account of the first revelations received by the Prophet.

Muhammad would seclude himself in the cave of Mount Hira and worship God in seclusion. He would, whenever he wished, return to his family at Mecca and then go back again, taking with him the necessities of life. Thus, he continued to return to Khadijah from time to time, until one day the revelation came down to him and the Angel Gabriel, or Jibreel, appeared to him and said: "Read!" But as Muhammad was illiterate, having never received any instruction in reading or writing, he said to the angel: "I am not a reader." The angel took hold of him and squeezed him as much as he could bear, and then said again: "Read!" The Prophet said: "I am not a reader."

The Angel again seized the Prophet and squeezed him and said:

> Read! In the Name of your Lord, Who has created (all that exists), has created man from something that clings. Read! And your Lord is the Most Generous, Who has taught (the writing) by the pen, has taught man that which he knew not. (Quran 96: 1-5)

He felt tremendous fear and ran back home. He thought the djinn had possessed him. Upon doing so, he heard a loud voice saying: "O Muhammad, thou art the Messenger of God, and I am Gabriel." He looked up at the sky, and he saw an angel filling the horizon. In every direction he turned, the angel was there, repeating: "O Muhammad, thou art the Messenger of God, and I am Gabriel."

He ran down the slope of the mountain in fear to his wife, "Cover me, cover me!"

Like the prophets before him, the truth did not resonate with him, nor did God read his mind. His response upon receiving the first revelation was fear and seeking comfort from his wife, Khadijah, may God be pleased with her. This was not due to his lack of confidence or because he was full of doubts, but rather because of his purity and tremendous humility before God as well as others. He did not make up or plan this event.

His people knew him as as-Sadiq, or The Honest One, and as al-Amin, or The Trustworthy One.

When he told his wife, she pointed to his attributes and his honesty and trustworthiness. She noted how he took care of the poor, and told him that God would help him.

> O you who covers himself [with a garment],
> Arise and warn
> And your Lord glorify
> And your clothing purify
> And uncleanliness avoid
> And do not confer favor to acquire more
> But for your Lord be patient.
>
> (Quran 74:1-7)

Muhammad began his mission calling people close to him in secret: family, friends, and neighbors. He is not aiming for controversy and attention, like some reformers who start their mission by verbally attacking those who they want to reform. After all, charity begins at home. That is, if we want to tackle racism, sexism, or any other social ill, then our practice must begin with family, friends, and those nearest to us. It doesn't begin by calling out to those far away, and bringing attention to ourselves, like as-Samiri did in the story of Moses, upon him peace.

In the fifth year after his revelation was received, the Prophet, upon him peace and blessings, sent a group of companions to Abyssinia for ten years. Some went alone and some went with their families. There were eleven men and fourteen women.

In the tenth year, the Prophet, upon him peace and blessings, lost his uncle Abu Talib. Three days later, he lost his wife, Khadijah. During the same period, he faced the worst form of torture from the people of Taif, who rejected him, upon him peace and blessings, and threw stones at him. His main support were gone, and the torture and trials increased.

People slowly enter Islam

The Prophet, upon him peace and blessings, met a group of the people of Medina at al-Aqaba a number of times. Who were they, and what was the significance of each?

At the end of the twelfth year, twelve men of Ansar made an oath of allegiance. They also made an oath that they would not associate partners with God, fornicate, engage in falsehood, or disobey the prophet, upon him peace and blessings.

Then Prophet Muhammad sent with them Musab Bin Umayr, God be pleased with him, to teach them the Quran. Two leaders named Saad bin Muadh and Saad bin Ubadah embraced Islam from his hands. And many of their people entered Islam after them.

The second pledge of al-Aqaba was at the end of the thirteenth year, during the hajj season, when 70 men and two women of the Ansar pledged an oath to him, upon him peace and blessings. They promised to protect him as they protect themselves and their wives and children. He, upon him peace and blessings, appointed for them 12 leaders.

Now, he was known as al-Mustafa or The Chosen one. He was chosen by God as the seal of the prophets and final Messenger to guide and lead humanity to the Divine Light.

Let Aisha Speak for Aisha

Allah and His angels send blessings on the Prophet: O ye that believe! Send ye blessings on him, and salute him with all respect. (Quran 33:56)

Our societies and institutions often don't believe women who say they've been abused. The #metoo movement has done a good job of bringing this to our attention, and of supporting investigations of women's accusations. Yet, just as it's important to hear women's calls for justice, it is also important to hear other stories: of praise, support, and love.

Historically, many people have refused to listen to Aisha. When the topic of Aisha is raised, many wave their arms and shout about her age. We know she was much younger than Muhammad when the two married, although her exact age is disputed. What is certainly wrong is that she is sometimes portrayed as a silent child-figure who cannot speak for herself.

I want to move away from the argument over her age, which often puts words in Aisha's mouth. Instead, we need to let Aisha speak for herself.

Aisha was not, as she is sometimes portrayed, a silent figure. Many of her sayings and her stories were recorded. We also know about her jealousy, and how she argued with Muhammad. We know she was a scholar and a leader, and how she opposed Ali, the prophet's cousin, in a battle after the prophet passed away.

Indeed, many of things that have reached us from Muhammad came from his wife Aisha. Because she outlived him, she had plenty of opportunities, after he passed away, to speak out. If he had secretly abused her, or manipulated her, she could have spoken out against him. Yet no stories like that have reached us. Indeed, Aisha always spoke about Muhammad in a beautiful way. A lot of the things that reach us about the prophet's household, and about how he was as a person, came from Aisha.

Even though Aisha was jealous of Khadijah, the prophet's first wife, much of what we know about Khadijah comes from Aisha, too.

Aisha was a vibrant woman, sometimes angry, and sometimes had strained relationships with other women. She struggled with jealousy and with the social ills she'd inherited from her society, but she also overcame them. In the end, she opened doors for other women instead of shutting them.

Although Aisha was a leader in her own right, she did have conflicts with other women. However, she fought for women's rights. As humans, it is important to recognize flawed role models with whom we can identify. And while Aisha was a woman of great strengths, she also struggled with pettiness, prejudice, and jealousy.

She particularly struggled with her prejudice against Muhammad's Jewish wife, Safiyyah, and the Prophet had to encourage Safiyyah to continue to take pride in herself and her identity. We all struggle to overcome prejudices we inherited from our society.

So instead of worrying about the age at which a long-dead woman was married, we should respect her enough to listen to the echoes of her voice. Because she had a strong and passionate intellect, Aisha was able to record details of the prophet's private life that weren't available to others. Because she was younger, she outlived him and was able to pass these stories down to teach the generations that came later.

The voice we have of Aisha—which was remembered by all those who knew her—is not the voice of a victim. She was a fierce and opinionated woman, and we should not impose a victim's narrative on her.

We know, for instance, that Aisha complained to Muhammad about how frugally they lived. We know that he gave her and his other wives the opportunity to leave him, and also be well-provided. We know that she chose to stay with him, and that she had power, a voice, and influence. We also know a great deal more about Muhammad's life than we would without her.

There is a story, narrated by Aisha, that says:

> One night, the Prophet was prostrated in prayer, and he stayed like that for so long, she thought he had passed away. Feeling thus, she stood up and shook his toe. She felt the movement, and then lay down again near his head, to hear

what he was saying, and he said: "I seek refuge in Your pleasure from Your wrath, and in Your pardon from Your punishment, and in You from You. I cannot enumerate Your praises as You praise Yourself."

Aisha also tells us that, before the Prophet would get up for the optional prayer in the middle of the night, he would seek Aisha's permission. Thus he balanced her rights with the rights of God.

An older woman

It is not only Aisha who people often paint as a silent, easily manipulated woman. Khadijah—the prophet's first wife—was significantly older than him. Instead of respecting the relationship between them, people refuse to listen to Khadijah, too, and claim he married her for money and used her. Yet, after Khadijah had passed away, Muhammad stayed in contact with her family. We also know from Aisha that Muhammad continued to speak highly of his first wife.

The Prophet had a loving relationship with Khadijah, who was the first to stand by him and support him, and who believed in him when the whole world stood against him. The Prophet clearly learned a lot from Khadijah, including how to nurture the women of his community into being leaders in their society.

He honored the contract he made with Khadijah in not taking another wife, and—with his other wives—he never pitted one against the other, but rather treated each as individuals and nurtured them each as individuals.

It is not up to us, now, to tell Khadijah or Aisha or any other woman of that era what they thought about the Prophet. It is for us to stay quiet enough that we can listen to the echoes of their voices, and to let women everywhere tell their own stories.

Why women leaders?

The Prophet Muhammad, peace and blessings upon him, helped change the opportunities available to women in many different ways. He came into a society that was strongly prejudiced against women. He could have simply told people: In the future, we need to live differently. He could have spoken for women, on their behalf.

Yet, as many studies have shown, in order to empower women, we need to be able to see women leaders. The simple existence of women leaders improves the self-esteem of women and girls. When women are in positions of leadership, this improves the self-worth of all women. Part of the wisdom behind nurturing many women leaders after Khadijah—who were of different personality types, and who often didn't see eye-to-eye—was to nurture and grow a range of future women leaders.

The Prophet could have spoken for women. He could have stood in as the voice of women. But instead, he wanted to nurture women who spoke for themselves and who were leaders in their community.

Leadership is a responsibility, and a Muslim who seeks leadership must recognize that they will be held to higher level of accountability before God. However, there is a need for leadership. The solution is to nurture and educate people of faith who enjoin moral conduct and forbid immoral conduct without regard for gender, class, or anything else but Allah. We must teach them not just the law, but the ethics and spirit of the law. Leaders must also be held accountable before a committee of their peers, and there must be some process to counter abuse of power, nepotism, and bias.

What is a successful role model for women? It is a woman who is both accountable and vulnerable as she leads. This doesn't mean simply flipping the roles, saying, "I believe women no matter what." It doesn't mean that women should blindly and uncritically defend one another, just as men have done. This is a false utopia and an unhealthy way of leading.

Neither should successful role models be "token" leaders, who were pushed forward by men in order to support an oppressive agenda. This is another type of unhealthy leadership for women.

Muhammad didn't support either of these two kinds of leadership. Aisha didn't exclusively support other women, but neither did she exclusively shut them down. Aisha was a flawed, fierce, and charismatic leader who engaged others and struggled to be better. She didn't always get along with other women in the community. But instead of stepping in and settling arguments himself, Muhammad nurtured and promoted the self-confidence and self-worth of all women, and he encouraged them to work things out themselves. When Aisha called Safiyyah a Jewess, as a pejorative, Muhammad nurtured Safiyyah and told her that she came from a line of prophets. Like all good leaders, Aisha learned from this.

Believing His Wives

Allah and His angels send blessings on the Prophet: O ye that believe! Send ye blessings on him, and salute him with all respect. (Quran 33:56)

Muhammad married many women after Khadijah. They were Zainab bint Khuzaymah, Aisha, Sawdah, Hafsah, Maymunah, Umm Habibah (Ramlah), Zainab bint Jahsh, Umm Salmah, Juwayriyah, and Safiyyah. All his wives were with him by choice. While Khadijah was the only one who proposed to him, all the rest were given a choice to leave and refused.

With his wife Khadijah, he fulfilled the agreement not to take another wife and did not violate the marriage contract. He was married to one woman at the height of his youth for twenty-five years, loyal and faithful. After Khadijah passed away, he married other women in a polygamous relationship.

The Story of Umm Juwayriyah

After Khadijah's death, Muhammad married other women. The characteristics these women had in common were their intelligence and their care for others.

Umm Juwayriyah was said to have been an exceptionally beautiful, intelligent and wise woman who was brought up in the lap of luxury. She had been educated and raised as a princess, but, during a time of war, was made a bondswoman to Thabit ibn Qays, who told her she had to pay ransom for him to let her go.

Courageously, Umm Juwayriyah pled her case to the Prophet. In this, she was thinking not just of herself, but of her family. The Prophet saw her intelligence and influence, and he offered to pay her ransom. It's often said that the Prophet was attracted to her beauty, and he might well have recognized her beauty, but that could not have been the only reason for his interest in her, as he was presented with many beautiful women in his lifetime.

Like Muhammad's other wives, Umm Juwayriyah was intelligent, something a womanizer would be repulsed by, as womanizers don't like intelligent women, but rather those they can easily manipulate. In any case, her father showed up with the ransom money and she was freed. Again, the Prophet made an offer of marriage, and she accepted even after she was freed and with her family.

Although Umm Juwairiyah was very beautiful, the marriage was a political move, to remove any desire for war of vengeance or feelings of humiliation. However, once the marriage took place, the war booty that had been taken from the Banu Mustaliq was returned, and the prisoners of war were freed.

Aisha once said of Umm Juwairiyah, "I know of no woman who was more of a blessing to her people than Juwairiyah bint al-Harith." May God be pleased with them both.

The "simple Bedouin woman"

There is, among Muhammad's relationships with women, the story of an innocent and gullible wife who was tricked by others. She was easily manipulated and told that, when the Prophet came to consummate the marriage, she should say, "I seek refuge in God from Prophet Muhammad."

If you want to know the character of someone, put God before him. This woman refused Prophet Muhammad, and he accepted her refusal and let her return to her family. None of Muhammad's wives were with him out of compulsion, but rather freely chose him.

Zaid and Zaynab

Indeed, following the choice of one's heart is important. Muhammad knew that Zaynab and Zaid were both good people, people of integrity and faith, so he tried to bring them together in marriage. However, marriage is not just about hanging out together—you also need to have some desire for the person you marry.

Zaynab accepted the marriage proposal because it was brought to her by Prophet Muhammad, peace and blessings upon him, but internally she was not receptive to Zaid. She respected him, honored him, but she wasn't interested in marrying him. This is another lesson: just because someone is a person of good character doesn't mean you have to find them attractive.

In the end, Zaynab married her heart's desire.

Ramlah bint Abu Sufyan

Abu Jahl was the leader of the Quraysh who were fighting the Muslim community. After Abu Jahl died, Abu Sufyan ibn Harb became the leader.

Ramlah was his daughter, also known as Umm Habibah or Mother of Habibah, after the name of her daughter. It is important to note that Abu Sufyan later became Muslim and is considered a companion of the Prophet, upon him peace and blessings. The reality of people is based on their exit from this world.

I want to explore the trials that Ramlah faced and how reflecting on such people helps us in evaluating our story and trials.

At the time, her father Abu Sufyan was a very powerful leader, fighting and torturing the Muslims. Yet she accepted Islam and opposed her father.

People assume that the war the early Muslims faced was a war of "us" vs. "them." What they fail to realize is that the battles fought in those times were parents against children, siblings against siblings, friends against friends. It was a war of truth against falsehood.

Ramlah was married at the time, and she migrated with her husband and a small group of Muslims to Abyssinia, to escape the persecution.

Abu Sufyan sent messengers to the Negus, the King of Abyssinia, to seek their extradition. The messengers tried to win over the Negus against the Muslims, but after examining the Muslims' beliefs and listening to the Quran being recited, the Negus concluded: "What has been revealed to your Prophet Muhammad and what Jesus the son of Mary preached came from the same source."

More trials followed.

After this, Ramlah's husband left Islam and gave her the choice of leaving Islam or divorce. She accepted the divorce and was now a single parent in a foreign land, living in a small community of Muslims, with no extended family. Her husband passed away, leaving her widowed instead.

Ramlah's life was full of choice after choice to love God and Prophet Muhammad, upon him peace and blessings. She loved them over her own self, her father, the life of wealth, influence and privilege, her homeland, and her own husband.

She went from wealth to poverty.

From power and influence to weakness.

From family and friends to loneliness.

From familiarity, belonging, and roots to being a foreigner.

From marriage to life of a single parent.

She made these decisions and faced these trials without holding God under any obligation to provide any particular result, but rather she simply had a good opinion of God.

What happened next?

Four months after the death of her husband, Ramlah had a dream in which someone called her the "mother of the believers," which was confirmed the next day.

Then Abrahah, a servant of the Negus, came to her with glad tidings. She told Ramlah that Prophet Muhammad, upon him peace and blessings, had sent a letter and appointed the Negus as his representative, and that the Negus should contract a marriage between Ramlah and him. If she accepted, she was to also appoint a representative to act on her behalf.

I have said it before: If you want to test a man's mettle, pretend to be weak. When Moses, for instance, came across two women whose father was old and ill and who were having a hard time looking over their flock, he didn't use this as an opportunity to lord over them or be their savior or protector. He didn't take advantage of their vulnerability. Instead, he gave them quiet and straightforward assistance. He did not act the "great" man, but instead was the man following his values.

Likewise, the Prophet did not take advantage of Ramlah's vulnerability. Instead, he communicated with her through a representative and gave her the advice of appointing a representative for herself to make a decision that was in her best interests.

Rather than getting into the details of the marriage that followed, I want to pause here and reflect on how the Prophet responded. Some argue that the Prophet treated Khadijah well because she was a powerful woman with a strong support system. However, the marriage to Ramlah and others shows that the Prophet always had a deep respect for women's autonomy and their choice to accept his marriage proposal or not. There was no manipulation whatsoever. It is in that spirit that he also accepted the marriage proposal of Khadijah in his youth.

And how did Ramlah feel about the proposal? She was overjoyed, appointed Khalid ibn Said ibn al-Aas as her representative, and accepted the proposal.

Safiyyah bint Huyayy

Safiyyah bint Huyayy, may God be pleased with her, was a Jewish woman who belonged to the tribe of Banu Nadir, a tribe that betrayed a peace treaty with the Muslims and attacked them. Some of her kin died in the Battle of Khaybar.

There were other Jewish tribes who did not betray their treaties and continued to have peaceful ties with Muslims. So, due to her relationship with the tribe that attacked Muslims, Safiyyah's loyalty was questioned by some, and she faced discrimination even by her co-wives. In response, Prophet Muhammad, upon him peace and blessings, said to his wife, "If they discriminate you again, tell them that your husband is Muhammad, your father was the Prophet Aaron and your uncle was Prophet Moses. So what is there in that to be scornful towards you."

We all look to our heritage, heroes of our past, to feel a sense of value and self-worth.

The Prophet did not engage in guilt by association, nor did he treat his wife with suspicion given her relationship to the tribe that attacked Muslims. There was no spying, nor watching her, nor questioning her loyalty. He continued to treat her with love, mercy and compassion.

As I mentioned before, all Muhammad's wives wanted to be with him out of choice. But it's also important to mention how he saw his spouses. He saw them as gifts from God. He used to say that God blessed him with the love of Khadijah. There is a hadith in which he asked permission from Aisha to get up and pray extra prayers during the night. She responded that she would prefer he be next to her, but wanted him to be happy, and what pleased him, pleased her.

As he stood up to prayer, Muhammad prayed to God in gratitude for this gift.

Often we treat every divorced woman as though she were Khadijah. But Khadijah is not the same as Ramlah. And neither of them were Umm Salama, Hafsa, or Sawdah. Each had a distinctive personality and distinct wisdom. We have to separate their stories.

Khadijah had power, influence and wealth. Ramlah, who was also divorced or widowed, was a refugee who was separated from her family because of her faith.

None of Muhammad's wives were compelled into marriage. None were treated with a lack of dignity or self-respect. All of them were with him by choice. None of them were manipulated socially, mentally, spiritually or otherwise to be with him or marry him. None of the women—when given choice to leave—chose to leave him.

He nurtured his wives to know themselves, to know him and his mission, and to know God.

Daughter of Hatim

We know, from hadith and from history, that the Prophet Muhammad, upon him peace and blessings, was mistreated by the tribe of Taif, where he was stoned and ridiculed by the community's youth.

Later, when the Muslims entered Taif, a prince named Adi fled the city, leaving his sister behind. There are stories of a woman pleading their case to the Prophet. He took one intelligent and influential woman, Umm Juwayriyah, as a wife. But what about those who wanted only to be set free?

The sister of Adi was one such woman. She came before the Prophet and told him:

> Messenger of Allah, my father is dead; my brother, my only relation fled into the mountains on the approach of the Muslims. I cannot ransom myself; I count on your generosity for my deliverance. My father was an illustrious man, the prince of his tribe, a man who ransomed prisoners, protected the honor of women, fed the poor, consoled the afflicted, and was deaf to no appeal.

First, the Prophet praised her father, Hatim. Then he declared: "The daughter of Hatim is free, her father was a generous and humane man; God loves and rewards the merciful."

This freedom came without any strings attached. Adi, touched by gratitude, returned to Medina and was received by the Prophet. But his sister—whose main desire was to be free—remained so.

Husband and Prophet: Resolving Conflict, Creating Choices

> *Allah and His angels send blessings on the Prophet: O ye that believe! Send ye blessings on him, and salute him with all respect.* (Quran 33:56)

What sort of spouse was Muhammad, peace and blessings on him? When, like all other married people, Muhammad had arguments with his spouse or spouses, how did he deal with them?

The prophets held themselves to a very high standard. Like Jesus, upon him peace, Muhammad lived a very frugal lifestyle. He didn't hide his wealth, nor did he refuse to spend what he had. But he kept little for himself, and he was always spreading what he had among those in need.

During the time of the early Muslims, there were many military battles. When the battles were finished, there was sometimes abandoned property or wealth, and Muhammad would take this and distribute it amongst the poor. Some of his wives complained about this, as they wanted to benefit from it. But instead of keeping it for his own family, Muhammad used this acquired wealth to repair feuds, soften hearts, or relieve the sufferings of the poor.

As to his own wives and children, Muhammad felt that, since they were married to a prophet, they should be held to a higher level of accountability and responsibility than others in the community. After all, they too were responsible for building a peace movement, a community, and a nation.

They weren't the only ones who had to hold themselves to such a high standard. Muhammad's companion Umar ibn al-Khattab, for instance, would take an hour each day to call himself to account and to go through everything he'd done in that day.

As the complaints of Muhammad's spouses grew louder, Muhammad was patient and forbearing in his explanations. Then, one day, he realized a choice had to be made. He left his spouses for a month and went to Mashraba, a place nearby, where he could be alone and reflect. While he was gone, rumors started up, suggesting he might divorce his spouses.

Live what you call people to do

In a real-life marriage, there is always conflict. What's important for us to look at is: What happened during this conflict? Did any party in the relationship threaten another, or did they negotiate and come to an agreement?

Although Umar ibn al-Khattab was one of Muhammad's most important companions, the two of them had very different personalities. Where the prophet was mild, gentle, trustworthy, and down-to-earth, Umar was tough, direct, and intimidating. When Umar went to visit Muhammad in his isolation in Mashraba, he found the Messenger of God on a mattress made of straw, with the mattress's marks on his body. The prophet was clearly in a state of sorrow, with only a handful of barley and a fleece hung on the wall.

At this sight, Umar wept. The Prophet asked him, "Why do you weep?" Umar explained that kings and sultans lived very luxurious lifestyles and yet, here was God's most beloved, living so rough and plain.

Muhammad explained that he had been called for a mission, and it was important for him to make a sacrifice. He couldn't be calling on the poor to be patient while also living in luxury. Whatever you call others to, you also have to be in that position. This is an important message for us today as well. Some Saudis, for instance, who live very luxurious lifestyles are calling on others to be patient. The Prophet's response, upon him peace and blessings, was to direct the attention of Umar to the next world where the kings would have ruin and the believers would be in luxury.

Conflict and resolution

At this, Umar asked the prophet if he was planning to divorce his wives. No, the prophet said.

Umar asked for permission to let the companions know, since rumors were spreading, and Muhammad granted him this permission. Indeed, they continued to talk until the Prophet's heart was lightened, and he laughed.

Prophet Muhammad, upon him peace and blessings, stayed in seclusion for a month, until he received the following revelation:

> O Prophet! say to thy Consorts: "If it be that ye desire the life of this world, and its glitter ~ then come! I will provide for your enjoyment and set you free in a handsome manner.
>
> But if ye seek God and His Messenger, and the Home of the Hereafter verily God has prepared for the well-doers amongst you a great reward." (Quran 33:28-29)

Now, Prophet Muhammad, upon him peace and blessings, visited his wives and shared the revelation. He couldn't change his lifestyle. But, if they weren't happy living in poverty, then he would wish them well in a different life.

He told each wife to consult with her family and make a choice. In today's terms, something similar would be consulting with a therapist or attorney. In this, Muhammad wasn't trying to play power games. He was giving each of the women a real choice.

Aisha responded immediately that she didn't need to consult anyone, that she preferred God and His Messenger. One by one, his other wives made the same choice. For them, this time of separation and seclusion had helped them realize what they loved most, and they chose God and His Messenger.

When we look at this story, we can see important lessons for our own relationships. If we're in a relationship where we're having a conflict—perhaps because of the mission we're being called to—we can offer our partner a choice to join us, or a choice to go their own way. Just as Muhammad didn't try to force or manipulate or guilt his wives into being part of his mission, neither should we. And whatever we're calling people to, we have to be the first to put it in practice.

Taif and Rejection

Allah and His angels send blessings on the Prophet: O ye that believe! Send ye blessings on him, and salute him with all respect. (Quran 33:56)

It is important to mention how Muhammad dealt with rejection. When the Prophet went to call people to God in the city of Taif, he was not welcomed.

One falsely assumes that if God is with you, He showers blessings upon blessings on you in material reward, and everyone loves you and applauds you.

Prophet Muhammad, upon him peace and blessings, was very sad at the loss of his beloved wife, Khadijah, may God be pleased with her, and the death of his supportive uncle, Abu Talib. He was not able to win the hearts of the people of Quraysh, so he decided to choose another town.

He chose Taif, a small town that was east of Mecca. He went with his companion Zaid. The tribe of Thakif lived in Taif, and they were very cruel to the Prophet. Besides their coldness, they rose against him and forced him to leave.

He went to Taif with complete trust in God. Yet they didn't show him respect or listen to him at all. His efforts yielded no results.

Not only did they refuse to listen to him, but they also kicked him out by letting the street urchins hiss, mock, jeer and stone him such that his feet were bleeding.

He was the chosen one and God's most beloved, and he faced this cruelty and suffering.

Here we can pause and ask: What is hope?

At times, people confuse hope with obligation. Hope is best defined as having a good opinion of God regardless the results, while obligation is when one is attached to the results. It is a form of emotional blackmail that seeks to abuse God, an attempt to compel and provoke God into action, as though one could control or overpower God's will with their emotional pleas.

A cry of need that's made while embracing one's vulnerability is different than a cry that is embedded in a desire for power and glory.

How does the Prophet respond in the face of rejection and hostility? And why is he facing this hostility and rejection from Quraysh in Mecca, and now the people of Taif, as well as trial upon trial?

In material things and with a material eye it appears that he is facing only rejection. But, in the reality of faith, he is gaining blessing upon blessing.

Listen.

Prophet Muhammad, upon him peace and blessings, responded with the following prayer:

> Ya Allah, to You I complain of my weakness, my lack of resources and my lowliness before men. Oh, most Merciful of those who show mercy! You are the Lord of the weak and You are my Lord. To whom will You relinquish my fate? To one who will misuse me? Or to an enemy to whom You have given power over me? If You are not angry with me I don't care what happens to me. Your favor is all that counts for me. I take refuge in the light of Your countenance, by which all darkness is illuminated. And the things of this world and next are rightly ordered. I wish to please You until You are pleased. There is no power and no might, save in You.

His main concern was that God was pleased, and that he was continually gaining the blessing of beholding God's beauty and Majesty. This does not need commentary. Rather, we should take a moment of silence to place ourselves emotionally, mentally, and spiritually in this place, and reflect on the inner beauty of Prophet Muhammad, upon him peace and blessings. He did not ask for power over his enemy, but he turned to God for protection. He understood that there was no power and no might save in God. Was this not a tremendous blessing in the face of such cruelty and sadness?

And yet there are more blessings.

His prayer reached the heavens and Angel Gabriel, upon him peace, appeared before Prophet Muhammad, upon him peace and blessings. The Angel Gabriel greeted him.

Muhammad was asked if he would like the service of an angel to crush the town for the horrible way he was treated and kicked out.

Muhammad, upon him peace and blessings, said:

> Even if these people do not accept Islam, I do hope from Allah that there will be persons from among their progeny who would worship Allah and serve His cause.

He refused the opportunity to punish the people who had made him bleed. Instead, his beautiful heart shunned this and chose not to give them any trouble. As the years passed, the progeny of many of his enemies and those who had mocked him came to accept Islam and to praise Muhammad, upon him peace and blessings.

His life was a totally sincere and true sacrifice to the one he loved, God.

After the Angels left, Prophet Muhammad, upon him peace and blessings, rested against a tree that was close to a garden owned by his enemies, Utbah and Shayba, the sons of Rabi'a.

Utbah and Shayba had watched the whole scene, and they had seen how the Prophet was pelted with stones and kicked out bleeding. They saw the Prophet make the supplication, and they saw how Zaid, his companion, was trying to keep him from fainting.

Now Utbah and Shayba, who had been mocking and torturing the Prophet and his followers for ten years, felt a wave of pity and sent their slave Addas to look after the Prophet and offer him grapes.

Addas offered the Prophet, upon him peace and blessings, grapes to eat.

The Prophet asked Addas his name.

Addas told him his name and who had sent him.

He could have rejected the grapes, but he was humble and in need, so he took a grape and said, bismillah, or, "In the name of God most compassionate and most merciful," and then ate the grape.

Addas was surprised, as he had never heard anyone say this before.

The Prophet asked him where he was from. Addas told him that he was a Christian from Nineva.

The Prophet told him that the Prophet Jonah, upon him peace, was from the same town.

Addas was surprised that Muhammad knew Jonah.

Prophet Muhammad, upon him peace and blessings, spoke well of Jonah and said that he was a Prophet like him, and that they were paternal brothers in faith. This surprised Addas, and he opened his heart to Prophet Muhammad, upon him peace and blessings.

Here we pause.

The owners of the grape field and his people had known Muhammad, upon him peace and blessings, since childhood, and they knew him as honest and trustworthy. Yet they had rejected him and fought against him for ten years.

The people of Taif rejected him and kicked him out without mercy.

God sent angels, yet the Prophet did not want the people of Taif to be punished, and the angels left.

He was in a very weak and exhausted state, and yet he took the opportunity to engage Addas in a conversation, explaining to him the connection between himself and Jonah, upon him peace.

Prophet Muhammad, upon him peace and blessings, never separated himself from the other prophets when calling to God. He always spoke of the prophets by acknowledging their station as well as their good character.

Then a small ray of hope, unexpectedly, came to strengthen his resolve and faith.

Addas kissed the head of Prophet Muhammad, upon him peace and blessings, and accepted Islam.

The Prophet rested for a while before continuing his journey to Mecca, to call to the one he loves: God. After he was mercilessly kicked out of Taif and returned to Mecca, then he was taken on a trip to the heavens. This trip is known as Israa and Miraj, also called the "Night of Ascension," which falls on the 27th day of Rajab, the seventh month on the Islamic calendar. Israa is the miraculous night journey of the Prophet, upon him peace and blessings from Mecca to Jerusalem in the 11th year of Prophethood.

Miraj is the miraculous journey of the Prophet from Jerusalem through the heavens where Allah made daily prayer obligatory upon us.

He was welcomed by the Angels, and the other prophets greeted him.

Then, there was a special meeting of lovers.

When God spoke to Muhammad, He said: "I have taken you as My beloved and I have expanded your heart and raised high the esteem in which you are held so that whenever I am mentioned you are mentioned with Me. I made your nation the best of nations and I made them the last and the first on the Day of Judgment. I made you the first prophet to be created and the last to be sent."

God spoke with his beloved, and He gave him the gift of prayers for his nation.

Nothing you do for God is ever lost, and every pain you endure will be relieved, and every humiliation will be compensated with elevation in the heavens.

What We Learn about Muhammad from Taif

Allah and His angels send blessings on the Prophet: O ye that believe! Send ye blessings on him, and salute him with all respect. (Quran 33:56)

The Chosen One or Al Mustafa

Prophet Muhammad, upon him peace and blessings, was chosen by God and received the first revelation at the age of forty. Another beautiful name that he is known by is al-Mustafa or The Chosen One.

There are three things non-believers say to minimize the life of the Prophet Muhammad, upon him peace and blessings.

One was that Muhammad must have been mentally ill.

Another is that he was a charlatan and a liar.

The third is that he was an "inspirational speaker" and influencer of his time, but not a Prophet of God.

All three can be addressed by the Prophet's time in Taif.

The Prophet Muhammad grieved deeply at the loss of his beloved wife, Khadijah, may Allah be pleased with her. She died in November 619 CE, around the same time that the Prophet also lost a beloved uncle. After their deaths, he decided to leave Quraysh.

In Taif, the townspeople were not only cold to his message, but they rose violently against him. They sent young people to throw stones, jeer and injure him.

The first suggestion—that the Prophet was mentally ill—crumbles under scientific scrutiny. Science has taught us a great deal about mental illness in the past fourteen hundred and forty years, since the time of the Prophet Muhammad. Using these tools, we can assess the suggestion that the Prophet Muhammad suffered from severe mental illness and that he hallucinated the revelations.

Those of us who have family members who suffer from a serious mental illness know about the fragility of people with a severe mental illness. Yet the Prophet Muhammad withstood rejection in Mecca, and then cruel rejection and attack in Taif, and yet this did not bow him.

Other types of mental illness impair one's ability to engage others compassionately, deal with rejection, and stay grounded in difficult situations. Although there are a wide range of mental illnesses that cause hallucinations, one thing is common among them: those with serious mental illnesses take a great deal of energy from family and friends. They may be wonderful, bright, giving people, but it is draining to care for someone who has a severe mental illness.

Yet over more than a decade of serious tribulations, no one described the Prophet as draining or exhausting, and indeed he gave energy to others. He led troops from the front lines in twenty-seven different battles, giving succor and encouragement to others. This does not fit the profile of mental illness as we understand it.

What about a charlatan?

Let's say, then, that Muhammad, upon him peace and blessings, was not mentally ill. He could have made up the story—about receiving messages from God—in order to reap the benefits of being a Prophet.

If things had gone well for Muhammad in Quraysh, perhaps this argument could be made. But someone becomes a charlatan in order to benefit from it. What is the incentive for Muhammad to continue on through more than a decade of disbelief, and then an even more violent response in Taif?

Muhammad experienced many tribulations: the death of his beloved wife and uncle, leaving Mecca, being greeted violently in Taif. And yet he withstood all of this with patience, in discomfort. Even when he was bribed—offered money and opportunities if he would only stop calling people to God—he did not return to a comfortable state. He continued with his mission. Thus we know he is not a liar, as someone who is a liar will move toward pleasure.

Indeed, Muhammad often said, according to hadiths that have come down to us, that lying destroys people's faith. In the face of lies, one is unable to be steadfast and determined. And yet Muhammad is one of the greatest examples we have of human determination and steadfastness.

A motivational speaker or influencer?

What if Muhammad—instead of being a prophet—was more of a problem-solver? He saw the many problems that faced his society, and he stepped up, as an inspirational speaker, to address them.

First, this doesn't wash with how Muhammad first learned he was a prophet, when God spoke to him, and he was overwhelmed by fear. He ran back to his wife, at first thinking he had been overpowered by djinn. It was only when he relayed the story to a beloved uncle that the uncle suggested: This sounds like what other prophets have experienced.

What he experienced was not something he sat down and scripted, the way a motivational speaker would. It's something that shook him to his core. Muhammad didn't choose to put himself in the position of prophethood. It was someone else who told him: You are being chosen.

Moreover, a motivational speaker or other influencer may be a noble person. But they are also getting benefit from their work. If their work didn't return results in one year, two years, three years, or ten—and if they were violently attacked—then it would be time to come up with another plan to solve the problems in Taif. But the Prophet withstood great pain, ridicule, and violent attacks, such that his soul was separated from his ego, and he continued until he was victorious.

In the face of rejection and the lack of hospitality of Taif, Muhammad, upon him peace and blessings, responded with this prayer:

> O God, to You I complain of my weakness, my lack of resources and my lowliness before men. Oh, most Merciful of those who show mercy! You are the Lord of the weak and You are my Lord. To whom will You relinquish my fate? To one who will misuse me? Or to an enemy to whom You have given power over me? If You are not angry with me I don't care what happens to me. Your favor is all that counts for me. I take refuge in the light of Your countenance, by which all darkness is illuminated. And the things of this world and next are rightly ordered. I wish to please You until You are pleased. There is no power and no might, save in You.

Instead of rejecting the people of Taif who rejected him, he said: Even if they don't accept Islam, I hope there are those among their children who will worship God and serve His cause. And indeed, as the years passed, the children and grandchildren of Taif came to accept Islam.

Healthy Power:
Enforcing Boundaries, Removing Barriers

Allah and His angels send blessings on the Prophet: O ye that believe! Send ye blessings on him, and salute him with all respect. (Quran 33:56)

One of the marks of healthy power is that it eradicates the sharp barriers between people of high and low status. It erases the barriers between people who have a great deal of money and very little, between people who come from traditionally respectable families and those who do not.

Muhammad, upon him peace and blessings, was known for bringing together people of high and low status, and for working to eradicate social and class transgressions between groups of people. This topic is one that requires an in-depth study with scholars. Influence and status in a society has its value, but when there are transgressions and abuse, this needs to be called out. We need leaders and we need people who will follow.

Abusive power sees people through the lens of class and status difference. Muhammad, on the other hand, brought people together. With him as a leader, people of varying social and economic backgrounds worked together, broke bread together, and talked together. While before they were separated, now they met each other on an equal field.

Muhammad not only spent time buying and freeing slaves, but also allowing them to take on roles that slaves were not granted in society. Bilal, for instance had a very beautiful voice and was given the role of muezzin, or of calling the faithful to prayer. The other muezzin was Ibn Umm Maktum.

They were given roles of honor and dignity, and could then marry without regard to previous status, race, or social standing.

Muhammad removed class boundaries in other ways, too. Zakat is not just a form of charity, but it is also taking from the rich and giving to the poor, so that those who are impoverished can stand on their own. When the Prophet Muhammad found someone who was in need, he would rally the community so that others would come and help.

Once, we're told, Muhammad heard of a man who didn't have enough money for his wedding. Muhammad came and bought the man's camel for a very good price, which thus provided the man with enough money to hold his wedding. And yet the man would be lost without his work animal. So Muhammad—after paying for the camel—left it with the man, along with his dignity and his money.

Divide and conquer

Abusive power doesn't listen. It creates barriers of class, race, social status, region, and others in order to give the powerful the illusion that they are the only ones in control.

Healthy power removes these barriers, and it tries to nurture a healthy society.

Abusive power, meanwhile, creates conflict and wars, as this keeps the people distracted. Indeed, all the people who the prophets were fighting were those who fomented and created classism. Jesus himself had to fight class divisions, as the Roman empire was deeply stratified.

Most of the time, abusive power is attached to wealth as well as power, and these leaders don't want to be brought down by people who are weak and of low status.

Leading by listening

As becomes clear in many stories about the Prophet Muhammad, upon him peace and blessings, he often led by listening, and he found out a great deal about the people around him through gentle conversation. He taught his followers likewise to listen to others and to find those who needed uplift.

There's a story we're told about the Prophet, upon him peace and blessings, in which he heard of a man who had both a son and a daughter. As is typical in many families, both then and now, the man treated his son better than his daughter. The man hugged the boy, praised and kissed him, but he scarcely acknowledged the little girl.

The Prophet called the man to account for this behavior, which was creating divisions and barriers. You're creating hatred between the children, the Prophet told the man. The girl is going to see that she isn't treated as well as her brother.

Thus, the Prophet listened to even the small things that went on, within homes and between children. Healthy power removes even these barriers, as it is a healing power.

Not fighting a name

It's very hard to fight abusive power, because you're not fighting a name or a figurehead. Instead, you're fighting what abusive power has built. At times, we become so attached to a name—attacking and ridiculing this particular name—that we forget what we're fighting against: abusive power.

We need to focus on what we really want to fall: racism, oppression, abuse, discrimination, and class division.

If we focus on fighting a name, then we can lose sight of what we're fighting and take on attributes of our oppressor. That's why even the oppressed must practice healthy power, particularly when engaging people at the margins and those who are poor.

The Story of At-Tufayl Bin Amr Ad-Dawsi

Allah and His angels send blessings on the Prophet: O ye that believe! Send ye blessings on him, and salute him with all respect. (Quran 33:56)

A companion of Prophet Muhammad, upon him peace and blessings, named At-Tufayl Bin Amr Ad-Dawsi was once told, before he had become a companion, that he shouldn't listen to Muhammad. Don't listen to him, at-Tufayl was told. He's a wizard. He's a magician!

The Prophet's enemies told at-Tufayl that the Prophet had fragmented the community, that his words were like magic, and that he severed the ties between father and child and between husband and wife. You must avoid him, the community told at-Tufayl.

At-Tufayl said that they insisted and insisted until he decided that he would not hear anything from the Prophet, and he inserted earplugs so he would not hear a word from him.

At-Tufayl went to do a mini-pilgrimage or umra at the sacred precinct in Mecca, the Ka'aba, with earplugs in his ears. Thus equipped, he went not to hear what the Prophet had to say, yet he saw him there at the Ka'aba and observed his presence. This way, he thought, he would be safe.

At-Tufayl reasoned with himself that he was an intelligent man, a poet, and one who could differentiate between the good and the bad. If what Muhammad said was good, he prepared himself to accept it. And if it was bad, he felt intelligent enough to reject it. So he decided to listen, to hear. Then he removed his earplugs and listened to what was being said.

One thing we know about the Prophet was that, before he was a speaker, he was a listener. So when at-Tufayl approached, he told him what others were saying about him, and he wanted to share his poetry. The man recited his poetry. And the Prophet listened.

So the Prophet knew what at-Tufayl had been told: This man is a wizard! He seeks to overpower and harm you! He's brainwashing you! But the Prophet didn't present arguments to the contrary. Instead, he shared verses with at-Tufayl that said: This is how you seek protection from those who would steer you wrong.

> Ikhlaas: Unique attributes of God
> In the name of God, Most Compassionate, Most Merciful
> Say: He is Allah, the One and Only;
> Allah, the Eternal, Absolute;
> He begetteth not, nor is He begotten;
> And there is none like unto Him.
>
> Al-Falaq: seek refuge with God from all evil
> In the name of God, Most Compassionate, Most Merciful
> Say: I seek refuge with the Lord of the Dawn
> From the mischief of created things;
> From the mischief of Darkness as it overspreads;
> From the mischief of those who practice secret arts;
> And from the mischief of the envious one as he practices envy.
>
> An-Nas: seek refuge from the hidden evil of mankind
> In the name of God, Most Compassionate, Most Merciful
> Say: I seek refuge with the Lord and Cherisher of Mankind,
> The King (or Ruler) of Mankind,
> The god (or judge) of Mankind,
> From the mischief of the Whisperer (of Evil), who withdraws (after his whisper),
> (The same) who whispers into the hearts of Mankind,
> Among djinns and among mankind.

The Prophet, upon him peace and blessings, knew that accusations cannot be met with counteraccusations. Many people will embrace the accusations, and there is nothing that can sway them. There are, as I write, many people who would suggest that Muslims are wizards who can take over the US, as though the country were some small island nation, and as though Muslims had not—since the 1500s—been an integral part of the growth of this nation.

There cannot be coexistence where there is chaos. When the public square is full of chaos and arguments, and when it is ambiguous on the rights of people, we cannot build or promote coexistence. When we have conversations, they must have boundaries to promote clarity and lift the chaos. At-Tufayl loved the surahs and asked the Prophet for a sign to help him be a missionary for his people. When he reached his people, he had a shining light on his forehead. He was worried that people might see it as a curse. He prayed that the light might move from his forehead to the wick he was holding.

At-Tufayl did not have religious outreach skills, and he had not kept the company of the prophet long enough to have his inner reality, and to move his people just as he was moved by the presence of the Prophet.

But he developed that inner reality.

And so lived forgetting himself and serving.

Muhammad and Aisha: Dealing with Slander

Slander is the revenge of a coward, and dissimulation of his defense.

—Samuel Johnson

Throughout history, people have slandered Aisha.

During her lifetime, Aisha faced slander so vicious it would have pushed a weaker woman to despair. But, as we'll see, Aisha knew herself and had a strong relationship with God. What's more, Muhammad, peace and blessings upon him, dealt with the slander aimed at his wife in a very healthy way.

Accusations leveled at women—then and now—are often treated differently from those leveled at men. When men are accused of sexual infidelity, people often find it possible to forgive. Yet when such accusations are leveled at women, people are usually quick to judge and quicker to punish. Just as people raced to judge Aisha more than a millennium ago, they raced to judge Monica Lewinsky twenty years ago, and they rush to judge women and girls today.

Every society has its injustices and inequalities. These social ills are the by-product of people measuring themselves not by how they stand in God's eyes, but by how they stand in the eyes of their fellow humans. Social ills flourish when people want to appear great in the eyes of their neighbors.

So what happens if a woman is slandered in a sexist society, as Aisha once was? This woman's friends and family will have two choices. If they judge by God's eyes, then they can tell the young woman: This is between you and God. If you are guilty, repent. If you are not, pray and be steadfast. But if they judge by the eyes of their neighbors, then they might condemn the woman. Or, if they feel shamed by the slander, they might even try to mete out their own "justice."

In these situations, those who are discriminated against will never be able to prove their worth. As Toni Morrison has said, if you worry about proving your worth in a racist society, "There will always be one more thing."

Just so, when Aisha was attacked, Muhammad didn't leap to proving her worth. He left it to God.

Inferiority complexes

Slanderers prey on people's feelings of inferiority. These feelings of inferiority grow and grow when our ego takes the lead, pulling the reins away from our soul. Thankfully, God sends trials and tribulations to test, elevate, and purify us—and to take the reins away from the ego and hand them back over to the soul.

Sometimes, it might seem as though feelings of inferiority can be resolved by material success, status, money, power, or privilege. But the more we have, the more we want. More leads not to more happiness, but to a more impressive façade of happiness.

We cannot throw away all human desires—they serve important functions. What we need to do is find the right balance between the ego and the soul. Trials and tribulations help us do this.

Aisha's trial

Trials often draw out the ugliness that is in people's hearts and minds. They bring these things out of the shadows, and this helps God to publicly purify the ills that have been in hiding. These trials also help teach important lessons.

In Aisha's case, she was traveling with the Prophet, upon him peace and blessings, as part of a caravan. During the trip, she lost a treasured necklace and went back to find it. Meanwhile, the group moved on without her.

When Aisha found she had been separated from the group, and realized she was stranded alone in the desert, she began to panic. There was nothing for her to do but wait and hope. Fortunately, she was found by an honorable man, Safwan bin Mu`attal. He offered Aisha his camel, and he led her on camelback until the two of them found her caravan.

One man, Abdullah bin Ubayy bin Salul, found this an excellent opportunity to spread lies and gossip about Aisha. First, bin Salul planted seeds of doubt about what Aisha had been doing in the desert. Slowly, some people began to believe his story and to repeat it. With each repetition, the rumors grew.

When the rumors began circulating, Aisha was ill. It wasn't until the rumor of her supposed "affair" was in full force that she heard of it.

The right responses

Prophet Muhammad, upon him peace and blessings, had a very simple and direct response to the slander. He told Aisha:

> If you are innocent, I expect that God will declare your innocence. But if you have committed the sin, you should offer repentance, and ask for God's forgiveness; when a servant (of God) confesses his guilt and repents, God forgives him.

Aisha also responded in the right way. She didn't crumble in the face of slander, and she didn't try to prove she was innocent. Instead, she said:

> You have all heard something about me and believed it. Now if I say that I am innocent, and God is my witness that I am innocent, you will not believe me, and if I confess something which I never did, and God knows that I never did it, you will believe me. I cannot but repeat the words which the father of Prophet Jacob, upon him peace, had spoken: I will bear this patiently with good grace.

Muhammad and Aisha did not suffer from an inferiority complex. They were not worried about how they appeared in the eyes of others. They didn't rush to give proofs. The accusations hurt them, of course. But they weathered society's blows without papering them over or trying to prove their greatness. What they did instead was to lead with the soul.

So this slander—which was meant to undermine the Prophet—actually elevated him. Trials like these can destroy marriages or relationships, but they can also separate the great from the ordinary. An ordinary abuser might hit his wife, or he might abuse her emotionally under the guise of joking about the slander.

Prophet Muhammad, upon him peace and blessings, did not harm Aisha, neither mentally nor emotionally. He did not even repeat the slander.

The Prophet was in a unique position. He could have rushed off to come up with verses to defend Aisha. Instead, he waited as the rumor went on, and it was more than a month before a revelation came from God.

The revelation of innocence

After more than a month, the Prophet returned with a revelation:

> Verily those who brought forth the slander (against 'Aisha) are a group among you. Consider it not a bad thing for you. Nay, it is good for you. Unto every man among them will be paid that which he had earned of the sin, and as for him among them who had the greater share therein, his will be a great torment. (Quran 24:11).
>
> Why then, did not the believers, men and women, when you heard it (the slander), think good of their own people and say: "This (charge) is an obvious lie?" (12)
>
> Why did they not produce four witnesses? Since they (the slanderers) have not produced witnesses! Then with God they are the liars. (13)
>
> Had it not been for the Grace of God and His Mercy unto you in this world and in the Hereafter, a great torment would have touched you for that whereof you had spoken. (14)
>
> When you were propagating it with your tongues, and uttering with your mouths that whereof you had no knowledge, you counted it a little thing, while with God it was very great. (15)
>
> And why did you not, when you heard it, say: "It is not right for us to speak of this. Glory be to you (O God)! This is a great lie." (16)

God forbids you from it and warns you not to repeat the like of it forever, if you are believers. (17)

At this point, you would expect Aisha to thank the Prophet, as indeed her mother told her to do. And yet Aisha said she wouldn't thank him, since it was God who had revealed her innocence. Thus did God send light to purify the hearts, minds, and souls of people and to teach Muslims how to deal with false accusations.

There are two other things we learn here about Muhammad. First is that he has no knowledge of the unseen—he knows only what God reveals to him. Second, if the Prophet had been dishonest, he would have divorced Aisha as he was pressured to do or run after the man who was falsely accused along with his wife. He did neither.

Aisha and Her Co-wives: Who Repeated the Rumor?

A rumor is a social cancer: it is difficult to contain and it rots the brains of the masses. However, the real danger is that so many people find rumors enjoyable. That part causes the infection.

—Criss Jami

It was not only the town's hypocrites who slandered Aisha. Even some noble people joined in the rumormongering. But it's also notable who didn't join in spreading the rumor.

Despite the deep jealousies that existed between some of Muhammad's co-wives, and the rivalries between them, not one of them took part in the slander against her. Aisha particularly had a rivalry with Zaynab bint Jahsh. Zaynab's sister even spread the slander against Aisha, yet Zaynab refused.

Zaynab was asked her opinion of Aisha, and she said: "O Messenger of God, I swear by God that I have perceived nothing in her except piety."

Thus Muhammad's wives could struggle with each other and disagree, but they would not take advantage of one another's misfortune.

As they say, rumors are carried by haters, spread by fools, and accepted by stupid people. But Muhammad's wives were none of these, and they passed this difficult test. While the slander aimed to humiliate the Prophet Muhammad, upon him peace and blessings, it actually became a means to further confirm his good character as well as the piety of all his wives.

What if your own daughter is accused?

It is not only the Prophet who has faced slander against a loved one. The same continues to happen to people today. So what should you do, if your own daughter is slandered just as Aisha was? God's answer is clear: You must support her against society. You must stand with your daughter. If you think she might have done something wrong, you can nurture her gently, suggesting she repent privately to God. But you shouldn't help create shame or a stigma that she might have to wear for the rest of her life.

Even if a young woman is "guilty," as Monica Lewinsky was, it is not healthy for society as a whole to attack her. We should not embrace a holier-than-thou judgmentalism, as this is used to oppress and control others.

The largest share of our attention should be on ourselves and our own sins, not on the sins or apparent sins of others. If we are in a close relationship with someone, then we can give them advice. But even in this case, we shouldn't make them our main focus.

In this way, we should embrace not the ego, but the soul.

Ego vs. soul

How do we know if we are letting our ego take the lead, or our soul? The ego is constantly in search of validation, of power, of greatness, of reassurance, and of material support. The soul, on the other hand, is always seeking its Creator.

The soul knows that contentment doesn't come from the sort of "success" where we aim to be better than others. Contentment comes from a state of being, or of spiritual peace, that only God can grant us. If you're not happy, then you need to seek happiness from God, and to open your heart to receive it through remembrance of Him, and through constant repentance. But being happy is not your main concern.

When we remember God often, we put our soul back in charge, and slowly God aids us in controlling our egos and polishing our hearts. When our hearts are polished, we begin to see egoism and materialism as unhealthy. Our love for guidance grows larger than our desire for external validation. We begin to love seclusion and moments of silence. We become conscious of the tremendous beauty of the universe.

Lessons learned

In this case, Aisha was innocent. In other cases, people might be guilty. But, in Islam, whether we're women or men, we can always repent our transgressions and continue forward. Islam is not a religion of self-hatred or despair. We make things difficult for ourselves if we measure ourselves in the eyes of others. If we, instead, measure ourselves in the eyes of God, then it's easier to repent and move on. Then, instead of proving that we're the best or most moral person in the room, we can focus on work that's beneficial to ourselves and others.

Welcoming Nobility

He said: "Here is a she-camel: she has a right of watering, and ye have a right of watering, (severally) on a day appointed." (Quran 26:155)

Prophet Muhammad, upon him peace and blessings, made Hijrah to Medina where he stayed for 10 years.

We do not need to dismantle powerful groups. Rather, we need to build our own power systems that serve our needs and allow us to tell our stories—systems that also give us a "path to the watering place."

Sometimes, people in power make this impossible. In that case, you must find another place to build.

As Malcolm X said, power respects power. But taking down people in power does not serve us. Instead, it creates further chaos. We don't want to create yet another system of tyranny that seeks to overpower others. We want to create one of peace and coexistence, not control and dehumanization.

Prophet Muhammad, upon him peace and blessings, had a favorite camel named Qaswa. He rode that camel on his journey to Medina. Along the way, he stopped for three days in a small town called Quba, where he laid down the foundations for the first-ever mosque to be built. He entered Medina with guards on both sides, drawn from the tribes of the town, who were there to protect him. He was also greeted by cheers of rejoicing and the welcome of the townspeople.

Many wanted to pull the camel toward their residence, but the Prophet commanded them to "let her go," as she would be commanded by God to stop at a location.

Where did the camel decide to stop and rest?

I find it helpful to find a good book which has a detailed biography of Prophet Muhammad's, upon him peace and blessings, life and read it in detail. Find one aspect of his life and focus on it.

Here, I want to focus on his migration to Medina.

When he got to Medina, Prophet Muhammad, upon him peace and blessings, did not try to dismantle the powerful groups around him. He started out alone and slowly attracted others, then built his own powerful nation. Of course, using this method meant other powerful groups might be threatened and try to fight him. In that case, one must fight the good fight. But as for Prophet Muhammad, he made peace treaties with other faith groups or nations with an aim of coexistence.

For instance, upon entering Medina, Prophet Muhammad, upon him peace and blessings, signed a peace agreement with the Jewish and Arab tribes in Medina and began building his nation.

So: What location did the camel Qaswa rest, and thus where did the Prophet Muhammad begin building? In *Muhammad: His Life Based on the Earliest Sources*, Martin Lings writes:

> At one point, it seemed as if she were making for the houses of the Prophet's nearest kinsmen of the 'Adi branch of the great Khazrajite clan of Najjar, for she turned into the eastern part of the city where most of the clan lived. But she passed by the place where he had stayed with his mother as a child and by all the other houses of those nearest to him, despite their earnest entreaties that he should make his home there. The Prophet gave them the same reply that he had given to the others, and they could only submit. He had now reached the houses of the Bani Malik branch of Najjar. To this subclan belonged two of those six men who had pledged allegiance to him the year before the First 'Aqabah, As'ad and 'Awf; and here Qaswa turned from the road into a large walled courtyard which had in it a few date palms and the ruins of a building. One end had been used at some time as burial ground. There was also a place set apart for drying dates. Slowly she made her way towards a rough enclosure which As'ad had set tip as a place of prayer, and there at the entrance she knelt. The Prophet let go her rein, but did not alight; and after a moment she rose to her feet and began to walk leisurely away. But she had not gone far when she

stopped, turned in her tracks and walked back to where she had first knelt. Then she knelt again; and this time she flattened her chest against the ground. The Prophet alighted and said: "This, if God will, is the dwelling."

He then asked who owned the courtyard, and Mu'adh, the brother of Awf, told him it belonged to two orphan boys, Sahl and Suhayl. They were under the guardianship of Asad, and the Prophet asked him to bring them to him, but they were already at hand and came and stood before him. He asked them if they would sell him the courtyard, and told them to name their price, but they said: "Nay, we give it thee, O Messenger of God." He would not, however, take it as a gift, and the price was fixed with the help of As'ad. Meanwhile Abu Ayyub Khalid, who lived nearby, had untied the baggage and carried it into his house. Others of the clan now came and begged the Prophet to be their guest, but he said: "A man must be with his baggage." Abu Ayyub had been the first of the clan to pledge himself at the Second Aqabah. He and his wife now withdrew to the upper part of his house, leaving the ground floor for the Prophet; and Asad led Qaswa to the courtyard of his own house which was close by.

Faith or fear?

What was the driving force behind the migration to Medina? Was it faith or fear?

If you reflect on stories about police brutality, fear is often used as a justification for fatal shootings. The officers, it's said, were afraid for their lives. They felt they were in danger and thus fatally shot an innocent person.

When we run in fear, that fear traumatizes us, and it might make us build solely for people like us, and for a feeling of protection and safety.

Fear drove Prophet Moses, upon him peace, to the Midian, and yet faith brought him back. Faith drove him to take his people to the Red Sea.

Hajar went to Mecca and stayed because of her faith.

What drove the migration to Medina?

The Muslims of Medina were given the title al-Ansar, or The Helpers. The Muslims of Quraysh—those who emigrated with the Prophet—were called the Muhajireen.

Let us pause here and reflect on a few things.

They say that, to help anyone, you must create an emotional distance between yourself and the one you want to help. In an oppressive relationship, it is often difficult to benefit the people around you—either the person directly, or those surrounding them, as this relationship is one of dependency or codependency.

During a migration or any separation, the focus should be on building you, your tribe, and those around you, in order to change relationships and break the cycle of oppression.

One can suggest that the Prophet left out of fear, or that his main concern was himself. However, his focus on building and using both al-Ansar and the Muhajireen together to build his community illustrates his wisdom, and how he was guided by God to build to benefit and guide all of humanity.

Another point is that, often, when we complain of powerful people and we rush to build, we take advantage of the poor in our midst. In the story of Muhammad's journey to Medina, we learn that two orphan boys offered him their courtyard. He refused to take it as a gift, but instead paid the full price.

Sometimes, we read of stories where people migrated from persecution only to persecute those in the land where they arrived. In this case, they migrated physically, but not mentally, emotionally, or spiritually. Unintentionally and unknowingly, they brought Pharaoh—or abuser—along with them.

It's important to read the story of how Muhammad migrated several times, and to reflect on it.

Making Peace: Between Fantasy, Reasoning, and Denial

Allah and His angels send blessings on the Prophet: O ye that believe! Send ye blessings on him, and salute him with all respect. (Quran 33:56)

Often, when people make peace, they attempt to do so in two extreme ways. One is to "play God." By this, I mean that they obsess over justice, revenge, and dominating others, while they themselves are out of control. Often such individuals are very rebellious, perverse, and insecure, and can only feel secure if they have power. Even with power, they remain insecure. Such individuals or groups often conduct investigations that justify all forms of torture and abuse including machinations, slander, false accusations, lies, projection, and hatred. They will wage war to take us to some utopian universe that never existed.

The other extreme is one that is in denial that any abuse exists. These individuals want to hug the abuser and believe that, somehow, they and the abuser will magically become best friends. You've heard the saying: all you need is love.

Yet peace is not denial, and neither is it fantasy reasoning.

Peace in Islam is also not utopia. Peace means making a commitment to a process of reconciliation and healing to face the challenges, trials, and tribulations that God places before us. In this process, you do not justify all sorts of abuse and indecency to promote utopia. You act within the framework of the values, faith, and ethics you claim to abide by.

Often, because people have a hard time dealing with reality, they are blind to their own transgressions and abuse of others.

When Prophet Muhammad, upon him peace and blessings, came to Medina, he made peace with the Arabs and the Jews of the town. Some stood by the peace agreements while others responded with discord.

Which chapter of the Quran was revealed during this time?

What lessons can we take from it today, as we make peace and seek justice to solve our problems?

Sometimes, people are confused by my use of the term "nobility." Does it mean that someone like Rep. Alexandria Ocasio-Cortez, who worked as a waitress, is not right for Congress? Do I support the critics who have attacked her working-class roots?

Good question, but quite the opposite: I actually find her very noble.

Rep. Alexandria Ocasio-Cortez entered the political field and fought the good fight. She did not start spreading rumors or playing games, but instead she presented her ideas and bold solutions openly and transparently. She did not take advantage of her supporters or stab others in the back in order to get elected.

What, then, is nobility? I wrote earlier about Bilal, the slave who was tortured after coming to Islam and who became known as the Caller to Prayer or Muezzin. Is he noble?

Nobility is about an inner reality or inner light that you use to face oppression, make peace, build your power base, engage with others, and other similar tasks. A noble person is one who does not engage in machinations or lies. This is a person who doesn't act treacherously or play games.

For example, in face of extreme oppression, Bilal bin Rabah, may God be pleased with him, responded "Allah is One, Allah is One." How many of us can do that? Most of us can preach it, but not practice it.

After embracing the message of Islam, Bilal was tortured by his masters, and he went from being an unprotected slave to a great hero. He was the only muezzin during the lifetime of the Prophet, upon him peace and blessings. Muslims view him with reverence and respect, given his heroism and the support he gave the Prophet.

Many believe that talking tough about one's oppressor is what makes them brave. They will cite this saying of Prophet Muhammad, upon him peace and blessings:

> A man asked the Messenger of Allah, peace and blessings be upon him, "What is the best jihad?" The Prophet said, "A word of truth in front of a tyrannical ruler."

What is a word of truth?

> *Those men, Allah knows what is in their hearts; so keep clear of them, but admonish them, and speak to them a word to reach their very souls.* (Quran 4:63)

"Stay clear of them" means you should not take them as companions, yet it also means you should not punish them. Admonish them and give them firm warnings—not to the ego, but to the soul.

What does that mean?

If Prophet Muhammad, upon him peace and blessings, was to go after them in a war, then the hope of reforming them would be over, and hypocrisy would remain in their hearts. Hypocrisy is when one's external behavior does not reflect the state of one's heart.

However, if you help them bear witness to the error of their ways, then you open a path for light to enter their hearts and souls and allow the purging of hypocrisy. If there is goodness in the person, then they will reform. If not, then they will kill the truthful person sharing the truth with them. One case in point is the Magicians in the story of Moses.

When you speak to the ego, you seek to dominate and control the behavior of others. You obsess over outward behaviors, which people will change openly out of fear or selfish interests, yet privately resist.

A truthful word comes from a heart connected to God. Although Moses, upon him peace, was known to be tough, harsh, and strong, what differentiated him from Pharaoh was that he was able to let go of the ego and listen. A word of truth that penetrates the soul can come only from a heart that listens to God, goes deeply into the argument of their opponent, then responds. Bravery is not in the speaking, but in the listening. Pharaoh, the Magicians, and Moses—upon him peace—all spoke on the Day of Festival. The Magicians and Moses, upon him peace, were able to listen to each other. Yet Pharaoh was not. The Magicians were then persecuted by Pharaoh.

When you speak a word of truth to penetrate the soul of another, you are putting God before them, as well as the teachings and the witnesses who want to testify.

The Light, the Illuminator, the One Who Reveals

All who obey Allah and the messenger are in the company of those on whom is the Grace of Allah, of the prophets (who teach), the sincere (lovers of Truth), the witnesses (who testify), and the Righteous (who do good): Ah! what a beautiful fellowship! (Quran 4:69)

Allah is the Light of the heavens and the earth. The Parable of His Light is as if there were a Niche and within it a Lamp: the Lamp enclosed in Glass: the glass as it were a brilliant star: Lit from a blessed Tree, an Olive, neither of the east nor of the west, whose oil is well-nigh luminous, though fire scarce touched it: Light upon Light! Allah doth guide whom He will to His Light: Allah doth set forth Parables for men: and Allah doth know all things. (Quran 24:35)

One of God's Names is an-Nur, which means The Light, The Illuminator, The One who Reveals.

Likewise, Prophet Muhammad, upon him peace and blessings, prayed, "O My Lord, render me Light," when he fully embraced the secret of the Quran, and, "Allah is the Light of the heavens and earth." One of Prophet Muhammad's names is also Nur, or the sacred light.

The Prophet's uncle, Ibn 'Abbas, said that one of the prayers that the Prophet made before the break of dawn was:

> O Allah, place light in my heart, light in my tongue, light in my hearing, light in my sight, light behind me, light in front of me, light on my right, light on my left, light above me and light below me; place light in my sinew, in my flesh, in my

blood, in my hair and in my skin; place light in my soul and make light abundant for me; make me light and grant me light.

From this, we can learn to turn to God if we wish to have this light within. We can seek it from Him, as He is the source of that light, not the ego, nor other people. It is important to take time to read the commentary on that verse in the Quran, as well as the beautiful name An-Nur.

"Let's be great again" syndrome

Earlier, I mentioned that Prophet Muhammad, upon him peace and blessings, was a man of high reputation and honor in the community. When he received revelations, he slowly lost this social standing. Yet he was more concerned with his principles, and with being true and sincere to God, than he was with being great again.

Muhammad went through many difficulties to demonstrate to us that his aim was not power, but rather to deliver a message to humanity from God. When all was lit up around him, and God took away that light, the light of his heart—which was strongly connected to God in humility—beamed and pierced through all the abuse and darkness from others.

At times, human hearts can be very hard. They can be so attached to status and wealth that they will reject God's message. However, we should never underestimate the value of planting a seed.

As Muhammad entered Medina, and as he started to build his community on principles and ethics, not all hearts reciprocated. Some who saw the message was spreading and being well-received began to feel threatened, and hence they began to make anonymous attacks on the Prophet.

It was at this time that the longest chapter of the Quran was revealed, al-Baqarah, or The Heifer. It is the second chapter of the Quran, and it starts with Alif Lam Meem, three letters of the Arabic alphabet.

The Meccan people fought the Prophet openly and transparently. In Medina, some—but not all—fought the Prophet and the community anonymously. These anonymous attacks hid behind mockery, innuendoes, and machinations; they were the types of attacks where a person says one thing in your face and another thing behind your back, professing to be with you while secretly undermining you.

The attacks came from both Arabs and Jews who had power and prestige, and who saw the Prophet rise in power and status while making peace agreements in good faith and goodwill. Whereas the Prophet was more concerned with delivering the message, they were more concerned with their greatness, power, and prestige.

It's important to reflect on this passage from the Quran:

> A. L. M.
>
> This is the Book; in it is guidance sure, without doubt, to those who fear Allah; Who believe in the Unseen, are steadfast in prayer, and spend out of what We have provided for them; And who believe in the Revelation sent to thee, and sent before thy time, and (in their hearts) have the assurance of the Hereafter. They are on (true) guidance, from their Lord, and it is these who will prosper.
>
> As to those who reject Faith, it is the same to them whether thou warn them or do not warn them; they will not believe. Allah hath set a seal on their hearts and on their hearing, and on their eyes is a veil; great is the penalty they (incur).
>
> Of the people there are some who say: "We believe in Allah and the Last Day;" but they do not (really) believe. Fain would they deceive Allah and those who believe, but they only deceive themselves, and realize (it) not! In their hearts is a disease; and Allah has increased their disease: And grievous is the penalty they (incur), because they are false (to themselves).
>
> When it is said to them: "Make not mischief on the earth," they say: "Why, we only want to make peace!" Of a surety, they are the ones who make mischief, but they realize (it) not.
>
> When it is said to them: "Believe as the others believe:" They say: "Shall we believe as the fools believe?" Nay, of a surety they are the fools, but they do not know. When they meet those who believe, they say: "We believe;" but when they are alone with their evil ones, they say: "We are really with you: We (were) only jesting." Allah will throw back their mockery on them, and give them rope in their trespasses; so they will wander like blind ones (To and fro).

These are they who have bartered Guidance for error: But their traffic is profitless, and they have lost true direction,

Their similitude is that of a man who kindled a fire; when it lighted all around him, Allah took away their light and left them in utter darkness. So they could not see. Deaf, dumb, and blind, they will not return (to the path). (Quran 2:1-18)

When God takes away light or greatness, what's really in people's hearts is revealed to them and others. The verse above emphasizes not people's inability to talk tough to others, but rather their inability to listen. They could not listen to God in humility, nor could they listen to the message they claimed to believe in, nor could they listen to the Prophet's message.

As we reflect on this, it's important to try to understand the history around this revelation and these verses. What lessons can you extract for yourself and others? One lesson is: Truth is spread through sacrifice, and falsehood through power.

It's good to look at examples of movement between darkness and light. We can appreciate the light of faith more when we reflect on those without faith. There are examples of hypocrites who accepted the faith and those who made agreements insincerely, with an eye to being great in the eyes of people. However, not all welcomed the Prophet with hypocrisy and envy. Some individuals did not harm or attack the Prophet, and they remained true to their agreements. These agreements did not require non-Muslims to accept the prophethood of the Prophet Muhammad, upon him peace and blessings. The agreements allowed each faith community to coexist and to build in peace, based on their convictions.

Still others accepted the faith sincerely.

I particularly want to reflect on two individuals who embraced the Prophet with sincerity and nobility. Both were noble people within their respective communities, and both were of high social standing. Neither sought the Prophet for a rise in status or prestige. They did not convert to be in a group that was quickly gaining influence in Medina, like some insincere converts who came to Islam seeking to be great in the eyes of people. The first was Salman al-Farisi, and the other was Rabbi Husayn ibn Sallam of Bani Qaynuqa'.

Salman al-Farisi gave up his prestigious life to find the Prophet Muhammad, upon him peace and blessings. No trials or tribulations were going to unmosque him. He ended up a slave under a Jewish tribe called the Bani Qurayh, but, after a funeral, he managed to free himself from work to meet the Prophet. Using his teachings and knowledge of what to look for to confirm whether Muhammad really was a Prophet, Salman found the Seal of Prophethood on Muhammad's back. He did not seek greatness from the Prophet, nor even to be freed from slavery. He just accepted Islam and went on with his life for the next four years with Bani Qurayh, with little contact with Muslims.

Rabbi Husayn ibn Sallam of Bani Qaynuqa's story was different. He came to the Prophet. Again, using his teachings and verifying things independently, he was able to sit with the Prophet and accept Islam. He was a noble rabbi within his tribe, a man of influence and prestige. Yet he came to accept Islam, and Rabbi Husayn came to the Prophet in secret and pledged allegiance to him. The Prophet named him Abd Allah, or Servant of God, a title that was also given to the Prophet.

The man asked that, before he revealed his conversion to his people, the Prophet first questioned them about the rabbi's character, knowledge, and position amongst them. Thus the Prophet called for the leading men of that tribe to come, and he asked them about Rabbi Husayn ibn Sallam. They said great things about him.

"He is our chief," they said in answer to the Prophet's question, "and the son of our chief. He is our Rabbi and our man of learning."

Then Abd Allah came out to them and said: "O Jews, fear God, and accept that which He hath sent unto you, for ye know that this man is the Messenger of God." He affirmed his own Islam and that of his household, and after this people reviled him, and they denied his good standing amongst them, which they had previously affirmed. But the rabbi was willing to sacrifice his greatness in the eyes of people, his status, and his title, in order to follow his convictions.

Like the Prophet himself, those who truthfully and sincerely came to Islam had to persevere through this test. All prophets have had to go through similar tests. There are many lessons to learn.

Seeking Greatness or Following Conviction?

Allah and His angels send blessings on the Prophet: O ye that believe! Send ye blessings on him, and salute him with all respect. (Quran 33:56)

Some converts to Islam say they have come seeking truth. Before Islam, they were just ordinary people, engaging in all the social ills of their culture. But after they became Muslims, they used Islam to promote themselves on the public stage and to launch themselves into positions of influence. Were they worried about the eyes of God or the eyes of fellow people?

One might ask: How can we tell? People who joined or formed ISIS, for instance, were not the most noble or great amongst their people, and they gave up what they had to form ISIS. They were the often uneducated people, who used religion and suffering to gain power or status in the eyes of people. If you look at their origins, they were not people of nobility who sacrificed their positions of influence. They were not following their convictions so much as they were following their egos.

Another thing to note is that while Prophet Muhammad, upon him peace and blessings, was building his nation in Medina, he and his followers were praying for the people of Quraysh in Mecca.

When Bilal would give the call to prayer, he would say:

"O God I praise Thee, and I ask Thy Help for Quraysh, that they may accept Thy religion."

Their hearts were not filled with the desire to seek power over Quraysh. Rather, their hearts were filled with the desire that the people of Quraysh be guided to the faith. Given their truthfulness and sincerity in holding to their convictions, God accepted their prayers.

War and self-defense

I've focused a good deal on people who seek power in order to dominate others. Next, I want to focus on war. Often, people assume that love can conquer hate.

However, domestic violence exists between spouses or partners who know each other well, and who have an intimate relationship. We cannot wait, expecting people will find their conscience and do the right thing. This is why war is allowed.

Some have used words of Gandhi and other civil rights leaders to criticize war.

However, political analyst Norm Finkelstein has said: "Gandhi's opinions on nonviolence are complex and not always consistent. But it should be clear that Gandhi ranked courage and bravery as high as nonviolence, and he repeatedly said that if you don't have the courage and bravery to resist the oppressor nonviolently, then you should use violence. He repeatedly denounced those who used nonviolence as a cover for their fear and cowardice."

Prophet Muhammad, upon him peace and blessings, was a threat to the Quraysh in Mecca and to some in Medina. His new nation had to learn to defend itself with valor and courage. It's also important to note that this was a community with a noble leader who built his nation within the boundaries of legality, decency, morality, and faith. It was built through conducting peace agreements with its neighbors and promoting security for all, not conspiring to ethnically cleanse anyone or to become a dominating force over others.

What verses were sent down to open the doors for the new community to fight in a battle?

> To those against whom war is made, permission is given (to fight), because they are wronged; and verily, Allah is most powerful for their aid; (They are) those who have been expelled from their homes in defiance of right, (for no cause) except that they say, "our Lord is Allah."
>
> Did not Allah check one set of people by means of another, there would surely have been pulled down monasteries, churches, synagogues, and mosques, in which the name of Allah is commemorated in abundant measure. Allah will certainly aid those who aid his (cause); for verily Allah is full of Strength, Exalted in Might, (able to enforce His Will). (Quran 22:39-40)

The Prophet led twenty-seven battles himself, and he sent his companions on forty-seven missions. After the Hijrah, several battles occurred, including: Badr, Uhud, The Trench, and the Conquest of Mecca.

The Battle of Badr occurred in the second year after Hijrah, on Friday, the seventeenth of Ramadan.

The Battle of Uhud occurred on the fifteenth of Shawwal, in the third year after Hijrah.

The Battle of the Trench occurred in the fifth year, in Shawwal.

In Dhul Qa'da of the sixth year, the Prophet, upon him peace and blessings, made the umra pilgrimage. The Quraysh had prevented him from making umra. At that time, the Prophet made the treaty of Hudaybiya and Quraysh, which was to last for 10 years.

Some of the agreements were that:

Muslims who fled Mecca and came to the Prophet were to be returned to Mecca.

Bani Bakr were allies of Quraysh and Khuza'a were allies of the Prophet, upon him peace and blessings.

The Prophet, upon him peace and blessings, would not be allowed to enter Mecca that year, but the following year. He shaved his head, slaughtered a camel, and returned.

Immediately after, Abu Basir escaped as a Muslim to Medina. The prophet, upon him peace and blessings, returned him. Yet Abu Basir killed one of the two men who were returning him to Mecca, and he escaped. Other Muslims fled and joined him. They cut off Quraysh's caravans to Sham. The Quraysh asked the prophet, upon him peace and blessings, to take them in, and they changed the treaty for that condition.

In the seventh year, the Prophet, upon him peace and blessings, wrote letters to the kings of the various regions. And the Conquest of Mecca occurred in ten nights, before the end of Ramadan, in the eighth year after Hijrah.

What event caused the conquest of Mecca? A violation of the treaty by the Quraysh. They assisted the allies of Bani Bakr against the Prophet's allies, Khuza'a. Then the Prophet, upon him peace and blessings, marched on Mecca with an army of 10,000. The Prophet, upon him peace and blessings, was honorable in conquest.

The farewell pilgrimage was in the tenth year after Hijrah. Prophet Muhammad, upon him peace and blessings, made hajj with all of his wives and many Muslims that year. Around 40,000 companions attended.

> If thou fearest treachery from any group, throw back (their covenant) to them, (so as to be) on equal terms: for Allah loveth not the treacherous. (Quran 8:58)

People speak of love and peace, but, at times, those same speakers will be behind the scenes, plotting and planning to undermine or betray you.

Often, when people manipulate us through lies of omission, they are not operating on a level playing field: emotionally, socially, or spiritually. They know more than we do, and they hold back key details while pretending—like Satan—to be a sincere adviser. Behind the scenes they are playing another game.

Prophet Muhammad, upon him peace and blessings, did not make peace with any group in this manner. Instead of making peace while weak, with the intention of changing gears when he got into power, his nobility is manifested in this verse above, as God taught him to throw back such treaties of deception in the face of the treacherous.

Either a person has genuine peace and goodwill—emotionally, socially, and spiritually—or they do not. There are no games, machinations, and deception in peacemaking. Like true love, peace refuses to play the games of treachery, but rather throws the false love and peace back in a false person's face.

Games of treachery are usually played by people who are attached to status and power, not values or faith.

In this manner, Prophet Muhammad continued to build his community. He did something that had never been done before in history—he made many peace treaties, promising to protect the people of the Book from any attacks.

Dr. John A. Morrow—an academic, researcher, scholar, teacher, activist, and member of the Canadian Métis community—came across an 18th-century text written by Richard Pococke that described and translated parts of the treaty the Prophet Muhammad had initiated with the monks of Mount Sinai.

In one section of the document, the text reads, "That whenever any of the monks in his travels shall happen to settle upon any mountain, hill, village, or other habitable place, on the sea, or in deserts, or in any convent, church, or house of prayer, I shall be in the midst of them, as the preserver and protector of them, their goods and effects, with my soul, aid, and protection..."

In addition, the parchment, which is signed with the Prophet's seal, bound the Muslims to honor these promises "for all time, even unto the Day of Judgment and the end of the world."

Below are some of the major treaties that he signed:

The Covenant of the Prophet Muhammad with the Monks of Mount Sinai

The Covenant of the Prophet Muhammad with the Christians of Najran

The Covenant of the Prophet Muhammad with the Christians of the World I

The Covenant of the Prophet Muhammad with the Christians of the World II

The Covenant of the Prophet Muhammad with the Assyrian Christians

The Covenant of the Prophet Muhammad with the Christians of Persia

The Covenant of the Prophet Muhammad with the Armenian Christians

The Covenant of the Prophet Muhammad with the Jews of Maqna

The Covenant of the Prophet Muhammad with the Yemenite Jews

The Covenant of the Prophet Muhammad with the Zoroastrians

The Covenant of the Prophet Muhammad with the Coptic Christians of Egypt

The Covenant of the Prophet Muhammad with the Syriac Orthodox Christians

The Covenant of the Prophet Muhammad with the Samaritans

The Covenant of the Prophet Muhammad with the Zoroastrians

As Dr. Morrow suggests in his book, *The Covenants of the Prophet Muhammad with the Christians of His Time*, "A visionary long-term planner, the Prophet understood that the spread of Islam could take centuries. What he sought to create were the conditions under which the seeds of Islam could be planted and watered, thus enabling Muslim seeds to sprout, grow, and spread. If a population preferred to remain heathen, Christian, or Jewish, they were entitled to do so as long as they entered into a covenant with the Islamic State as protected people."

Even as a victor, listening

Perhaps it's easier to listen when one is an underdog and an outsider. Indeed, Muhammad was known as a listener when people were first attracted to his teachings. When Abu Sufyan, one of the elders of Quraysh, went to Rome to complain about the prophet, he ended up praising the Prophet's character and the way he treated orphans and strangers.

But perhaps even more importantly, after two decades of fighting—after an exceptionally long battle—Muhammad entered Mecca with his head bowed, in a state of listening and humility. That is a very difficult thing to do.

How many of us could face twenty years of torture from those close to them, and then, at the moment of victory, respond with attentive forgiveness? That takes a lot of love. And listening is at the core of that love.

Lessons of Badr and Uhud

> *When the victory of Allah has come and the conquest, And you see the people entering into the religion of Allah in multitudes, Then exalt [Him] with praise of your Lord and ask forgiveness of Him. Indeed, He is ever Accepting of repentance.* (Quran 110:1-3)

Badr

The Battle of Badr was the first large-scale engagement that Muslims had to prepare for and face. Before that, they mainly resorted to speaking truth to power, which resulted in an increase of oppression in various forms. In this battle, the offensive army was sure of its power, sure that it could wipe out the small but growing Muslim community.

While war is not the first answer to oppression, there comes a time when war is the only answer the oppressors put on the table.

The Muslims who were treated like Habib an-Najjar lived to see a win that strengthened their faith in God and removed some of the years of trauma and suffering embedded within their souls. They saw the Battle of Badr, which took place on the seventeenth day of the month of Ramadan.

Coming out of the battle, witnessing the miracle, and knowing their true state of weakness and powerlessness, their internal dialogue would've been as such: If God hadn't helped us, we would have been wiped out. It would have nurtured strong God-consciousness.

We must first fail, and bear witness that the false logic and idols in our hearts and minds are a falsehood, and then accept the gift of faith and bear witness to God's power over all. The falsehood within must first come out and be denied and rejected before the truth and gifts that God is constantly showering upon us can be recognized and accepted.

Later, history records how the ruler Umar ibn al-Khattab entered Jerusalem, which we can compare to how other groups entered Jerusalem.

In this, we don't see the signs of just a military victory. If we look at Iraq and elsewhere where tyrants fell, we see that chaos emerged. But here, under Muhammad, we see a community emerge that is organized under a noble leader, connected to their humanity, and driven by values, God-consciousness and gratitude.

Muhammad shows evidence of divine aid, not military genius. If we want divine aid, we should do the same.

Uhud

Sometimes, when we witness a miracle or a triumph, we forget our former days and feel we've arrived. Although the Prophet had not wished to enter the Battle of Uhud, he followed the consensus after consulting with others.

During the Battle of Uhud, fifty archers were placed at the mountain, to prevent and protect the Prophet from being hit from behind. At one point, an assumption was made that the battle was over, and some of the archers disobeyed and ran after war booty, leaving the area behind the Prophet open for the enemy to go forth and attack. The Muslims had been winning, but they were severely wounded because of this.

Prophet Muhammad, upon him peace and blessings, was deeply hurt during the battle and many of his companions were killed.

> Behold! ye were climbing up the high ground, without even casting a side glance at anyone, and the Messenger in your rear was calling you back. There did Allah give you one distress after another by way of requital, to teach you not to grieve for (the booty) that had escaped you and for (the ill) that had befallen you. For Allah is well aware of all that ye do. (Quran 3:153)

Prophet Muhammad, upon him peace and blessing, was a nurturer, and that is the embedded reality of love and mercy. In a later verse in the same chapter:

> It is part of the Mercy of Allah that thou dost deal gently with them Wert thou severe or harsh-hearted, they would have broken away from about thee: so pass over (Their faults), and ask for (Allah's) forgiveness for them; and consult them in affairs (of moment). Then, when thou hast Taken a decision put thy trust in Allah. For Allah loves those who put their trust (in Him). (3:159)

Despite the heavy blow during the war, the Prophet, upon him peace and blessings, nurtured his fellow Muslims to turn to God, and he sought their opinions on his decisions. Whereas in the Battle of Badr, they went in fully relying on God, in Uhud, some were relying on their victory at the Battle of Badr. Such self-confidence can cause us not to take precautions or follow instructions.

The Prophet acknowledged their human condition and vulnerability. Instead of letting them run in shame away from God, he brought them to God to seek His forgiveness and mercy.

The Prophet was of such an exalted station that he asked God's forgiveness for them, and He forgave them. The Prophet did not hit them with humiliation or shame, but instead turned to them with mercy and forgiveness, and he consulted them on decisions.

Beautiful Names

The resemblance between me and the other prophets is like a beautiful house that is complete except for a last brick. All who see this marvel at its beauty, but they are also shocked by the missing brick. With me, that building of prophethood is completed.

—Prophet Muhammad,
upon him peace and blessings

Muhammad's stories connect all the prophets with one another, and they also connect us with ourselves and with all of creation. Through his stories, we are better able to understand ourselves and others.

It's well-known that God has many names, at least 99 of them. We also know that learning God's names is an important way of getting to know Him. Just so, the Prophet Muhammad, peace and blessings upon him, also has many different names for us to know.

All these names aren't known to us, as only God knows the Prophet Muhammad fully and completely. None among us can know Muhammad as God knows him. But we can pray for God's help in knowing Muhammad as the Prophet would like to be known, and for help knowing how God would like us to connect to Muhammad.

Part of this journey is learning the Prophet Muhammad's names.

"Seal of the prophets"

One of Muhammad's titles is "Seal of the prophets."

Muhammad once said: "The resemblance between me and the other prophets is like a beautiful house that is complete except for a last brick. All who see this marvel at its beauty, but they are also shocked by the missing brick. With me, that building of prophethood is completed."

The lives and experiences of all the prophets who came before Muhammad were used to nurture him, and thus, at last, he became the final brick in the building of faith. This happened at the moment when he summoned the souls of all the prophets, upon them peace, to al-Aqsa Mosque in Jerusalem. There, all the other prophets, peace and blessings on them all, prayed behind him.

In this way, the beautiful house was sealed.

Abd Allah

Another of the Prophet's names is Abd Allah, which means "servant of God." He was given this name because Muhammad has the honor of being God's truest servant. Muhammad once said that, when he is resurrected on the Day of Judgment, he will be prostrating before God.

No one else is going to reach the level that Muhammad has reached in serving God. Thus we call him Abd Allah, the true and sincere servant of God.

In The Most Beautiful Names, Tosun Bayrak Al-Jerrahi Al-Halveti notes that Abd Allah "is a servant who has received the highest level and honor which is possible to attain within creation." It's in the chapter Djinn verse 9 that Muhammad is identified as "the servant of God" who "stood up praying to Him."

Safiyullah

This name of the Prophet's means that Muhammad has been chosen by God out of the whole of creation.

Muhammad's father died before he was born, and his mother died when he was still young. This left Muhammad with no parent to rely on, so that he could rely fully on God. Thus Muhammad was in a state of wandering until he came to God, and his strongest emotional attachment is not to another human or anything else; only God.

"Haris Alaykum"

This name means "the one filled with solicitude for you," or "the one filled with care and consideration for you."

Some so-called religious people talk as though they want to throw every last person into Hell for some transgression or another. But Muhammad is the opposite: he is constantly praying for humanity, pleading with God to pull people from Hell.

From the chapter Tawbah, Verse 128 of the Quran:

> ...It grieves him that ye should perish; ardently anxious is he over you; to the believers is he most kind and merciful.

Ash-Shafi'

Ash-Shafi', or "the intercessor," is another of Muhammad's names.

The name ash-Shafi' is related to Haris Alaykum, his care of us. This name means that Muhammad is always worried on behalf of his people. He is concerned about their path, and he is concerned about getting them to heaven. It pleases Muhammad to intercede with God on our behalf, and thus Muhammad will be able to intercede on behalf of his nation on the Day of Judgment.

Taha

The name Taha is made up of two Arabic letters, Ta and Ha.

Some say the name means "the chosen one," and some say it means "the pure or purified one." The essence of the name is in the two Arabic letters, Ta and Ha, which come from a chapter in the Quran.

Here, Ta stands for purity or blessings, and Ha for hadi, or guide, and thus Taha is something like "the purified guide," or the one who is purified by God to guide humanity.

The Taha chapter in the Quran addresses the intimate relationship between the prophet Muhammad and God. Some commentators say Taha is also one of the names of God. In this way, God honors the Prophet with one of his own names and its attributes.

Muhammad, Ahmed, and al-Mahmoud

The three names Muhammad, Ahmed, and Mahmoud are all very similar, and all three have the same root letters. Their meanings are intertwined.

The name Muhammad means "the most praised one," the one who is most praised in all the worlds, and who we can never praise enough.

The name Ahmed means that its bearer is constantly praising God. No one praises God as much as Prophet Muhammad, and that's why he's also known as Ahmed. In the history of humanity, no one has praised God, or can connect to God, as much as Muhammad.

In the Saff chapter, in verse 6, it says:

> And remember, Jesus, the son of Mary, said: "O Children of Israel! I am the messenger of Allah (sent) to you, confirming the Law (which came) before me, and giving Glad Tidings of a Messenger to come after me, whose name shall be Ahmad."

It became clear that Muhammad was truly praising God when God's revelations stopped coming to him. When the revelations stopped, the Prophet also stopped. When God didn't say anything, Muhammad didn't say anything. Many people attacked the Prophet when he went silent. But during that time, he didn't respond to his accusers. He didn't simply shout at them: I am a Prophet and Messenger, God loves me.

Many mocked him, and his spiritual and emotional state grew anxious, as the Quran talks about in the short Duha chapter:

> Consider the bright morning hours, and the night when it grows still and dark. Thy Sustainer has not forsaken thee, nor does He scorn thee: for, indeed, the life to come will be better for thee than this earlier part [of thy life]! And, indeed, in time will thy Sustainer grant thee [what thy heart desires], and thou shalt be well-pleased.

Duha comes right after the darkest moment, when light very gradually begins to rise horizontally in the sky.

But first, Muhammad had to live through the darkness. This he did as one who is truly praising God. If a person truly loves God, and is truly praising him, then they will find time to pause. If God goes silent, they will try to discover whether God is displeased, as Muhammad did. It's just as in a human relationship. If you love another person, and that person goes silent and people tell you this person is displeased with you, then what do you do? If you truly love them, you will stop and see if you did or said something to displease them.

Real praise means you're concerned about whether the person is pleased or not. When the revelations stopped coming, Muhammad stopped and worried: Was God displeased? This worry showed that his love of God was genuine.

Just as Ahmed means its bearer is constantly praising God, Mahmoud means "the praised one" and "God's beloved." Mahmoud is also the name by which the Prophet is called in the Psalms of David.

Yaseen

The name Yaseen is made up of the letters "Ya" and "Seen," which together mean "ya" and "insaan," or "o man." This represents the whole man, the perfect man, the master of all men. God gave the prophet this name because he is seen as the perfect man.

As human beings, we know that we're not perfect. Yet we all seek and search for perfection. In order to come to terms with our flaws, we comfort ourselves by saying "I'm not perfect." Yet the heart always seeks perfection. It's a normal human desire, and we all love to see perfection. The prophet is that perfect man.

Just as the prophet is the perfect man, his first wife Khadijah was a perfect woman. She reached such a station that, it was said, God sent greetings to her. Mary, the mother of Jesus, also reached that station of perfection, as did Asiya, the adoptive mother of Prophet Moses.

The Friend Most High

The farewell pilgrimage was in the tenth year after Hijrah. Prophet Muhammad, upon him peace and blessings, made hajj with all of his wives and many Muslims that year. Around 40,000 companions attended.

Muhammad died in Medina when he was 63 years old, and he was buried in his beloved wife Aisha's apartment, which is now inside his masjid.

Our prophet, upon him peace and blessings, went to God ten years after his Hijrah, on what we believe was Monday the twelfth day of the month of Rabi al-Awwal, by consensus. However, Ibn Hajar said it was the second day of Rabi al-Awwal. The Prophet was buried at Asr on Tuesday, and Ibn Hajar said it was not possible for the twelfth to be on a Monday, so he argued it was the second instead. The final words of the Prophet, upon him peace and blessings, were "ar-Rafeeq al-A'la" or "The Friend Most High," referring to God.

Muharram, Ashura, and Stopping Cycles of Violence

> *O you who have believed, be persistently standing firm in justice, witnesses for Allah, even if it be against yourselves or parents and relatives. Whether one is rich or poor, Allah is more worthy of both. So follow not [personal] inclination, lest you not be just. And if you distort [your testimony] or refuse [to give it], then indeed Allah is ever, with what you do, Acquainted.* (Quran 4:135)

Although the faith is complete, lessons will be needed. There was no utopia before the Prophet's life, during his life journey, or after his life. The Quran will be guarded as well as its teachings. Yet, human trials and tribulations will come our way, inviting us to review our lives and reflect on the lives of the prophets, the teachings of Islam, and to answer the call of faith.

The month of Muharram is the first month of the Hijri calendar. The tenth day of this month is known as the Day of Ashura, or the day when God saved Moses and his followers from Pharaoh. On this day, we fast in gratitude as well as in humility, as, when we fast, we are reminded that it will wipe out our sins of the previous year.

This isn't the only major event in Islamic history that happened on the Tenth of Muharram. Imam Husayn, the prophet's grandson, also died in this day, just as Muslims were beginning the new year. Muharram symbolizes a new chapter in life, when we turn away from the many to the one God, from the shadows to light, from sin to guidance.

When the people saw the end of Pharaoh in that month, and the end of his oppression, it brought a new chapter and a new way of life for all those who had suffered under his rule. But a clear end to oppressive rule isn't the only way to have a new beginning.

"Husayn is from me, and I am from Husayn"

There is a famous hadith, a saying collected from the time of the Prophet, upon him peace and blessings. It goes: "Husayn is from me and I am from Husayn."

This hadith, which refers to the Prophet's grandson Imam Husayn, means that not only was he descended from the Prophet, but he also had the true Islamic spirit. Husayn is like me, the Prophet is saying. Husayn's line is my line, Husayn's message is my message, Husayn's principles are my principles, Husayn's mission is my mission.

After Husayn's father Ali was killed, the Muslim community was put to a great test. What would they do now? Would there be a bloody struggle for power? But Husayn's brother Hassan, who didn't want civil war, made a treaty with Muyawiyyah. After twenty years of ruling the new community of Muslims, Muyawiyyah also died.

Instead of a new leader being elected, as the righteous companions were, Muyawiyyah's son Yazid seized power. Many saw him as a tyrant who cared nothing about the lives of his people.

Some people decided to strike and boycott the new leader, as conscientious objectors. Imam Husayn left the city of Kufa, where the rulers were, and he and a few other young people refused to give their allegiance to Yazid. This was a powerful statement from the grandson of the Prophet.

Both Sunni and Shia alike see Yazid as a tyrant, and Imam Husayn as a role model of how we truthfully and conscientiously object to tyrants. Truth and freedom are a part of faith, and tyranny emerges if we don't hold those in power in check.

Unfortunately, those loyal to Yazid went from home to home to hunt Husayn down. Once a tyrant sees someone objecting with valor and honor—as President Trump saw Colin Kaepernick objecting, for instance—it exposes and enrages them. The followers of Yazid, who had divorced the faith from its spirit, captured Husayn and cut off his head.

What Imam Husayn did forced the tyrant to see himself. You don't need to tell a tyrant, Hello, you're a tyrant. It's when you valiantly object that an unjust ruler feels they've lost control, because you've projected that ruler's reality back at them.

Imam Husayn also had the credibility of being the prophet's grandson. Yazid's followers had tried to bribe him, but Imam Husayn refused, as he knew Yazid wasn't qualified to rule. Imam Husayn thus had to leave town, just as Moses once had to leave during Pharaoh's rule.

Different kinds of victory

At times, like Moses, the oppressed will see the crushing defeat of their oppressor and his soldiers. That's one sort of victory. At times, like Imam Husayn, we'll be victorious, but in a spiritual sense.

The victory here is that Imam Husayn was able to use his life to promote his message—not just that Yazid was a tyrant—but that one must stand up to a tyrant and conscientiously object.

After all, if you want to show the crookedness of something, the best thing you can do is show the correct way to act. Here, Imam Husayn shows us the right way to follow Islamic law and spirit in the face of tyranny. As Charles Spurgeon has said, "If a crooked stick is before you, you need not explain how crooked it is." You simply need to lay a straight one down beside it, and the work is done for you.

An eye for an eye?

The Prophet and Imam Husayn show us one way of achieving justice, through making themselves vulnerable. But not everyone in the world has been nurtured by a prophet. Many of us have a weakness for vengeance and vindictiveness. Such is the nature of humans.

During one battle, while fighting against the first Muslims, a woman named Hind was so angry at the death of her brother that she swore she'd go after the Prophet and eat from his liver. By comparison, when Muslims died in battle, the Prophet asked them to grieve quietly and without feeding a desire for revenge. These Muslims realized that justice did not end with their lives, and that the arc of justice continued.

Yet the common human being often responded as Hind had. When Islam began, there were many blood feuds that had been going on for decades.

The Prophet offered one model on how to end feuding. He lost his uncle and other family members, and he saw them mutilated. But the Prophet didn't answer this with vengeance. But the Quran doesn't say "turn the other cheek," either.

Verse 45 of chapter 5 in the Quran reads:

> And We ordained for them therein a life for a life, an eye for an eye, a nose for a nose, an ear for an ear, a tooth for a tooth, and for wounds is legal retribution.

In a discussion in one of my classes on restorative justice, some commented on how much effort it takes, when peacemaking, to convince the victim not to "burn down the village" of their oppressor. After all, when someone hurts us and our loved ones, over the course of many years, it is difficult not to want to hurt them in return.

We can see these cycles of violence playing out in many places around the world. Revenge and vengeance can feed on each other. Once they are put into place, it's exceptionally difficult to break the cycle, which takes a life of its own and can drag on for decades, causing the bloodshed of many people.

When the Quran says "an eye for an eye," this is meant to facilitate a limit—and end—to cycles of violence. What the Quran says is that you may only take out an eye in exchange for an eye, and you may not burn down the entire village. You cannot deny a victim's right to justice, nor can you turn away from their suffering and pain. But justice also shouldn't be blind revenge. We must open a door to patience and forgiveness, and for the victim to make a choice.

It's an eye for an eye, not an eye for a village, or torture, or starvation, or genocide.

This choice is also a way of nurturing the oppressed to take the high road. Verse 45 deals with reality, not a fantasy world. People respect Gandhi, as they should, but it's very difficult to apply that ability to turn one's cheek in every case. It's important to calm down the process and purge that desire for bloodshed.

That's the purpose and the spirit for the Quran's "eye for an eye."

In various other verses, God encourages people to show forbearance and forgive. Yet not everyone can accept that, and many plan their enemies' downfall or else want a double revenge.

The Islamic spirit is similar to what we read in Matthew 5:38-39:

> Ye have heard that it hath been said, An eye for an eye, and a tooth for a tooth: But I say unto you, That ye resist not evil: but whosoever shall smite thee on thy right cheek, turn to him the other also.

Yet how many of human beings can turn this cheek? Very few, which is why we see a middle ground in the Quran, of helping to gradually nurture humans to follow the spirit of the law. First, people need to have their pain acknowledged, and a path to justice within boundaries, and then an invitation to forgive.

In the Quran, again in Verse 45, there is an invitation to forgive. After the "eye for an eye," it continues:

> But whoever gives [up his right as] charity, it is an expiation for him.

PRAISE IS FOR GOD ALONE

Glory to thy Lord, the Lord of Honour and Power! (He is free) from what they ascribe (to Him)! And Peace on the Messengers! And Praise to Allah, the Lord and Cherisher of the Worlds. (Quran 37:180-182)

Gratitude is important. But *hamd*, or praise, is a state that's even higher than gratitude. Indeed, when God breathed life into Adam, upon him peace, Adam's first words were: "Alhamdulillah," or Praise and Glory to God.

As a species, our first word was *hamd*.

Praise in good times and bad

When I think about praise, I remember a moment in 1999, when I'd recently experienced my second miscarriage. Around the same time, I received news of a family member who was in the hospital with leukemia, about to have her first dose of chemotherapy. I had to remind myself to say Alhamdulillah. Then I read a scholarly commentary about a conversation between the angels and God, wherein God asks them: What did my servant say after he was afflicted? The angels reply: Alhamdulillah. And so God tells them to reward this servant with a palace in heaven.

Later, I was visiting my relative in the hospital. I wasn't sure how to comfort her, and I struggled with what to say. Then I was reminded of that passage, and I told her about it, and about how I'd praised God while recovering from my miscarriage. She looked at me and said, Alhamdulillah. She repeated it a few times, as it comforted her soul. Shortly afterwards, she went into a coma and passed away.

Her final words were Alhamdulillah, or Praise be to God.

Every time I open the Quran and come across verse 10 in the Yunus chapter, I shudder.

Their call therein will be, "Exalted are You, O God," and their greeting therein will be, "Peace." And the last of their call will be, "Praise to God, Lord of the worlds!" (Quran 10:10)

Alhamdulillah, or Praise be to God, is one of the greatest badges of the believer. We praise God no matter what state we find ourselves in, whether it be joy or sorrow, sickness or health, strong faith or doubt, wealth or poverty, married or single, with children or childless.

A commitment to work "Praise be to God" into the folds of our lives means putting God in control and trusting that God is able to do all things. This phrase enables and builds trust, particularly if we say it always, silently, and to ourselves as we watch the sun set or rise, or birds fly, or flowers bloom, or snow fall, or a loved one exit the world.

Saying "Praise be to God" brings us nearer to God. By saying it, we recognize Him not at our own station but His station, as Our Lord, Our Creator, and the One Who Loves Us More Than Anyone, including ourselves. We start to nurture feelings of love for Him and to bear witness when we are ungrateful.

Scholars have said: Praise is a settled matter, but for whom?

God said: for God.

When we praise other people, we become blind supporters of human beings who are not perfect. There's nothing wrong with thanking people, and we should express our gratitude to others. But praise belongs to God, as perfection is His alone.

Praise as a way of learning

Yet we can't praise God if we don't know Him—so praising God also pushes us to know the one we're praising. When a person is celebrated in society, we often want to find out more about them. Just so, when we commit to praising God, we push ourselves into that mode, of knowing and seeing the beauty around us, the signs of His greatness. We start to want to know His words as they appear in the Quran and what they mean. As a fan follows a celebrity, we'll start to seek the one we praise, and we'll begin to cultivate awe in our hearts.

Words of praise become a light in the heart, and what we seek seeks us. The heart was created to praise, so if we do not praise God, we'll be praising someone or something else—whether we're conscious of it or not.

We look to Prophet Muhammad, upon him peace and blessings, for guidance on how to praise God. His name "Muhammad" means "the most praising," and there is no creature who praised God more than His messenger Muhammad, peace and blessings be upon him.

We learn from Muhammad that praise is the means we have of approaching God the Almighty. Other names— "Ahmed," "Muhammad," and "Hamed,"—are also derived from the word "praise." Prophet Muhammad, upon him peace and blessings, used to say: "Glory be to You, we cannot count the praises for You, as You have praised Yourself."

Moses, upon him peace, is told to go to Pharaoh. After this, he asks for many things in preparation: the expanding of his chest, aiding his speech, and to be accompanied by his brother as minister. Then he says to God: "So that we may glorify you much and remember you much, for indeed You behold us constantly."

It's natural to praise

If we don't praise God, many of us will seek out other humans to praise, and praising other people can often lead to idolizing them. We often seek out people who have voice, influence, and power. If we've been traumatized and abused, we might not be able to tell that we're praising a narcissist.

A major difference between praising a human and praising God is that God does not benefit from our praise of Him. The praise, instead, benefits us. If we praise God instead of a celebrity, then we'll have the strength to stand up to the abuse of power, as we can see Rep. Ilhan Omar standing up to the abuse of power. Praising God protects us, by helping us not to be misled, used, and abused.

Thus we can thank Rep. Omar, but praise is for God alone. That way, if an individual travels, disappoints us, or dies, we still know who stood behind them and sent us the blessings that came through that individual.

The benefits of praise

Prophet Muhammad, upon him peace and blessings said:

> How wonderful is the believer! All of his matters are good and this is not for anyone but the believer; if he had good fortune he gave thanks, then it was good for him; and if he had a misfortune he endured it with patience, so it was good for him.

And if Muhammad was faced with something that he disliked, he would say: "Praise be to God for everything."

Praise centers and grounds a person. It turns them into a mountain in the face of the winds of the trials and tribulations we all face.

This doesn't mean that, if we're in a bad or unpleasant situation, we shouldn't try to fix it. But praising God will help us to avoid falling into despair. Praising God also helps us not to grow narcissistic. In good times, we also praise God in order to humble our ego and strengthen our soul. This praise helps us to internally assign our blessings to God instead of to ourselves. That way, when we see people deprived of this blessing—whether it be wealth or skills or health—we don't look down on them, but rather thank God and seek to help them however we can.

Although results are always with God, we shouldn't fail to study for a test and then praise God when we get a bad grade. That's not praising God, but rather evading hard work. That's what we mean when we say that praising God isn't about words on the tongue, but takes on a number of dimensions, including words. We can say:

> "Praise be to God - for creating us."
> "Praise be to God - for our breath."
> "Praise be to God - for water."
> "Praise be to God - for food."

A Torch to Light the Way

So exalt the name of your Lord, the Most Great. (Quran 56:96)

This verse is also part of the Muslim prayer. When you see Muslims bowing, they are responding to this verse. Again, Prophet Muhammad, upon him peace and blessings, taught Muslims to put this verse as part of their prayer.

In prayer, during prostration, Muslims recite the first verse of Chapter 87 of the Quran: "Glorify the name of thy Guardian-Lord Most High." In a hadith, or saying of Prophet Muhammad, upon him peace and blessings, it has been reported by Uqbah bin Amir Juhani that the Prophet had enjoined this verse during prostration.

Much as worshiping God protects us from narcissists and abusers, it also protects us from idolizing other people, from escapism, and from oppressing others. The chapter called al-Fatiha begins with "Alhamdulillah." This phrase is our torch in the journey of life, and as the chapter explains, it guides our steps. It allows us to turn to God for guidance during every trial, sorrow, and difficulty—and in the good times, too.

Just so, the Prophet, upon him peace and blessings, said: "Every verse has its share of bowing and prostrating." And we say: "Glory be to my Lord the Great," which means that we submit to and acknowledge God. In prostration, we say: "Glory be to my Lord the Most High."

When we prostrate, we are seeking help and guidance to live out His commands. The bowing and prostration is also an acknowledgement of our human weakness, as well as our need for His help and guidance.

> Allah wants to make clear to you [the lawful from the unlawful] and guide you to the [good] practices of those before you and to accept your repentance. And Allah is Knowing and Wise. Allah wants to accept your repentance, but those who follow [their] passions want you to digress [into] a great deviation. And Allah wants to lighten for you [your difficulties]; and mankind was created weak. (4:26-28)

In the chapter of the Quran called al-Fatiha, or The Opening, we can read: "It is You and You alone Whom we worship and you alone we seek for help."

> It is You we worship and You we ask for help.
> Guide us to the straight path,
> The path of those upon whom You have bestowed favor, not of those who have evoked [Your] anger or of those who are astray. (1:5-7)

I like to think that we will all face moments when our faith and values will be difficult to practice, where our feelings might not be in sync, or we no longer feel like it. This is a time when we are challenged to practice not because it makes us feel good, but because we genuinely believe in the message. I always felt that praising God was the medicine for such moments or times.

Praising God is also important when facing the oppressor, as you cannot face them alone, without God.

While doing so, we can join the symphony of every living thing that is praising God.

A companion of the Prophet, Ibn Abbas narrated:

I heard the Messenger of Allah saying: "O Allah, I ask You of Your mercy, that You guide by it my heart, and gather by it my affair, and bring together that which has been scattered of my affairs, and correct with it that which is hidden from me, and raise by it that which is apparent from me, and purify by it my actions, and inspire me by it with that which contains my guidance, and protect me by it from that which I seek protection, and protect me by it from every evil.

O Allah give me faith and certainty after which there is no disbelief, and mercy, by which I may attain the high level of Your generosity in the world and the Hereafter.

O Allah, I ask You for success [in that which You grant, and relief] in the Judgment, and the positions of the martyrs, and the provision of the successful, and aid against the enemies.

O Allah, I leave to You my need, and my actions are weak, I am in need of Your mercy, so I ask You, O Decider of the affairs, and O Healer of the chests, as You separate me from the punishment of the blazing flame, and from seeking destruction, and from the trial of the graves.

O Allah, whatever my opinion has fallen short of, and my intention has not reached it, and my request has not encompassed it, of good that You have promised to anyone from Your creation, or any good You are going to give to any of Your servants, then indeed, I seek it from You and I ask You for it, by Your mercy,

O Lord of the Worlds. O Allah, Possessor of the strong rope, and the guided affair, I ask You for security on the Appointed Day, and Paradise on the Day of Immortality along with the witnesses, brought-close, who bow and prostrate, who fulfill the covenants, You are Merciful, Loving, and indeed, You do what You wish.

O Allah, make us guided guiders and not misguided misguiders, an ally to Your friends, an enemy to Your enemies. We love due to Your love, those who love You, and hate, due to Your enmity those who oppose You.

O Allah, this is the supplication (that we are capable of), and it is upon You to respond, and this is the effort (that we are capable of), and upon You is the reliance.

O Allah, appoint a light in my heart for me, and a light in my grave, and light in front of me, and light behind me, and light on my right, and light on my left, and light above me, and light below me, and light in my hearing, and light in my vision, and light in my hair, and light in my skin, and light in my flesh, and light in my blood, and light in my bones.

O Allah, magnify for me light, and appoint for me a light. Glory is to the One who wears Glory and grants by it. Glory is to the One for Whom glorification is not fitting except for Him, the Possessor of Honor and Bounties, Glory is to the Possessor of Glory and Generosity, Glory is to the Possessor of Majesty and Honor."

— At-Tirmidhi Hadith No. 3419

The prophets and Messengers were established with proof that they had been sent and directed by God. They did not compel anyone to these truths, and neither should I or anyone be compelled by a person's personal experience with God. Nor should anyone be compelled with my personal reflections of faith. They are mine and I share them for others to investigate and take what they find of benefit and disregard otherwise.

However, I see it both ways or more. As a Muslim living in the West, and belonging to a minority group, I see groups from all directions seeking to control the will of others, obligating people to their beliefs or worldview, justifying discrimination, abuse, and disrespect as well as scapegoating others. They do not know how to give advice in good faith, establish healthy boundaries with people with whom they passionately disagree, or respect people who do not share their worldviews. No one is asking you to marry them. They're just asking that you respect them as human beings, recipients of the Divine Breath. You do not have to respect their ideas or personal experiences.

Yet some will justify all manner of abuse while claiming to be fighting abuse and discrimination.

Ibn 'Abbas narrated from Prophet Muhammad, upon him peace and blessings:

> When you go to a powerful ruler and fear that he will attack you, say, "Allah is greater. Allah is mightier than all His creation and Allah is greater than all that is feared and all that you are wary of. I seek refuge with Allah. There is no god but Him, the One who keeps the seven heavens from falling

onto the earth by nothing except His permission, from the evil of your servant so-and-so [mention the names] and his armies and followers and supporters, both among jinn and men. O Allah, be my protector against their evil. Your praise is great and Your protection is immense, Blessed is Your Name. There is no god but You."

—*Al Adab al-Mufrad*, Imam Bukhari

We don't turn to ourselves, the way Satan did, when he worshiped God from a sense of egoism. Instead, we worship God the Almighty by asking help from God the Almighty. When we bow to Him, we announce our submission to Him, and in prostration we ask Him for help.

"Alhamdulillah" gave strength to the Prophet Joseph, upon him peace, to stand against the calls from all the women of the kingdom. It gave him guidance, strength, and willpower so that he was elevated to a station of power over them when he was released.

When he was released, he did not attribute his release to anyone other than God.

We can see the "Alhamdulillah" in this verse:

And he raised his parents upon the throne, and they bowed to him in prostration. And he said, "O my father, this is the explanation of my vision of before. My Lord has made it reality. And He was certainly good to me when He took me out of prison and brought you [here] from bedouin life after Satan had induced [estrangement] between me and my brothers. Indeed, my Lord is Subtle in what He wills. Indeed, it is He who is the Knowing, the Wise." (Quran 12:100)

One of my favorite forms of praise was given to Juwairiyah one morning. The Messenger, upon him peace and blessings, left while she was in prayer, and he returned while she was in prayer.

He asked her, "Have you been sitting in the same place since I left you?"

"Yes," she replied.

The Prophet said, "I recited four phrases three times after I left you, and if these were to be weighed against what you have been reciting since dawn, they would still outweigh them. They are: 'Glory be to Allah and Praise be to Him as much as the number of his creations, and His pleasure, and the weight of His Throne, and the ink of His words.'"

I have always liked these words praising God, even though I had not been aware of the story behind it. The beauty of this story is how the Prophet praised God and glorified Him in his actions as well as his words. And so "Alhamdulillah" is the torch we need to keep us moving forward on the path of faith and guidance, from our first breath to our last.

Amenah Abdel Jawwad Wazwaz: How to Praise God in Illness?

And lower to them the wing of humility out of mercy and say, "My Lord, have mercy upon them as they brought me up [when I was] small." (Quran 17:24)

My mother Amenah Abdel Jawwad Wazwaz had a stroke on November 30, 2009. She lost all the abilities we take for granted: the ability to breathe, to eat, to drink, and even to use the bathroom. We had to teach them to her all over again, as one teaches a baby. This was an experience through which we learned to be thankful for the ability to eat without the need of a feeding tube, to breathe without a breathing tube, to drink without an IV, to raise our hands, to walk, and more.

But this is different from gratitude. That is a state of praise, through which we exalt God as Lord, regardless of whatever state we find ourselves in. It's a state of beholding God and acknowledging His attributes. It's not a feeling, and we should praise Him regardless of how we feel.

When we praise God, it also helps us to be patient while God unfolds His decree and helps us understand His wisdom behind an event. While we are alive, our knowledge is limited, and praise helps to nurture the certainty of faith.

When we're not seeking God, then we're seeking to fulfil our desires or the desires of others. "Alhamdulillah," on the other hand, grants us true freedom. Through it, we can see others as instruments in God's hands who He uses to benefit us or test us. We were created for the purpose of worshiping God, so "Alhamdulillah" nurtures us to embrace our purpose.

My mother used to read the Quran all the time. She learned as a youth to read the Quran, although she did not know how to read anything else besides the Quran.

When she had her stroke, we tried to get her life back to normal. We bought a Quran which had a pen that would read the word for her when she put the pen on the word. However, she could not recognize any words or read. She started to cry profusely as she looked at the Quran and could not read. We calmed her down and tried to help her just listen to the Quran. Her favorite reciter is Shaykh Abdul Basit Abdul Samad, and I purchased a beautifully made 30 CD set for her to listen to. Later, we used YouTube videos of him reciting the Quran for her to watch.

Since she could no longer speak, we had to figure out how to get her to pray the five daily prayers.

This became her recitation during prayer for ten years:

SubhanAllah - "Glory be to God."
Alhamdulillah - "Praise and thanks to God."
La ilaha illallah - "There is no deity except God."

La ilaha illallah is very easy on the tongue and she held on to it with determination. It was almost as if she was worried that she could not recite it as she lost the ability to read and speak. She reminded me of the verse:

[Allah] said, "O John, take the Scripture with determination."
And We gave him judgment [while yet] a boy. (Quran 19:12)

For the next ten years, she remained determined to listen to the Quran throughout the day, and she prayed, not only her five daily prayers, but continued all the optional prayers: Duha (mid-morning), Qiyam (first part of the night), Tasbeeh (mid-evening), Tahajjud (late part of the night), and Nafl (extra), during the day and night as well.

Everyone who visited my mom or called her would repeat after her what she said. She could only say:

La ilaha illallah - "There is no deity except God."

People would respond:

La ilaha illallah, muhammadun rasūlu-llāh
(There is no deity except God and Muhammad is His Messenger.)

So I would comfort my mom, and I let her know that she was calling to God. She was reciting the shahadah, and others were reciting after her. Everyone that talked or visited with her kept reciting the Muslim declaration of faith after her, without anyone shoving it down their throat. For some, the only time they ever said it was when they visited my mom; for others, it became a reminder to say it more often.

> Allah and His angels send blessings on the Prophet: O ye that believe! Send ye blessings on him, and salute him with all respect. (Quran 33:56)

My mother used to love Prophet Muhammad, upon him peace and blessings. She saw him in a dream more than once, and she would always tell us stories about him. She told stories that, as a young person growing up in the US, I found hard to believe, until I was able to verify them.

She told stories about how even the trees and animals loved him.

Once we'd helped my mother settle into a new routine of prayers, listening to Quran, and saying la ilaha illallah, we started to look for lessons on Prophet Muhammad, upon him peace and blessings.

We found many that were lighthearted stories about his life as a father, husband, and neighbor. For instance, we used to watch "A Day with the Prophet," by Rufaida AlHabash. I would put the coffee on and remind her the program was starting. Her face would light up, and she would come and watch the program with me.

Since she could not send peace and blessings upon the Prophet, given her stroke, I felt that listening to stories about his life, as well as the teacher sending peace and blessings upon him, would help her act on this verse.

I continued to look for programs for her to watch, and she would listen and watch them.

Prophet Job, upon him peace, is known for his patience. There is a famous prayer he makes to God, but many have misunderstood the prayer:

> For verily we found him full of patience in adversity: how excellent a servant [of Ours] who, behold, would always turn to Us! (Quran 38:44).

The prayer he makes is:

> And [remember] Job, when he cried out to his Sustainer, "affliction has befallen me: but Thou art the most merciful of the merciful!" Whereupon We responded upon him and

removed all the affliction from which he suffered; and We gave him his family, doubling their number as an act of grace from Us, and as a reminder unto all who worship Us. (Quran 21:83-84)

How do we reconcile how God found him in difficulty and his prayer? On the outside, it appears like a complaint. It is said however, that Prophet Job, upon him peace, used to praise God and remember Him often. When the stage of his illness reached a level that made it difficult for him to praise God, that is when he made the prayer. He was not worried about his illness as much as his inability to praise God or worship Him as much.

I reminded my mother of this prayer and would say it to her as the stages of her illness advanced. She used to listen to the Quran nonstop and could only say "La ilaha illallah" or "There is no deity except God," the Muslim declaration of faith. However, in the final stages of her illness, she could not listen or speak much, so I would recite the prayer of Prophet Job, upon him peace, for her.

This doesn't mean we do not pray for good health or a cure from an illness. Prophet Job, upon him peace, is used as an example to those who are afflicted with a chronic illness or a difficult sickness, when relief is not in sight. The story is meant to nurture faith and patience, and to use the time in that state to worship God and increase one's worship, recognizing that the illness might be the means that God is using to bring one closer to Him or elevate their station to one of excellence in God's Knowledge and Eyes.

She saw the Prophet, upon him peace and blessings, before she passed away on November 29, 2019. She loved to tell us the dream using signs and gestures. I pray she is now in his company.

I pray she heard this call when she breathed her last, and we will hear it when we take our last breath:

> (To the righteous soul will be said:) "O (thou) soul, in (complete) rest and satisfaction! Come back thou to thy Lord, well pleased (thyself), and well-pleasing unto Him! Enter thou, then, among My devotees! Yea, enter thou My Heaven!" (Quran 89:27-30)

Farewell, my beautiful mother.

Hearts united in pain and sorrow
will not be separated by joy and happiness.
Bonds that are woven in sadness
are stronger than the ties of joy and pleasure.
Love that is washed by tears
will remain eternally pure and faithful.

—Khalil Gibran

To God we belong, to God is our final return.

O God, the Unique, the Master of all Greatness, Majesty, and Generosity, Creator of the heavens and the earth, the Living, the Self-Sufficient, the Most Kind and Generous. In the name of your Exalted Essence, we beg that you envelop Amenah Abdel Jawwad Wazwaz with Your Mercy, Forgiveness, and Love and that you raise her station with your beloved, Prophet Muhammad, upon him peace and blessings, whom she loved and taught us to love. Ameen.

And the last of their call will be, "Praise to Allah, Lord of the worlds!"

Sources

Al-Jerrahi Al-Haveti, Shaykh Tosun Bayrak. (1985). *The Most Beautiful Names*. Putney, Vermont: Threshold Books.

Al-Mubarakpuri, Safi-ur-Rahman. (1996). *The Sealed Nectar*. Riyadh, Saudi Arabia: Dar-ul-Salam Publications.

Al-Imam Ibn Kathir. (194-256 A.H. or 810-870 A.D.) *Stories of the Prophets*. Translated by Shaykh Muhammad Mustafa Geme'ah, Office of the Grand Imam, Shaykh Al-Azhar: El-Nour For Publishing Distribution and Translation.

Haneef, Suzanne. (2002). *A History of the Prophets of Islam: Derived from the Quran, Ahadith and Commentaries Vol. 1 & 2*. Chicago, Illinois: Kazi Publications.

Lings, Muhammad. (2017). *Muhammad: His Life Based on the Earliest Sources*. Islamabad, Digital Deen Publications.

Al-Buti, Dr. Muhammad Said Ramadan (2007) *The Jurisprudence of the Prophetic Biography and A Brief History of the Rightly Guided Caliphate*. Translated by Nancy Roberts. 2nd edition: Damascus: Dar al Fikr.

The Quran: Arabic Text with Corresponding English Meanings (Saheeh International). Almunatada Alislami, Abul Qasim Publishing House (1997).

The Holy Quran: Translation and Commentary (Yusuf Ali). Reprinted by Islamic Vision (2001). First published 1934.

    The writings and reflections in this book were inspired heavily by the commentaries and teachings of Shaykh Muhammad Metwalli al-Sha'rawi and Dr. Muhammad Said Ramadan al Buti. Most of the thoughts and reflections came from their teachings.

    I have listened to answers of many counselors as they respond to questions of people in need of help. These questions were great to reflect on and extract insight from. While I appreciate all those counselors, I want to recognize notable thanks to Dr. Abdul Lateef Krauss Abdullah and Counselor Hwaa Irfan whose counseling questions were exemplary to reflect on and beneficial.

Shaykh Qays Arthur, I worked with him on a project as a Star Tribune blogger. Parts of this project were polished and edited in this book.

Dr. Jamal Badawi and Jeewan Chanicka, I read many of their writings. The Hajj reflections were inspired by their teachings.

Mohammed Rateb al-Nabulsi, I read his writings on al Fatiha, and was inspired by his commentary.

Acknowledgments

To the beautiful teachers who have exerted their efforts to learn the religion and teach it, with generosity pass it down to later generations until it reached me and benefitted and was a source of inspiration while writing this book.

First and foremost, Prophet Muhammad, upon him peace and blessings, his family, his companions, and their followers, who without their sacrifices we would not be Muslims. To all the Prophets and Messengers of God, whose stories were used to nurture Prophet Muhammad, upon him peace and blessings, and are a source of benefit for us today.

Shaykh Ayman and his wife Sanaa, who were role models in Knoxville, Tennessee and inspired me to know my faith more. Shaykh Muhammad Metwalli al-Sha'rawi and Dr. Muhammad Said Ramadan al Buti, whose online teachings made this book possible. Hwaa Irfan, whose patience and forbearance helped me to see things differently. Dr. Abdul Lateef Krauss Abdullah, whose wisdom was inspirational.

Amenah Abdel Jawwad Wazwaz and my daughter, Maryam Laid, who were my companions in this journey.

Marcia Lynx Qualey, who edited this book and helped me clarify my thoughts and ideas, as well as raised challenging questions to help me better research and present my work.

About the Author

Fadwa Wazwaz was born into a family of 10 children in Jerusalem, Palestine. A mother of one daughter, she is a Palestinian Muslim American who was raised in Chicago, Illinois, who began her college years at Knoxville, Tennessee, and who graduated from the University of Minnesota. She has used her time in Minnesota to help build and strengthen the United States' Muslim communities, as well as those communities' ties to other marginalized groups. She co-founded an educational outreach organization, through which she gave talks to local groups, dispelling negative stereotypes about Islam and Muslims. She has also been trained in Restorative Justice at the Center for Spirituality and Healing and has given workshops to social workers on how to work effectively with youth and Muslim patients.

In 2003, she was a community columnist for the Pioneer Press. In 2006, she helped start up a civil rights organization, through which she mentored young leaders. From 2008 to 2009, she was a policy fellow at the University of Minnesota's Humphrey Institute of Public Affairs, and, in 2009, she started as a blogger for the *Star Tribune* and worked on helping Minnesotans understand Islam and Muslims. Also in 2009, she and her siblings began a new journey, taking care of their mother, who had suffered a major stroke. In 2015, she formally began work on this book, bringing together writings from over the past twenty years.

Wazwaz is a social commentator on issues that affect Muslim communities, Palestinian affairs, faith and values, coexistence, and ethics. She currently blogs at EngageMN.com.

www.ingramcontent.com/pod-product-compliance
Lightning Source LLC
Chambersburg PA
CBHW071221080526
44587CB00013BA/1449